Praise for *The Experience-Centric Organization*

"Organisations have understood the importance of customer experience, but still struggle to organise to deliver great experiences. Finally a book that fills this gap, packed with many examples and based on extensive experience. I recommend it highly."

-MARC STICKDORN
COAUTHOR AND EDITOR OF *THIS IS SERVICE DESIGN THINKING* AND *THIS IS SERVICE DESIGN DOING*

"Product based companies need to embrace the world of experiences and develop experience rich services around the product. This book shows how you can make this transformation, and gives clear advice about the journey you need to take as an organisation to develop and maintain experiential leadership."

-JESSE OLSON
CONSUMER STRATEGY DIRECTOR, ADIDAS

Customer obsession and delivering a great experience is something that connects today's winners, and is key for organizations that want to be successful in the next decade. To be able to take a leading position, companies need to support both the customer experience and the employee experience. For many, this is a strategic challenge that requires a rethink of organizational models and structure. This book is a great way to kick-start that process.

-BRIAN WHIPPLE
CEO, ACCENTURE INTERACTIVE

The Experience-Centric Organization

How to Win Through Customer Experience

Simon David Clatworthy

Beijing · Boston · Farnham · Sebastopol · Tokyo

The Experience-Centric Organization
by Simon David Clatworthy

Printed in the United States of America.

Published by O'Reilly Media, Inc., 1005 Gravenstein Highway North, Sebastopol, CA 95472.

O'Reilly books may be purchased for educational, business, or sales promotional use. Online editions are also available for most titles (*http://oreilly.com*). For more information, contact our corporate/institutional sales department: (800) 998-9938 or *corporate@oreilly.com*.

Development Editor: Angela Rufino	**Cover Designer:** Graham John Mansfield
Acquisition Editor: Melissa Duffield	**Interior Designers:** Graham John Mansfield, Ron Bilodeau, and Monica Kamsvaag
Production Editor: Katherine Tozer	
Copyeditor: Rachel Monaghan	**Illustrator:** Graham John Mansfield
Proofreader: Rachel Head	
Indexer: Lucie Haskins	

July 2019: First Edition

Revision History for the First Edition:

2019-06-26	First Release
2020-03-13	Second Release

See *https://www.oreilly.com/catalog/errata.csp?isbn=0636920218104* for release details.

978-1-492-04577-9

[GP]

Contents

Part 2 The How

Preface

Who This Book Is For

This book is for anyone who understands the importance of the customer experience and is looking to take the next steps toward delivering truly great experiences. It offers a framework for how to get your organization structured to be able to deliver upon the experiences you want to provide. The book allows you to find your position on the stepwise transition toward experience centricity, and guides you in what you can do as an organization to make the next step up.

Why I Wrote This Book

I have been fixated upon delivering memorable customer experiences for 30 years and have come to understand that this is an organizational imperative, rather than something that can be fixed through a single project mandate. As a voracious reader, I found myself increasingly frustrated that many books talked about the importance of the customer experience, but few actually helped you design these experiences. Not only this, but they neglected to describe how you should transform your organization to deliver the great experiences you want to deliver. I kept finding myself working with leadership teams who were saying, "We know this is important, but how can we do this? How can we design the company to be able to comfortably deliver great experiences?" There, the literature comes up short, and that is the reason why this book was written.

I am a join-the-dots kind of person, seeing connections, patterns, and trajectories all around me. I have seen several waves of technology and organizational paradigms come and go, and this got me asking a fundamental question:

> *The customer experience has been important for many years, but what comes after the customer experience?*

This question bugged me for a long time because the answer was always more and better experiences! However, I recognized that providing more,better experiences requires organizational capabilities. Finally, I realized that the customer experience is not a wave that we will pass through, but instead a trajectory with an endpoint. Organizations compete on customer experience, and the endpoint of this trajectory is when an organization makes the customer experience their "reason to exist." That is, they become an experience-centric organization. Suddenly a lot of dots came into focus as I realized that we are on the edge of a step change in terms of how the customer experience is viewed. This has enormous consequences for business in the next decade and I hope that as a reader, you will see its relevance for your organization. I strongly believe that it is relevant and important for the future of service. I sincerely hope you find it useful, and that it arms you to engage in the competitive landscape of customer experience today.

How This Book Is Organized

This book is divided into three parts about the why and how of the experience-centric organization.

Part I focuses on leadership and presents the case for the experience-centric organization, the stepwise transformation toward it, and organizational characteristics needed to become experience-centric.

Part II is about the how of the experience-centric organization. It goes into detail about the customer experience itself and how to design for it.

Part III presents two guest chapters that describe new, evolving areas of competition and competencies that you should aspire to develop,once you have become experience-centric.

Each part gives you the knowledge to understand your position on the experience-centricity maturity scale, and provides valuable information about what you can do to transform as an organization toward experience centricity.

Part I: The What and the Why

Chapter 1: The Experience-Centric Organization

This introductory chapter summarizes the whole book. It starts by explaining why the customer experience is now the main arena of competition and how this will intensify and evolve during the next decade.

The chapter then introduces the experience-centric organization as the endpoint of this trajectory, and explains what this means for an organization.

Chapter 2: Five Steps to Becoming Experience-Centric

Chapter 2 presents a five-step transformation model that outlines the path organizations usually take on their transformational journey toward experience centricity. This allows you to benchmark your own position, and begin thinking about a transformation roadmap.

Chapter 3: The Structure of the Experience-Centric Organization: The Wheel of Experience Centricity

This chapter describes the underlying structure of the experience-centric organization. It identifies key parts of the organization and their role in supporting the design and delivery of memorable customer experiences. Understanding this structure, and how the parts fit together, is key to unlocking the potential of the experience-centric organization.

Chapter 4: The Core Behaviors of the Experience-Centric Organization

How does an organization behave when it has become experience-centric? This chapter gives you an answer, describing the key behaviors of an experience-centric organization. This allows you to identify behaviors you already exhibit, and those that you need to develop.

Chapter 5: Organizing for Experience Centricity

Great experiences are provided by the whole organization, where everyone has their part. This chapter describes how you can structure the organization and develop an organizational logic that is focused upon delivering truly great experiences.

Part II: The How of Great Experiences

Chapter 6: Starting with the Experience

To be able to deliver great experiences, you need to know what a customer experience is and how customers experience your offerings. This chapter includes recent knowledge gained from neuropsychology about how we experience the world, and what makes for a great customer experience. It also describes how you can use this knowledge to design for memorable customer experiences.

Chapter 7: Experiential Translation: From Experiential DNA to Customer Experience

This chapter introduces the concept of *experiential DNA* and describes how it evolves from your brand DNA. It shows how to identify your experiential DNA and how you can use it as a platform to develop relevant and desirable offerings that will deliver extraordinary customer experiences.

Chapter 8: Experience Fulfillment: Designing the Experiential Journey

A key thing about the customer experience is that value is created through use. Until a product or service is used, the customer only has expectations, and you have only made promises. This makes fulfilling experiential expectations vital to the organization. This chapter describes how experiences are fulfilled together with customers through interactions with the touchpoints of the experiential journey over time. It then describes how you can become expert at experience fulfillment.

Part III: Going Further

Chapter 9: Design for Meaning

Chapter 9 takes you deeper into how to get a black belt in experience centricity, by understanding the deeper meanings that customers attach to their experiences. It goes into detail about how we instinctively read meaning into an experience and shows how, contrary to many initiatives about individually tailored experiences, collective experiences are more memorable and important to us.

Chapter 10: Trendslation

Customer relationships go two ways. As customers develop a relationship with you and your services, they extend the personality and behavioral characteristics related to your organization into expectations related to the broader world of culture and even politics. Chapter 10 introduces *trendslation*, an approach to help you become a proactive leader in this process by translating cultural trends into experiences.

Chapter 11: Conclusion

The conclusion wraps up the book and looks back at the chapters as a whole.

Chapter 12: Further Reading

This book summarizes the knowledge and experience from many different areas. It can only scratch the surface of some areas, however, so this chapter offers plenty of suggestions for you to go further.

Deviations from the Script

At different points in the book, you will find text boxes with different symbols. These give different kinds of in-depth detail related to the chapter, and you can choose to follow them or just hop over them.

An academic deep dive

This symbol invites you to indulge in an academic half-hour to link this work to relevant research.

Related and interesting

This symbol indicates a slight but relevant diversion from the text. If you are short of time, you can skip these, but I hope you stay and read them, because they contextualize many of the points in the text.

Tools and approaches

This symbol indicates the use of tools and approaches that encourage an experiential way of thinking.

Examples from real life

This symbol designates real-life examples to show how others have utilized the approach toward experience centricity.

Interview

Here, you will find interviews with and insights from key people regarding their experiences of working with experience design.

O'Reilly Online Learning

For almost 40 years, O'Reilly Media has provided technology and business training, knowledge, and insight to help companies succeed.

Our unique network of experts and innovators share their knowledge and expertise through books, articles, conferences, and our online learning platform. O'Reilly's online learning platform gives you on-demand access to live training courses, in-depth learning paths, interactive coding environments, and a vast collection of text and video from O'Reilly and 200+ other publishers. For more information, please visit *http://oreilly.com*.

How to Contact Us

Please address comments and questions concerning this book to the publisher:

O'Reilly Media, Inc.
1005 Gravenstein Highway North
Sebastopol, CA 95472
800-998-9938 (in the United States or Canada)
707-829-0515 (international or local)
707-829-0104 (fax)

We have a web page for this book, where we list errata, examples, and any additional information. You can access this page at *https://oreil.ly/experience-centric*. There is also a website with companion files available for download at *www.experience-centric.com*.

To comment or ask technical questions about this book, send email to *bookquestions@oreilly.com*.

For more information about our books, courses, conferences, and news, see our website at *http://www.oreilly.com*.

Find us on Facebook: *http://facebook.com/oreilly*

Follow us on Twitter: *http://twitter.com/oreillymedia*

Watch us on YouTube: *http://www.youtube.com/oreillymedia*

Acknowledgments

Although this book has my name on the cover, it is the result of collaboration with a great many organizations and people during the past years. First off, a big thank you to Judith Gloppen and Berit Lindquister, who encouraged me to work on this, when I developed the term *experience-centric organization* and who worked together with me on this path some years ago. Second, thanks to Ted Matthews and Claire Dennington, who not only have guest chapters in this book but also are part of the R&D team at AHO, working with design and experience-rich services. I would also like to thank the Norwegian Research Council, particularly Lise Sund, who has embraced the role of design in service innovation and helped finance the Centre for Service Innovation (CSI), which helped produce this book. Finally, thanks to AHO's Institute for Design (IDE).

To the reviewers, who helped me get my message across, thank you for sharpening the message and the book. I hope to repay the favor to you. To the supportive people at O'Reilly, who helped get the book out, a thank you for your help and patience. And a large tip of the hat to Graham, who developed the layout and illustrations for the book, and who put up with the continual frustrations of text changes at the last minute.

Then, over to family. To Charlotte, who has encouraged me and been a supportive home editor, and to my four kids, who have listened positively and with a smile when I have gone on and on about the book: you are all wonderful, and I promise to now shut up about it.

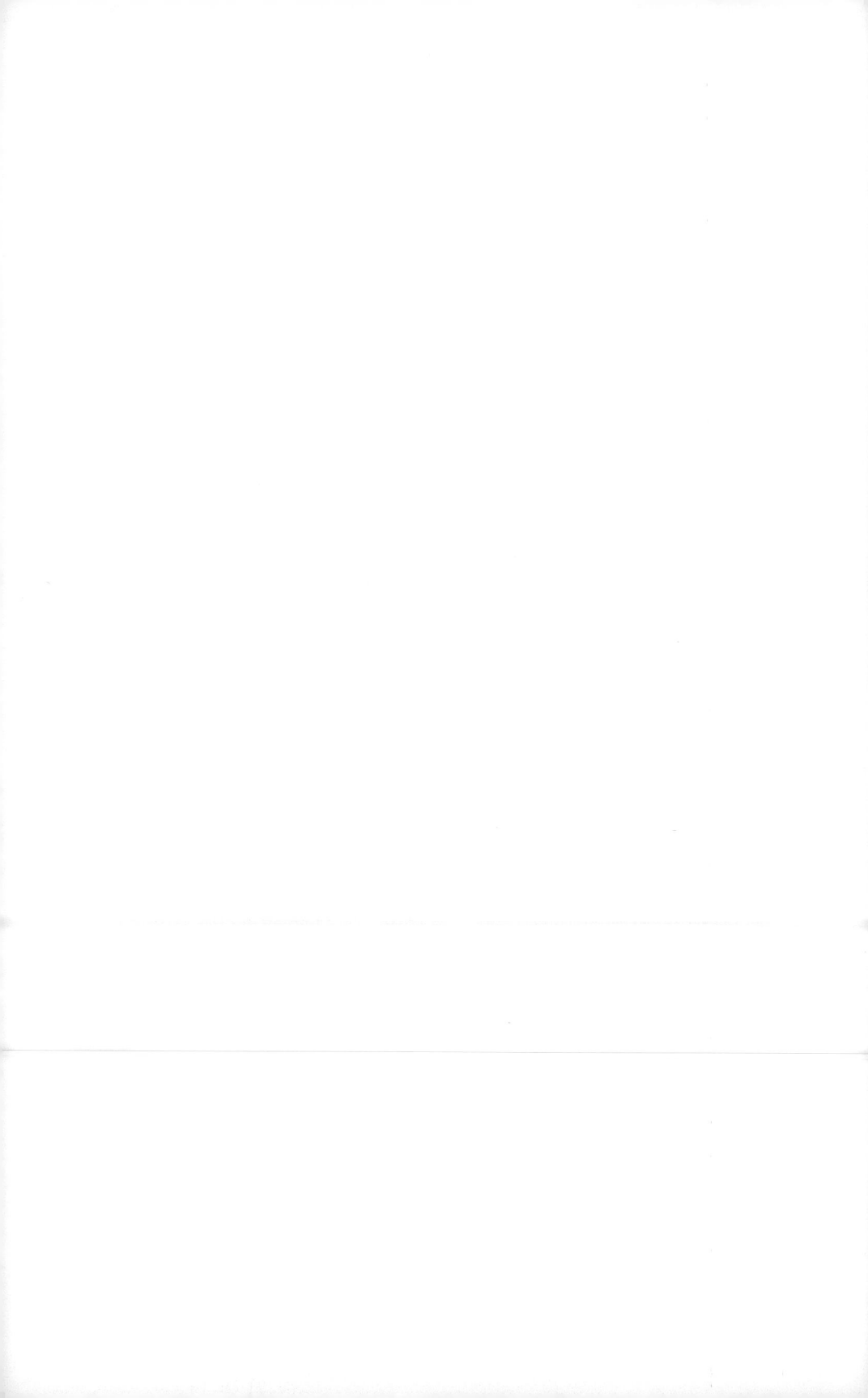

PART I

The What and Why

1

The Experience-Centric Organization

This introductory chapter shows that the customer experience is now the key driver in the market, and will be the main competition arena for the next decade. It describes what it means to compete through customer experience in a market where meaning is the new currency, and explains why the trajectory toward the experience-centric organization is one that you cannot avoid.

What Is an Experience-Centric Organization and Why Is It Important?

There's a transformation under way in organizations, one that puts the customer experience at the heart of the enterprise. Its endpoint is the experience-centric organization—an organization where there is total alignment around experiential delivery. All organizations are on a trajectory toward experience centricity, and it will become the defining characteristic of organizations during the next decade. This book introduces the characteristics of the experience-centric organization, explains its core behaviors, and outlines the steps you need to take to elevate your organization to the final, ultimate level of customer experience.

The market is driven by the customer experience. The first trillion-dollar company in the world has embraced it, experts describe it as the number-one business priority, research in cognitive neuroscience is explaining its importance, and your competitors are putting effort into it. The customer experience has now become the major source of competitive advantage, and one that you cannot ignore.

You're not going to stand out at customer experience if you don't prioritize it, and with the bar being continually raised, this means making it your central company mission. It's time to bring the customer experience into the core of your organization and place yourself on the path to becoming an experience-centric organization. Becoming experience-centric does not mean dropping everything you have done, but rather placing it in perspective, behind what matters most: how customers experience using your products or services.

This book will help you understand why you should embrace the customer experience, what it means to become experience-centric, and how to get there. If you are reading it, then you already have an interest in making this happen. This book describes how to distinguish your organization from your competitors through an experiential offering, and gives you a roadmap to optimize your organization for the future. Together this knowledge will give you a unique advantage that your competitors will be unable to match.

The experience-centric organization builds on a current trend: the customer experience is the key driving force in consumer choice and the key competitive arena in business. Every offering, whether it be a discount airline ticket or a luxury holiday, is judged experientially by customers. Everything is experience, and where there is competition, it is the experientially better service, as perceived by the customer, that wins. As a business, you need to respond to this trend by making the customer experience your number-one priority, and embark on the journey toward experience centricity.

This message is not totally new and you, like me, might ask, "Why have we not fixed the customer experience and moved on?" The reason is as simple to explain as it is complex to implement: experiences have been considered a feature of a product or service instead of an organizational imperative. We have not taken the customer experience seriously enough, assuming that we can just bolt it on at the end of a project, instead of using it as a starting point. Now is the time to move from considering experience simply as a feature to making it your core organizational mission.

Why Customer Experience Is King

In a world where there is competition, customers choose services based on their experience using them.

Recent statistics show that:

- Fifty-three percent of consumers have scrapped a planned purchase or transaction because of bad service.[1]
- Seventy-four percent are likely to switch brands if the purchasing process is too difficult.[2]
- Forty-nine percent say that companies are providing a good customer experience today.[3]
- Americans tell an average of 15 people about a poor service experience.[4]
- A total of $62 billion is lost by US businesses each year following bad customer experiences.[5]

These statistics have drawn the attention of CEOs, who have started to consider the lifetime value of the customer experience. David Reibstein, a marketing professor at the Wharton School, has translated customer experience into hard cash value. The lifetime difference between satisfied and dissatisfied customers at Starbucks is estimated at $2,800 per customer. The lifetime value of a satisfied BMW customer is estimated to be $143,500.[6]

It seems like we have had a kind of collective amnesia during the past 20 years, as a result of which we've ignored the customer in the design of products and services. The commoditization and technologification of services has been the priority, and the customer experience has lost out. The focus has been on digitalization, technology platforms, value chains, and call-center costs, and organizations took their eye off their customers as a result. Demos (a UK government think tank) describes the consequence as "a fundamental disconnect between services and people" and says that society has changed faster than service organizations. When they say this, they mean that customers have embraced brands, luxury, symbolic value, and design when it comes to products, but with services, the offerings simply haven't

> **"Oh my God, we have ignored our customers for the past 10 years!"**
> —*Insight from an executive with a national betting company, after realizing that their huge investment in technology platforms meant that they had stopped thinking about the customers.*

been available. More recently the customer experience has been on the agenda in many organizations, but as I've mentioned, it has been considered a feature of a product or service—something to be *added to* the design process, rather than something that *drives* it. It's time, therefore, to catch up and focus the organization on the customer and the customer experience.

According to a RightNow Technologies survey, 85% of respondents revealed that they've had customer experiences so dreadful that they've yelled, cursed, hit and broken things, suffered headaches, felt their chests tighten, and even cried. Only 3% of respondents reported that they have never had a negative experience with a company.[7]

So why are customer experiences so poor? Because organizations are not oriented toward the customer experience, responsibility for it is fragmented, it is cross-silo, and there are few key performance indicators (KPIs) that target experience explicitly. Jot down who has responsibility in your organization for the customer experience. You will probably find that responsibility is fragmented and lies with a multitude of people, spread across the many silos of your organization. Is there a culture of discussing the customer experience at management meetings or around the coffee machine? Do you listen to what your customers have to say about their experiences? The answer is most likely that it is on the agenda, but it is not the central theme for discussion. A new paradigm for service has arrived, one in which the customer experience is a primary driver of innovation in service organizations. According to a study, 95% of senior business leaders believe that the next competitive differentiator is customer experience,[8] and in 2018 the *Wall Street Journal* pronounced, "Customer Experience Is the Key Competitive Differentiator in the Digital Age."[9]

We will soon see the emergence of experience-centric organizations across all areas of business. These are organizations in which digitalization, technology platforms, value ecologies, and business models will all become means to achieve the unique experiences that customers value. Organizations will become experts at orchestrating their offerings in order to co-create memorable experiences with customers. Now's the time to get a jump on your competitors by embracing the customer experience and making it your main company mission.

Why This Is a Trajectory You Cannot Ignore

This book is the outcome of many years of working in the field of customer experience, through which a logical trajectory, discussed next, emerged. When the main market differentiator is the customer experience, delivering a superior experience becomes increasingly prioritized within the organization. Over time, as competition increases around the customer experience, and organizations focus more on it, it will inevitably become the company's main mission. The organizational imperative will then be to refocus and align the company around the customer experience. When this occurs, the organization can be termed *experience-centric*.

Embracing experience centricity allows for an immense clarity of purpose for an organization, and for disparate parts of the organization to understand both this trajectory and their role in making it happen. It simplifies and mobilizes the organization around a simple concept—simple to understand, but requiring ambition and a deft touch to implement.

The Inevitable Endpoint of a Long Journey

We are on multiple converging paths toward the experience-centric organization. On the one hand, hypercompetition means that customers have their choice of providers and thus can choose the experience they prefer. Differentiation in the market comes, therefore, from a superior customer experience. On the other hand, companies are investing in improving their customer experience, and there is now a race to differentiate experiences.

A second, parallel development relates to branding. Corporate branding has been emphasized for many years in many organizations, and companies are working hard to combine internal and external branding to create a consistent solution. Branding is moving from *promising* a customer experience to *delivering* a customer experience. This shifts the focus of the brand toward customer interactions with your service or product and how to deliver on the experiential promise you make. This new focus requires understanding the interactions that the customer has each and every time they use your service, as well as a different organizational structure. That is, it demands an alignment within the organization around the experience you want the customer to have.

A third experience trajectory is the experience economy itself. This is deepening every day. We have entered a period in which the experiential is central to our lives. We are not rational economic beings; we value experiences, and we seek them out. As Soren Kierkegaard clearly stated, life is not a problem to be solved, but a reality to be experienced. It seems that we, as a society, are in a stage where we have embraced this and are now willing and able to see the experiential in everything.

There are also economic and market explanations as to why the experience economy is expanding and deepening. We have more disposable income than past generations. Earlier, it was a big deal in a household to get a functional product, such as a washing machine or a dishwasher. These appliances are taken for granted now, and we expect more. We have opened our eyes to experiences, and at the same time, better experiences are available. Competition is now evaluated through customer experience.

 ### When a Washing Machine Provided Family Entertainment

This story not only shows the range of entertainment available in the English countryside in the '70s, but also what captivated us at that time. When I was a kid, our family couldn't afford an automatic washing machine, and my mother, a working mother, still used an old, secondhand manual washing machine with rollers to squeeze the water out of clothes. She would use a whole day to wash clothes, on top of her demanding job.

In 1970 we bought an automatic washing machine. A Hotpoint automatic! We were amazed by the technological marvel that promised to dose powder, wash, rinse, and spin clothes, without us even having to be anywhere near it. It was so exciting that we all placed chairs in front of the machine and watched a full cycle—90 minutes! We were in awe the whole time at how it could do all of this.

OK, we only had two black-and-white TV channels at that time, and it was winter in the country, but looking back, it still seems crazy. There are several things to learn from this story, though. The experience of the machine was new and amazing, and entertaining. It came from new technology for the time; and for many years after, technological advancement was the reason for buying products. Now we just assume the technology works, and we look for experiences from the use of a product, not from its technology. In contrast to my childhood experience, we now have experiential overload: Instagram, Facebook, Messenger, hundreds of TV channels, YouTube, films, cafés, and more. Most families now have a higher standard of living and expect to have a washing machine (and a dishwasher), so the novelty effect is not there. Our economy today stretches to other experiential things such as holidays, services, socializing, and the like. Technology has delivered and moved on, and it frees us up to look for other things in our lives: valuable experiences.

Finally, technological advances mean that today almost all products and services function adequately. This was not the case 30 years ago, when we often made choices based on technical performance and reliability. We no longer need to expend the effort to do this; we understand when buying a dishwasher that it will wash our dishes, or when buying a toothbrush that it will clean our teeth. This frees us up to focus on how it makes us feel, rather than what it does.

Together these developments have created a new paradigm in society, one in which the customer experience is the main motivator of our choices and therefore the key differentiator in the market. This applies not only to luxury consumption, but to each and every consumer decision we make. We make experiential evaluations of our purchases, and we judge them based on the experiential outcome. As we will see in Chapter 2, our brains are wired to continually estimate and evaluate our experiences—a fact we are only now realizing. Buying a budget airline ticket is a trade-off between experience and cost, and we make a decision based on our perception of the total experience, which includes all aspects of our customer journey: ordering tickets, checking in, traveling, and ending our journey. This doesn't mean that cost is unimportant, but rather that cost is weighed in terms of experience and we experientially evaluate both the offering and its delivery. The choice, even for low-price solutions, is based on an experiential cost-benefit judgment. This judgment helps us make decisions: we consider how differing competitive offerings rate according to our expected experiences, our earlier experiences, and the opinions of others in relation to price.

Why Has It Taken So Long?

Society is well into the experience economy, as described by Pine and Gilmore in their book from 1999. This is an economy in which desirable customer experiences are key to value. *The Experience Economy* (Harvard Business School Press) was a groundbreaking book for me. It identified one of the central truths of the economy—that we are driven by experiences, not functions. It used Starbucks as an example, showing how it is possible for people to functionally make good coffee themselves for a few cents, but they instead prefer to spend several

Interview with Olof Schybergson

As CEO of Fjord, Olof Schybergson knows a lot about digital transformation. Fjord is a part of Accenture Interactive, and now has over a thousand designers spread over 27 offices. This makes them one of the largest design and innovation consultancies in the world. Olof believes strongly in design as a strategic resource and argues here for its role in the transformation of whole industries.

I agree 100% with the trajectory described in this book. Experience fundamentally is the single trait that most clearly links the most successful companies in the world. Customer obsession and taking a human lens and really delivering a great experience is a red thread that connects the organizations that are winning in the world. At Fjord we simplify the term *customer experience* and talk just about experience, so that it also includes the employee experience. Business tomorrow is built by delivering excellent experiences, whether toward end customers or employees.

I like the term *experience-centric organization*. When you say "customer-focused," it assumes that the constituent is the customer and their purpose in life is to consume and buy things. Experience can be applied to all people and includes the employee, the customer, the patient, the citizen, all categories. It starts with the customer experience, then moves to the customer-facing employees and progressively back through the organization.

At Fjord we have seen a shift at work, where more and more of the requests from clients are looking at the customer and employee experience or purely the employee experience. There is a trend in this direction to compete for talent. You need to offer a strong value proposition for employees and a strong employee experience. When the project focus is upon a superior customer experience, companies realize they also need to change the employee experience. This is especially true for the customer-facing employees, so it is important to enable them. This causes great challenges for companies that are competing for talent.

Q: Do you think organizations are prepared for this transformation?

A: Organizations are wholly unprepared. Woefully. Most large organizations are set up under an industrial model, with business units and KPIs, and the goal is optimizing within them. To provide a fantastic customer experience across everything the customer does, you need to reorient the organization around the customer. Instead of talking about marketing and sales as different business units, you should obsess over customer moments.

Most organizations are not set up or organized for experience and are unprepared or structurally incapable of collaborating across business units. The experience needs to become strategic and used to reorient how the organization thinks. Those who don't face up to the need for transformation toward an experience focus will disappear and be quickly replaced. It will become a game of survival. When we worked with Sprint, [CEO] Marcelo Claure said, "I have never thought of my organization like this. I thought of my organization as 12 different channels to market. Now you have reoriented how I think. To provide the best possible experience, we need to put the human in the center and orient around key moments that matter across channels. That is where it becomes very real."

> **"Those who don't face up to the need for transformation toward an experience focus will disappear and be quickly replaced. It will become a game of survival."**

Q: What is the experiential DNA of an organization?

A: The evolution of brand DNA is experiential DNA. A brand is built through a set of experiences and the collection of those experiences becomes the brand. If there is a mismatch between the experience and what the brands advertising is telling you, you will intuitively trust your experiences more than the advertising. So marketing and advertising have evolved into becoming experiential.

Many organizations cannot express their org DNA. A lot of CEOs recognize that they have a challenge doing this, and they look toward other organizations that are experience-obsessed. They know that they have to do the same, but don't know how to go about it.

Instead of "Here are a bunch of products to push out," the thinking should be "Who are my customers and how can I best be relevant to them and provide an experience for them?" This is a monumental battle and takes time. Short-term crises and the trench warfare of the everyday get in the way of significant, long-term improvements and delay this [shift].

The concept of loyalty is radically changing. Companies should ask, "How can I be loyal to my customers rather than make them loyal to me?" The answer is to sustainably, over time, ensure that every moment and every interaction is relevant and meaningful depending upon customer need and expectation.

dollars going to a coffee chain. Why would economically rational people choose to spend over 10 times as much on something like this? Now, we are all familiar with the coffee experience, we understand that Starbucks is not in the business of selling coffee; it is in the business of providing experiences.

It has been 20 years since *The Experience Economy* was published. The rational economic human being has now been put to rest (see more about this in Chapter 6), and even economists now understand that human behavior, emotions, and feelings are central to how we function as people. This all seems obvious; however, the journey, which in many ways was signified 20 years ago, has not reached its end.

The Experience Economy Is Central to Our Lives

In 2018, a newspaper journalist called Elle Hunt decided to find out if ditching avocado toast lunches and café lattes would allow her to save enough to buy a flat. This was based on criticism from real estate agents berating millennials for spending money on fancy sandwiches rather than buying apartments. Hunt went to a financial advisor, who told her it might just be possible to save up a deposit if she changed her lifestyle and became frugal for a period. After trying for several weeks, Hunt found she was saving a lot of money, but concluded that the experiences she gained from her social activities, coffees, and avocado toasts were more valuable to her than saving toward an apartment. That is, the experience economy, the economy of here and now, was more important for her than delaying gratification for later home ownership. Experiences have become a central part of our lives.[10]

The Power of Desirable Experiences

If I asked you when Apple last launched a new iPhone, the majority of you would be able to give me a fairly precise date, and even probably tell me something about the expectations for the one coming up next. If I asked you about when Hewlett Packard last launched a printer, few of you would know. Why? One is desirable, the other not. Desirability is currency, and distorts the normal rules of marketing.

Instead of having to subsidize to get customers over to your service, if you offer a desirable experience, customers will seek you out. They will switch because they want to. You will not have to bribe them, and you will not have to incite them to come over to you. People will gravitate toward your service, because it is something that they want, rather than the solution that may be different, but is no better than a competitor's. The ability to deliver a consistent and memorable user experience is the most important strategic asset a business can have.

Customers are looking for emotional connections through experiences, but ones that they might not always be able to explain, even though they understand and identify with these experiences when they have them. This is a key part of experience-centric solutions: delivering something that "hearts and souls identify with," and that resonate with something in the consumer's being. To quote Howard Schultz, CEO of Starbucks, "We are not in the business of filling bellies, we are in the business of filling souls."[11]

> "The minute they set eyes on it, they feel something that they might not be able to define. But it's something that their hearts and souls identify with. It's something they want to be a part of."
> —*CNET*[15]

If such experiences are now a key driver in the market, then delivering them should become the focus of organizations acting in this market. Putting this in the context of the CNET quote, organizations should focus on developing and delivering services that inspire feelings that customers might not be able to define, but that they identify with on some deeper level and that they want to be a part of—desirable experiences. Doesn't that sound like something your company needs to deliver?

Even Low-Cost Solutions Can Be Experiential

In the experience economy everything is judged experientially, even low-cost solutions. Returning to an earlier example, when you evaluate a low-cost airline, you make experiential judgments based on cost related to the expected experience: Can I live with the discomfort and hassle of the low-cost airline? Would I prefer less transfer time? How difficult is it to change a ticket? All of these are experiential decisions that you consider as a whole based on previous experience and expectations. As stated previously, where there is competition, it is the experientially better alternative that wins. However, some believe that the customer experience is evaluated on the degree of entertainment included. This comes from viewing Disney as a leading provider of experiences and wanting to copy their model. This is wrong and has led a lot of organizations in the wrong direction. There are many situations in which the customer is looking for a functional solution, and focusing on functional experiences can create great value. As we will see later in the book, the "extraordinary ordinary experience" can be low-cost and still offer high experiential value.

Airbnb Focused on the Experience from the Start

From the first minute, Airbnb as an organization was focused on the guest experience, and that turned out to be their route to success. At the time, there were many other rental sites offering accommodations, yet the competitors focused on the functional aspect of listing rentals as objects, and not on the experiential aspect of what it felt like to be a guest. Both Airbnb and its competitors listed apartments, but only Airbnb focused on delivering the experience of staying in one.

The experiential focus was there from the start, and is part of Airbnb's DNA. During the company's founding period, when the founders rented out beds in their own apartment, guests each found a small pile of coins by their beds so that they could buy subway tickets. This was because the founders, as hosts, knew how difficult it could be to arrive in a country with large notes and be stuck at a subway machine that needs small coins for travel. This was a small but practical gift that had little impact on the profit margin, but an immense impact on the guest experience. It was a clear benevolent act, and communicated that Airbnb had your best interests at heart. Perceived benevolence, as we will see later, has a massive effect on our experience, and let's face it, how many companies can you think of that are benevolent toward customers?

Shortly thereafter, the founders focused on the photography of Airbnb apartments because they wanted guests to "experience the experience" before arriving, and good photographs offer that opportunity. They understood that the first part of the experiential journey for a tourist was not the stay itself. People want to stimulate that buzz you get before you travel, the expectation of something great, and Airbnb tapped in to that.

This was the company's experiential value proposition—"to experience the experience"—and at the time, it jumped out and caught your attention. Compared to other sites offering apartments, holiday stays, and couch surfing, what set Airbnb apart was the experience that it offered. At the same time, this was supported by touchpoints and platforms that made it easy to sign up and book.

It has taken a lot of deep thought and great design work to get Airbnb to where it is now. The company's recent focus on linking apartments to experiences and developing experiential guides shows that its trajectory is becoming even more experiential. Airbnb is stealing a lead by bringing the experience into everything it does. It is experience-centric.

The extraordinary ordinary experience (more on this in Chapter 6) is a way of providing exceptional yet functional experiences without adding entertainment. It focuses on getting the job done, and shows that even highly functional solutions can be designed to be memorable. It's all about knowing the experience you should give, rather than adding entertainment. As we will see later, memorable experiences and entertainment are not always the same thing. For example, I hate having to pick up packages at my (not so local anymore) post office, and if the post office clerk tried to entertain me, I think I would hit them. The experience of picking up a package does not need to be entertaining, but it can be enjoyable and memorable: that is, it can be an extraordinary ordinary experience.

Aarstiderne's Experience-Centric Approach

Aarstiderne (pronounced "Orrstiderna") is an award-winning Danish thought leader in the area of ecological food delivery and ecological transformation. They have an experiential vision, an idealistic mission, and a drive for change that translates into a successful experiential offering and permeates everything they do. This has made them the first profitable ecological food delivery service, and in the past five years they've seen a whopping 600% increase in profits. However, not everything in their development has been easy: they have learned the hard way about getting the organization to fit around the experience they want to provide.

Aarstiderne has always had a mission to change what we eat, and to move people toward ecologically sourced and local produce. What is interesting is that they have created an experiential offering that is not only successful, but also has an interesting service ecology. The offering is built up from several smaller offerings, each operating synergistically with the others to center the experience around the family: there's a focus on parent-initiated family meals, another around children as future meal makers, and a third emphasizing children's closeness to nature. The main offering rotates around delivering ecological food boxes to customers' homes. This was Aarstiderne's first offering and is their most successful today, although it has evolved from selling a set of in-season vegetables to also offering ingredients for a set of meals that a family can make together. This changes the company's role from one of sourcing and distributing high-quality produce to one of curating home experiences. The key is in the combination of high-quality produce and family collaboration, with the idea being that everyone in the house can take part in preparing the food that is delivered.

When it comes to children, way back in 2003 Aarstiderne split up part of their original farm near Elsinore in Denmark into small plots of land where school classes prepared the soil, sowed seeds, nurtured the land, and picked their vegetables each year. Aarstiderne developed a clear, dramatic curve

Source: Aarstiderne and Have til Mave.

for farming activity, culminating in a harvest festival. The children fired up outdoor pizza ovens, rolled out outdoor kitchen units, and prepared vegetable pizza (among other things) to bake and eat—all based on what they had grown themselves. Not only did this give them an understanding of where food comes from, but it also highlighted the quality of homegrown food, demonstrated the ups and downs of a season, and gave them the fantastic experience of preparing, cooking, and eating their own vegetables in a festival atmosphere. What could be a better experiential closure than that?

Then, as there should be, the Aarstiderne experience had a neat little trick in the tail. The kids each received a cookbook, with the recipes for the food they had made. Each cookbook contained a preformatted letter for the child to sign and give to their parents, saying that they would like to take part in making food more regularly at home.

Together, this created an experiential world of interlocked offerings, all aimed at heightening the experience of the participants, and with a mission of changing food consumption for the better. The school gardens were so successful that they became a separate entity in 2006 and were scaled up from 2014. Have til Mave ("From Garden to Stomach"), as they are now called, has 40 school gardens in Denmark and has started a national initiative to develop culinary school gardens.

The success of Aarstiderne and Have til Mave is a great example of an experiential focus that works at multiple levels. At the functional level it teaches about the life cycle of plants and about food production, and it delivers high-quality produce to people's homes. At the emotional level, through its dramatic curve, it produces mastery and pride in children, delivers aesthetic and olfactory experiences, supports family integration, and fosters children's independence, confidence, and respect for the outdoors. At the self-expressive level, it allows families to express their family values to others (e.g., through the highly visible packing boxes outside their homes), and at the idealistic level, it allows people to be a part of a movement. All of this should identify these two companies as experience-centric, and I would agree. However, they have done this the hard way and probably would not identify themselves as being experience-centric. They would more likely describe themselves as idealists with a successful commercial solution, and this has led them to struggle through some of the structural and organizational challenges identified later in the book. They have a desirable offering, but they have struggled with experience fulfillment, enabling, and structure. Yet, despite all of these struggles, their experiential focus has driven them forward and made them stand out, making them a household name in Denmark.

Experience-Centric Goes Far Beyond Customer-Centric

Many organizations confuse customer-centric and experience-centric, and their first instinct when deciding to focus on customer experiences is to look at how they can add something to their existing customer-centric initiatives. This is a tempting thought, but it's wrong. There is a very different attitude and approach in the experience-centric organization than there is in the customer-centric organization. The following table shows how the experience-centric organization is a step change away from customer-centric:

CRITERIA	CUSTOMER-CENTRIC	EXPERIENCE-CENTRIC
Value goal	Customer satisfaction	Experiential desirability
Basic philosophy	What do our customers want	What do we want our customers to feel
Basic approach	Reactive	Proactive
Organizational structure	Siloed according to business processes	Experientially aligned
Key terms	Value proposition, segments, brand promise	Experiential value proposition, individuals, brand experience
Orientation	Services as products	Experiences delivered through services
Brand orientation	Broadcasting a brand promise	Delivering a brand experience

As you can see, there are very different approaches taken by the experience-centric organization, right down to the value goal of the organization itself. Moving the goal from customer satisfaction to experiential desirability requires a very different approach within the organization—one that has structural implications. The experience-centric organization impacts the ways of both thinking and doing within the organization.

Experience Centricity Challenges Institutional Logics

All organizations have internal logics that describe their shared values, beliefs, and practices. These are hard to identify and difficult to describe when viewed from the inside, but often are obvious from the outside. They are a core part of the organization's DNA, and can be difficult to change. Certain logics can persist in an organization a long time after concerted organizational change efforts.

When working with organizations, I have experienced product-centric logics in a global footwear manufacturer, technology-centric logics in a global telco, and process-centric logics in a major Nordic logistics organization. The experience-centric organization challenges these institutional logics and often requires transforming embedded values, beliefs, and practices. This might seem daunting, but in my experience there is a clarity of purpose that comes with the experience-centric approach. Experience centricity is something that everyone in the organization can identify with, and it encourages organizational alignment.

Common to all of the organizations I have worked with is a recognition that a transformation toward experience centricity is necessary and that the organization needs assistance to achieve it. The book shows different strategies, based on my research and collaboration with many different organizations, that can be applied to change institutional logics.

Wait—Haven't I Heard This Before? What's New? Why Should I Read This Book?

The theme of customer experience is not new, and you have probably heard about it through several converging areas—corporate branding, cultural branding, the experience economy, design thinking. All of these areas are complementary to the message in this book.

The value of this book is threefold. First, it identifies and gives a name to the phenomenon that we are experiencing in the market and in business. Just giving it a name has great value, and I have seen several light-bulb moments where people have immediately grasped the term and adopted it as a North Star. Second, the book brings different areas together into a unified focus that gives organizations clarity of purpose. Finally, it offers advice on how to transform your organization to become experience-centric. There are clear stages and levels to this process.

Put another way, the book describes the bigger picture, puts it into perspective, and helps you make the transformation that is necessary to embark on an experience-centric trajectory.

Hopefully this book can contribute to important conversations and will help people realize, "Yes, that is what we need to do, and we need to do it together." Further, I hope it will give you an internal terminology to facilitate those discussions. Finally, I hope the book gives you an approach to and an understanding of how to implement experience centricity throughout your organization.

Where Do I Look for Best Practices?

When we're at our best, we don't wait for external pressures. We are internally driven to improve our services, adding benefits and features, before we have to. We lower prices and increase value for customers before we have to. We invent before we have to.

—JEFF BEZOS, AMAZON CEO [12]

At this stage, you will have to look carefully for best practices, as there are perhaps only a handful of truly experience-centric organizations. Few organizations could claim to have had an experience-centric approach from the start, but several have arrived there through sheer doggedness. They are the companies that have had a visionary leader who has imposed that vision on the organization. However, many more are on their way and getting close, without necessarily using the term or having the overarching model for how to do it. They all share a clarity of purpose—that the customer experience is the driver of their organization—but they differ in their ways of approaching experience centricity and making the organization work. Some have become experience-centric through strategic and tactical thinking, but most have approached it the hard way. They have developed highly experiential offerings as a start-up, had success, and afterward had to painfully forge an organization that can scale the offering or support it.

I present examples of organizations that I consider to be experience-centric, or at least experience-focused. Some are high-end, such as Aesop, while others are more everyday. Common to all is an attention to detail, and the ability to align around the customer experience. This is the key success factor, and one that is not easily achieved. Apple, unsurprisingly, is the star performer, and although it's overused as an example, there is an important message here: the first trillion-dollar company in the world has had an experience-centric strategy for about 20 years, and has achieved great success during this period. Apple's success has not come through luck, but by having a crystal-clear vision of starting with the experience and working backward throughout the organization. This is something Steve Jobs explained in 1997.[13]

Amazon is another example, and at the time of writing, it is tipped to become the second trillion-dollar company in the world. Jeff Bezos is perhaps the one person who, from the start, has been totally fixated on the customer experience. The largest innovations in online shopping came from Amazon, and now, the greatest recent innovation in brick-and-mortar stores is coming from Amazon too, with the walk-in, walk-out supermarket project. It is no surprise that Amazon is held up as a model, then, because it has done the work to continually improve the experience of its customers. A recent article by CB Insights shows that for Amazon, building a high lifetime value among its customer base through proactive delight has been a powerful differentiator, and it has paid off. The average lifetime value of a Prime customer was estimated at $2,500 in 2017.[14]

Keywords for Experiential Transformation

Naming things is really important, and having a good descriptive name for something, when it fits the context, can actually contribute to organizational change. I found this when introducing the basics of service design to one of Scandinavia's largest insurance companies. Terms such as *touchpoints* and *customer journeys* were new, but they rapidly became integrated into everyday conversations in the company and thereby rapidly became a part of people's way of work. So, terms do matter, and I hope that the following terms help initiate change in your organization by giving different perspectives on some familiar concepts. I introduce them up front so that when you meet them later, you will have some idea of what I mean.

The *experiential value proposition* (EVP) is the perceived value of your service *offering* when viewed through an experiential lens by the customer. Since it is a proposition, it has not yet been experienced, and therefore represents expected experiential value. The EVP comprises a mix of functional, emotional, self-expressive, and idealistic factors, which both include benefits but also costs, and risk.

The EVP can be broken down into two main parts: what you want to offer and what your customers perceive as being offered. The first should be your design target, an essential part of every project. The second is what customers think you offer them from an experiential point of view and is the more important of the two. This includes individual, social and cultural factors and can only be understood through dialog with customers.

In this book, I use the term *offering* rather than *value proposition*, because it is more down-to-earth and customer-focused. While *value proposition* might be the academically correct term, it reflects a company-out direction, and encourages you to focus on what you are proposing to the customer. The term *offering*, on the other hand, is viewed from the customer's side: "What are you offering me?" When you find people in your organization using the term *offering* from a customer's point of view, particularly in terms of experience, then you know your organization has shifted its weight and begun to view itself through the customer's eyes.

Your *experiential DNA* is the core building block that your organization uses for working with the customer experience. Similar to human DNA, it defines you and what you can and cannot offer as a customer experience. Your experiential DNA is a mix of who you are, who you have been, and who you want to be. It is balanced between the customer's perspective and the organizational perspective. In other words, internal culture plays an important part in your DNA, but it is balanced by the external customer view, which is based on earlier experiences and expectations. Experiential DNA is a mix of your mission, vision, and values, your brand strategy and history, how you view yourself, how you are viewed by your customers, and your heritage.

Experiential DNA includes a large degree of storytelling, in which heroes, myths, and key historical events are woven together. But it is not a fiction; it is something everyone within the organization can identify with, because it is authentic, shared, and felt. The term *experiential DNA* should be well understood and cherished in the organization because it defines what you can and cannot offer. Understanding your experiential DNA is not always easy, and can require considerable soul-searching. However, it is crucial to delivering the right experience, and identifying it is one of the important steps in translation (see Chapter 7).

A question that should regularly be asked within the organization is whether a project, an investment, an offering, or even an employee is a good fit with the DNA of the organization. This can even be turned into a regular organizational mantra: "Does it fit our DNA?" Everything the organization does should fit its experiential DNA.

The *experiential journey* is the journey that a customer takes in relation to their use of your product or service. It can often be divided into prepurchase, purchase, and post-purchase phases, and further divided up into use phases with discrete *experiential moments*. The experiential journey can be fine-tuned to incorporate expected *touchpoints* along the way—the tangible and intangible points of contact between the customer and the service/product. Touchpoints can be direct (e.g., a letter, a welcome package, signage inside a building, a logo, an SMS, a company employee) or indirect (e.g., word of mouth). Understanding the touchpoints along the experiential journey, and the experience customers have when interacting with them, is one of the first stages of becoming experience-centric.

Experience *orchestration* is pretty self-explanatory. You can imagine an orchestra either playing together or playing discordantly and transfer that thought to your customer experience. There is a need for orchestration within the organization, to get people to work together to deliver the experiential value proposition. A shared company vision, shared direction, and shared humility are required to develop an organizational culture. The company's leadership is key to developing, sharing, and living this culture. In addition, the term *orchestration* should be used regularly within the organization—for example, "How do we orchestrate this service experience, and who is responsible for orchestration in this project?"

The company needs to have an *orchestrator*, a person responsible for the customer experience. That person should be part of the leadership and may be given the title of chief orchestrator, chief experience director, or similar. In addition, each and every project needs to have an orchestrator who is responsible for the experience of that service, and this person should report to the chief orchestrator. Finally, the experience itself requires orchestration during delivery to tailor the experience to the customer and ensure that the experiential journey functions as required.

Infusion refers to spreading a certain way of thinking and doing throughout the organization. Imagine placing a tea bag in a cup of hot water and watching the color and flavor spread in the water. That is what infusion is about in experiential terms—spreading the experiential focus everywhere in the organization. Infusion doesn't happen on its own and requires constant effort to maintain its momentum. Infusion is a positive process and requires optimism in the organization. Without this optimism, infusion is blocked, so before making the change (i.e., placing the tea bag in the water), you need to make sure the organization is ready for it. This preparedness might come from identifying your place on the path toward experience centricity (see Chapter 2), and moving at the right speed through those steps.

The fastest and shortest way from A to B is a straight line. In an organization, this means getting everyone aligned with and contributing toward experience centricity. This creates a readiness throughout the organization for the experience you want to deliver. *Alignment* means getting the whole organization behind the experience you want your customers to have. It means everyone giving 100% toward supporting the experience that you want to deliver, and not least, understanding their role in this. Alignment, infusion, and ownership all interrelate. Whereas infusion is about the shared understanding of the experience, alignment is about applying the capabilities to make it happen.

Ownership is an individual and collective feeling of participation in and influence on the experience to be delivered, and is vital to its success. Ownership brings pride, and these two aspects go hand in hand. Ownership and pride motivate people, encourage collaboration, and make people go the extra mile when needed. Ownership has a strong intrinsic element, meaning that people self-motivate toward the common good. However, ownership also requires that the individual is recognized in the organization, that they become visible and are openly rewarded. Ownership can be seen as the result of infusion and alignment working together. When you know and are confident in your role in the organization, then infusion has been successful and you can align your contribution to the whole.

One of the challenges to ownership is that peripheral parts of the organization, those furthest from the experience delivery, might not see their role. This is not because they are not important, but mainly because they themselves cannot see their contribution. Internal symbolic gestures, specific activities, and internal storytelling all help to bring peripheral roles into the organization and encourage ownership.

Behavioral authenticity describes how well the behaviors of your touchpoints fit with your experiential DNA. We all know that people have a tone of voice and behaviors, but so do apps, web pages, and almost all other touchpoints. Identifying the correct behaviors for your DNA, and ensuring behavioral authenticity, is a key part of developing and maintaining experience centricity.

Endnotes

1   American Express, "American Express 2017 Customer Service Barometer," *https://amex.co/2VVRvqD*.

2   Devon McGinnis, "Research Shows Customer Loyalty Hangs in the Balance: 'State of the Connected Customer Report'," Salesforce, October 24, 2016, *https://sforce.co/2JHJP9V*.

3   David Clarke and Ron Kinghorn, *Experience Is Everything: Here's How to Get It Right* (New York: PwC, 2018), *https://pwc.to/2XagMio*.

4   American Express, "American Express 2017 Customer Service Barometer," *https://amex.co/2VVRvqD*.

5   Chris Bucholtz, "The $62 Billion Customer Service Scared Away" (NewVoiceMedia blog), *http://bit.ly/2Xafrbd*.

6   Knowledge@Wharton, "Connecting Marketing Metrics to Financial Consequences," November 17, 2004, *https://whr.tn/2WcXIU7*.

7   RightNow Technologies (later acquired by Oracle), "2011 Customer Experience Impact Report Getting to the Heart of the Consumer and Brand Relationship," *http://bit.ly/2WsfYZa*.

8   Colin Shaw, *The DNA of Customer Experience: How Emotions Drive Value* (New York: Palgrave Macmillan, 2007).

9   Irving Wladawsky-Berger, "Customer Experience Is the Key Competitive Differentiator in the Digital Age," *Wall Street Journal*, April 20, 2018, *https://on.wsj.com/2HEwqNw*.

10 Elle Hunt, "Can You Really Save for a Deposit by Ditching Coffee and Toast?" *The Guardian*, January 29, 2018, *http://bit.ly/30OqgBY*.

11 Daniel Schorn, "Howard Schultz: The Star of Starbucks," CBS News, April 21, 2006, *https://cbsn.ws/2I89l58*.

12 Jeff Bezos annual letter to shareholders 2012, *http://bit.ly/2VSx8e8*.

13 Mike Cane, "Steve Jobs Insult Response," posted June 8, 2011, *http://bit.ly/2Xitw6N*.

14 CB Insights, "21 Lessons from Jeff Bezos' Annual Letters to Shareholders," October 16, 2018, *http://bit.ly/2I6BY2B*.

15 Chris Matyszczyk, "Why Apple Keeps Winning in Style," CNET, February 1, 2015, *https://cnet.co/2worGFt*.

2

Five Steps to Becoming Experience-Centric

This chapter places the previous chapter into the context of organizational transformation and experience maturity. It describes the five steps that organizations take to become experience-centric. After reading this chapter you will be able to position yourself on the experience-centricity maturity scale and develop a roadmap for the transformation of your organization.

Both a Sprint and a Marathon

After working with organizations and observing their challenges with customer experience, I have seen a pattern emerge in the steps they take, both in terms of how they understand experience centricity and in terms of activities and organizational change. These are summarized here as the five steps to becoming experience-centric (see Figure 2-1). Every company I have worked with has followed these steps quite closely, and you can use this process in your own organization as both a way of benchmarking your progress and a planning tool for development.

During the first stages, it is possible to sprint and get a fast foothold by taking a customer journey approach, but from then on, change becomes a longer-term process of organizational development to alter the internal logics of the organization (unless you are a start-up). This chapter describes the five-stage transition model to experience centricity and the characteristics of each stage.

CUSTOMER ORIENTED

Adapt existing offerings to the customer

Experience seen as top layer

JOURNEY ORIENTED

Understand service as a customer journey

Experience seen as process outcome

CUSTOMER CENTRIC

Reorient the organization toward the customer

Experience seen as important

EXPERIENCE ORIENTED

Understand service as experience

Experience seen as a key success factor

EXPERIENCE CENTRIC

Align around the experience

Experience is an organizational imperative

Figure 2-1. The five steps to experience centricity.

I am often asked if it is possible to jump over some steps or combine them. The answer is that you can leapfrog certain steps, depending on your organizational DNA, your flexibility to change, and the degree of change needed. If you are an incumbent with a long heritage, perhaps even an old monopolist (post, telecom), then you likely have a marathon ahead. If you are a newer organization, with a charismatic leadership team and a dynamic spirit as part of your DNA, then it is possible to move through the steps quickly. The main insights I have gained from organizational change are to plan carefully, get design onboard at an early stage, and don't do too much too soon. What this means in practice is unique to your organization.

The following sections describe each of the steps, its characteristics, and possible ways to fast-forward through the stage.

Stage 1: The Customer-Oriented Organization

Since you are reading this book, you are most likely past this first stage, but there are a surprising number of organizations that are still here. The customer-oriented organization looks at the world from the inside out, toward the customer. It has great belief in itself, possibly due to a history of earlier success. It views customers as segments and its offerings as products to be sold, taking a transactional view of relationships with customers. The customer-oriented organization uses Michael Porter's value-chain model and is deeply siloed as a result.[1]

A customer-oriented organization sees its product offerings as being fixed, and asks for customer input as a means of improving them, rather than considering changing the offerings altogether based on customer feedback.

Although the customer-oriented organization views the customer experience as one of several important factors, it's akin to a top layer of icing on a cake that has already been baked. When it comes to services, this type of organization has not yet embraced the customer journey as an important innovation tool, although it might (wrongly) consider its process flows to be customer journeys. The main characteristic of a customer-oriented organization are described in the following table:

CRITERIA	CUSTOMER-ORIENTED
Focus	Organizational efficiency, units shipped
Basic philosophy	How can we adapt our products to suit the customer?
Basic approach	Organizationally focused
	Incremental adaptation of existing solutions
Organizational structure	Strongly siloed according to business processes
Key terms	Value chain, segments, internal metrics
Orientation	Services as products
Brand orientation	Broadcasting a brand promise
Customer experience seen as...	An add-on—really there in name only
Typical quote	"We have a new service; could you look at it and improve the customer experience?"
Tactic to progress	Introduce customer journey thinking and visualization
	Develop concept service ideas

Ways to Fast-Forward as a Customer-Oriented Organization

To progress quickly from the customer-oriented organization stage, introducing customer journeys works well. This is because the journey approach encapsulates a customer view, time, touchpoints, and

Insights from Nicholas Ind

Nicholas Ind is a branding guru with several books to his name. He has worked with and advised a broad range of commercial organizations such as Adidas and Patagonia, as well as nonprofit organizations such as Greenpeace and UNICEF. As he explains, it is important to him that an experience focus is part of the culture of an organization.

It is a deep consumer desire to have interesting, positive experiences. There is a pleasure in buying a product, and the experience of using it gives pleasure also. Customers are increasingly demanding, and those companies who do not understand this will underperform.

An experience focus needs to be in the culture of the organization. You need responsibility from the top and commitment from all senior people. You need a chief executive and others in the leader group to work together on the experiential focus. If not, then details will be wrong and things will go wrong. My fear would be that you create a customer experience department and that would marginalize it.

Transformation toward experience centricity means a focus on:

- Leadership
- Emphasis and strategy that is centered on the experience
- Reevaluation of what you measure, what you reward, the people you employ, how you train them, and how you reward them

This is how I would prioritize them.

The CEO has to be a chief experience officer and the head of the organization. Orange, the telco that launched in the UK, is a good example. Hans Snook, as CEO, was completely focused on customers. When they got sold, Orange fell asleep when it comes to the customer experience. The set of values changed, and its experience focus became less clear. Snook had left.

Understanding customer experience is all about understanding what people feel. To be experience-centric you should never let customers become a piece of data in a market research report. This is not a surface thing, and when you dig below the surface, you uncover important aspects and thinking behind what people really experience. These are often existential needs that are not captured by numbers. Often organizations have barriers around them and learn about customers through the dead hand of research. The scientific approach to brand building in many organizations gets in the way of customer centricity. [Organizations] are often not structured around the customer, and a focus on data means that they often prevent themselves from understanding customers. Quantitative questions often give superficial answers when it comes to the customer experience.

"To be experience-centric you should never let customers become a piece of data in a market research report."

Most projects require a business case based upon a quantitative study to proceed, and that is more difficult to do with experiences and desires. There is a need for something to balance this quantitative focus. I recently compared two brands: one a fashion brand and the other a large telco. The fashion brand said that everything they do is based upon gut feelings, while the telco said it was all based upon quantitative decisions. My conclusion was that the quantitative approach often prevents an organization from really understanding customers.

During implementation, things get compromised in organizations. Convenience and expedience for company benefit will often trump the customer experience. For example, an airline brand I know focused upon the travel experience, but then the call center was only staffed between 10 a.m. and 5 p.m. The expediency detracts from experience and customers end up disappointed. Therefore, there is a need to follow the experience all the way through and ensure it's implemented in practice.

experience. In addition, the division of a journey into periods of before, during, and after use introduces a relationship concept rather than the transactional buy/sell model. Together, the journey and touch-point approach introduces some key elements of-experience-centric thinking: seeing through the customer's eyes, considering the experience before, during, and after a journey, and recognizing that customers move across silos during their journey. It also introduces design as an approach that facilitates collaboration between team members through co-design. As we will see in the next section, moving toward the journey-oriented organization is a step both the customer and the organization will notice. It creates huge momentum in the customer-oriented organization and propels it in the direction of experience centricity.

Stage 2: The Journey-Oriented Organization

This stage starts with some relatively small but successful projects to map the customer journey. At this stage, the journey is called a *customer* journey, rather than an *experiential* journey, although the customer experience should be reflected in your journey visualizations.

The journey-oriented organization recognizes the huge potential of the customer journey as a new view on innovation and invests quickly in developing this competence. The organization understands the value of customer journey mapping and is hungry for more.

The journey-oriented organization develops an appreciation of what design offers in this context. It is in the early phases of using design thinking and service design, and the journey orientation offers it several advantages:

1. It introduces the view and voice of the customer and often can result in a light-bulb moment regarding the value of a customer's perspective on a service.
2. It introduces an emotion-based view of the organization's service, showing how the customer travels across touchpoints (and silos).

3. It introduces touchpoints and highlights the way that customers interact with the service. Initially the organization may feel that touchpoints have limited value, but they quickly realize how many touchpoints they have, and how poorly coordinated they are across the organization. As a result, they come to understand how the offering as a whole is experienced through its parts.

4. Branding and marketing teams begin to take a more active role in service delivery and move from advertising and visual identity toward touchpoints. The idea of journey orchestration begins to take hold.

5. It introduces the visual and integrative skills of the designer. This is the start of an understanding that designers, particularly service designers, add value and have relevance for the organization.

6. It raises awareness that the customer experience is not simply good or bad, but can be nuanced and shift over time. The idea of using Net Promoter Score (*http://bit.ly/2ZKbLhf*) gains traction due to this heightened awareness.

The journey-oriented organization quickly starts to use terminology such as *customer journeys* and *touchpoints* and deploys journey mapping as standard practice, although at first without any clear specifications regarding what format the journey maps should have. For some of this innovation work, the organization uses external designers, who are seen as a valuable addition. The designers introduce four valuable aspects, which are then used to further develop the organization itself. First, designers bring *creativity* in that they are oriented around what can be, rather than what is. Second, they bring a visual approach to collaboration, and by visualizing they make tangible many of the aspects discussed in team workshops. Third, they bring a customer view, often introducing customer insights and voice into the organization in a different way than the norm. This galvanizes a customer perspective, which later leads to a customer-centric initiative in the organization. Finally, designers bring an *experiential focus* to their work and proposed solutions. They focus on the experience of customers (and staff), and not only have a terminology for it, but also prototype it at an early stage. In addition, they do a limited but relevant translation, matching the customer experience to the brand strategy of the organization.

The following table describes the key characteristics of the journey-oriented organization:

CRITERIA	JOURNEY-ORIENTED
Focus	Service delivery and consistency
Basic philosophy	How can we improve our products using a customer journey approach?
Basic approach	Organizationally focused
	Incremental adaptation of existing solutions
Organizational structure	Strongly siloed according to business processes, but now with some collaboration across silos
Key terms	Terms such as touchpoints, journeys, and voice of the customer are introduced
Orientation	Services as products delivered over time and across touchpoints
Brand orientation	Still focused on broadcasting a promise
Customer experience seen as...	Something that can be considered during the design process
Typical quote	"It really helps to see the whole journey and the individual parts."
Tactic to progress	Introduce the customer to customer journey thinking
	Develop a customer-centric initiative
	Develop concept service ideas

Ways to Fast-Forward as a Journey-Oriented Organization

To move through this phase as fast as possible, you need to do three things. First, invest in service design and look to develop a long-term relationship with a good service design company. At this stage, you need to find some designers that you feel you can work with, including over the long term. Second, introduce experiential mapping as a standard tool within the organization. As part of this, I recommend you focus on experiential fulfillment (see Chapter 3) and create your own templates for describing experiential journeys (see Chapter 6). This introduces a customer-oriented explanation of your services that is also visual. Third, establish a way of gaining customer insights as part of your projects, which means making sure that the teams start listening to customers (you can read about seeing, hearing, and being the customer in Chapter 4). If you do these three things, you will rapidly move through the journey phase toward the customer-centric phase.

To accelerate faster, establish a function in your organization related to customer journeys and customer experience. With careful planning, you can later develop this into the area responsible for experience design. However, the skills you need at this stage of maturity will be different and more functional than those needed later, so be prepared to change the mandate and leadership of this group once it's established.

At this point the journey-oriented organization will have developed a momentum and positivity toward change that will quickly orient them toward customer centricity.

Stage 3: The Customer-Centric Organization

The customer-centric organization has a very different worldview from the customer-oriented organization. Instead of asking how its existing offerings can be adapted to customers, the organization asks, "What offerings do we need to provide to satisfy customer needs?" This might sound like a subtle shift, but it is a profoundly different position. While the customer-oriented organization is still focused on itself as its main interest, and customers simply take what is offered, the customer-centric organization is genuinely focused on understanding the customer. This is a huge change, not only of leadership mindset but of organizational logics, in which the organization's "reason to be" is transformed into serving customers (which is what service is really about, right?). To do this, the organization has to go on a collective journey of understanding the customer.

This step toward customer centricity is usually sparked by journey mapping and involving customers in that process. The journey mapping approach brings customers in as co-designers, and the organization realizes that there are huge benefits to be gained from listening to customers and placing their voice at the heart of the organization.

The customer-centric organization augments journey thinking with a customer focus and a customer mindset. One of the main priorities of the customer-centric organization is satisfying customer needs, and large-scale initiatives are introduced to identify those needs and then convert them into services. As part of this process, there is a push to measure to what extent the customer's needs have been satisfied with quantitative metrics, such as Net Promoter Score.

The goal of this organization shifts from directly identifying the customer's needs to understanding their lives and lifestyle. The organization recognizes the importance of identifying latent customer needs, and the fact that customers are not always good at articulating what they want or need. This broadening of the view of customer need is an important precursor of the move toward experience centricity, since it introduces a social and cultural view of customers (although at this stage, it is latent and not explicitly discussed throughout the organization).

The customer-centric organization has a deeper understanding of what it means to deliver service, and this leads to a desire for long-term relationships with customers. However, it also makes the organization aware of its collaboration with external actors and how this relates to the customer. The organization begins to view the world using an actor network lens rather than a value chain one, and thus becomes aware of the importance of key internal and external actors as essential contributors to the customer experience. Further, the organization may realize it needs to develop new actor configurations to satisfy the customer needs that are identified, and establish strategic collaborations around customer needs as a result. This shift also introduces the customer as a key co-producer of value, as well as the customers' own networks as an important source of insight.

When it comes to the customer experience, there is a growing understanding of its importance within the organization, but this is framed in terms of satisfying needs, and by developing consistent and satisfactory experiences. There is still, as yet, poor terminology regarding customer experience within the organization, and the brand is still not fully focusing on the customer relationship or on translating the brand into experiences.

The following table summarizes the key characteristics of the customer-centric organization:

CRITERIA	CUSTOMER-CENTRIC ORGANIZATION
Focus	Value is created by providing what customers want, including over the long term
Basic philosophy	What services should we offer to make our customers loyal and satisfied?
Basic approach	Externally focused
	Development of customer-initiated solutions

CRITERIA	CUSTOMER-CENTRIC ORGANIZATION
Organizational structure	In flux from earlier siloed organization; customer responsibility visible on organizational chart
Key terms	Customer insights, voice of the customer, Net Promoter Score, life stages, customer lifetime value
Orientation	Services delivered over time and across touchpoints to provide relevant experiences and satisfy customer needs
Brand orientation	Early orientation toward service delivery
Customer experience seen as...	Something that supports customer satisfaction
Typical quote	"We need to offer something customers need, if we are to survive."
Tactic to progress	Move the conversations with the customer from "What do you want?" toward "Tell us more about yourself."

Ways to Fast-Forward as a Customer-Centric Organization

Moving through this phase of development takes longer than the previous stages. This is because it requires a fundamentally different organizational logic, one that takes time to infuse into the organization. Therefore, the emphasis here should be on developing and encouraging both formal and informal organizational structures to facilitate this step change. Storytelling, and sharing myths and examples within the organization is a strong way to accelerate this stage, especially when combined with images of customers, customer insight quotes, and repeated internal rewards for customer-focused activities. Stories about the time an employee went the extra mile for a customer become epics, and they help cement the new mindset.

KPIs for customer centricity should be developed. This is not an easy task, but it leads to important cross-silo reward mechanisms that recognize that achieving requires collaboration. There should be active discussion regarding the destruction of silos to create a new, cohesive structure based on customer needs. These can be customer journey-based structures, or customer life stage structures that are contextually dependent on your organizational DNA.

The organizational DNA plays a key role in this phase of development. There is a real danger of becoming entranced by your customer insights, so much so that you start to develop solutions from customer insights that do not fit with your DNA. Be aware here of your limitations as an organization, and spend time discussing and raising awareness of your organizational DNA. This can be framed as a return to the heritage of the organization, getting back to the basics of what you are good at, or a celebration of your heritage. However, you might genuinely identify a customer need that can radically innovate on your existing offerings. In this situation, you have a difficult choice between stretching your organization to change, or starting up a new organization to exploit this potential, possibly as a joint venture with other key actors.

The customer-centric organization works to create alignment around customer centricity, and it becomes the organization's mantra. This is important priming for the next step toward experience centricity.

Stage 4: The Experience-Oriented Organization

The experience-oriented organization builds on the customer-centric approach and forms a stepping-stone toward experience centricity. This is a relatively short-lived stage, because the organization realizes quite quickly that it needs to take a more radical approach to truly deliver desirable experiences.

In many ways, the previous stages have started a transformation that, like a supertanker, has a momentum that is difficult to stop. This move toward a greater focus on the customer experience comes from having closer customer contact. During the customer-centric stage, the organization realizes that customer centricity is not just about listening to customers. Indeed it is about *understanding* customers, and doing so in a much wider context. This fosters a greater focus on the lives of customers outside of the transactional sphere, and the addition of a cultural understanding of the customer (for more about this, see Chapter 10). The organization increasingly realizes that the customer-centric phase has perhaps focused too much on the functional aspects of the experience. The emotional aspects have also been considered, but the dominant logic in the organization is still centered on functional benefits.

The integration of design into the organization brings design and marketing closer together, and creates a shared understanding of the importance of the customer experience during this phase. This initiates a deeper discussion about designing for experience, and brings the brand closer to an involvement in experiential delivery.

In organizational terms, the customer-centric organization began to stretch the existing organizational logics and structure without radically changing them. The customer-centric phase required more of an organizational paradigm shift rather than radical organizational change. The experience-oriented organization stage incrementally adds to this by deepening the focus on the experience. It is at this stage that the organization begins to realize that transformational change is required to be able to adequately embrace the customer experience. At the same time, the organization is primed to make this transformation, since many realize that change is due. In this way, the momentum that has built up almost demands the organizational transformation that is about to happen.

The following table describes the key characteristics of the experience-oriented organization:

CRITERIA	EXPERIENCE-ORIENTED ORGANIZATION
Focus	Value is created by providing experiential benefits based on what customers want
Basic philosophy	How can we adapt our services to provide experiences based on what customers say they want?
Basic approach	Externally focused
	The addition of experiential benefits to functional benefits
Organizational structure	An incremental change from customer centricity that brings marketing and design closer together; increased focus on experiential metrics
Key terms	Experiential benefits, customer insights, Net Promoter Score, customer lifetime value
Orientation	Services delivered over time and across touchpoints to give emotional, in addition to functional, benefits
Brand orientation	Orientation toward customer experience as part of service delivery
Customer experience seen as...	Something that is central to customer satisfaction
Typical quote	"We need to add something experiential to customer's needs."
Tactic to progress	Shift from customer needs to customer experience as the starting point for all discussions

Ways to Fast-Forward as an Experience-Oriented Organization

The experience-oriented organization already has a customer focus and now has integrated an experiential orientation. This organization is therefore almost ready for the last step toward experience centricity. To accelerate this process, it is time to focus all development work on the customer experience and to initiate projects with an experiential brief. Customer contact should now be supplemented by an understanding of what customers feel, in addition to what they want. Further, the organization needs to discuss how best to organize to deliver on its experiential promise. This discussion should involve a closer collaboration between design and marketing, particularly brand management.

Stage 5: The Experience-Centric Organization

Welcome to the experience-centric organization! You have gone from customer orientation through a journey phase and customer phase and are now in the final stage: optimizing your organization to deliver valuable customer experiences. This section briefly describes the experience-centric organization. It is brief because there is a separate chapter (see Chapter 4) dedicated to the core behaviors of the experience-centric organization.

The experience-centric organization is a logical next step for a customer-centric organization because the customer-centric stage developed an organization with an extreme customer focus. This will have revealed the importance of the customer experience in their decision making, and make it clear that an experiential focus is the natural next stage of development.

Harder, Better, Faster, Stronger

The experience-centric organization knows the experience it wants to provide for its customers, and knows how customers perceive its offerings and brand. This kind of organization tries harder to deliver the experience that it has defined, since everybody there knows what experience to deliver and how to do so. The offering clearly differentiates itself as being better than its competitors and provides an experience that fits the DNA of the organization, making it difficult to copy. This organization is faster, because it has a natural ability to adapt to changes in outside culture and to any technological or market disruptions—it has an internal alignment around flexibility. And this organization is stronger, because it has a shared vision and cohesive reason for being, and a clear focus to work toward.

The following table describes the key characteristics of the experience-centric organization:

CRITERIA	EXPERIENCE-CENTRIC ORGANIZATION
Focus	Experiential desirability
Basic philosophy	What do we want our customers to feel?
Basic approach	Proactive and experiential
Organizational structure	Experientially aligned
Key terms	Experiential value proposition, translation, trendslation, experiential journey
Orientation	Experiences promised and delivered along an experiential journey
Brand orientation	Transparency of organizational DNA delivered through a desirable customer experience
Customer experience seen as...	The core source of value
Typical quote	"How does that suggestion impact our desired experience?"
Tactic to progress	Improve your cultural interaction

Ways to Fast-Forward as an Experience-Centric Organization

The experience-centric organization is something that you develop into, becoming deeper and wider as you proceed through the stage. This is because the more you understand experience, the more you find that you have to integrate new areas of competence into your organization. You have already implemented new ways of working through the previous stages, and you can shoehorn these into an existing organizational model without making radical changes to your organizational logics. Now, however, as you enter the experience-centric world, you are changing the organizational logics. The degree to which you are challenging these logics depends on the journey thus far. If your whole organization has a customer journey approach, and genuinely is focused on understanding customers, then it will be ready for an experience-centric approach. If, however, the work until now has not been organization-wide and has not genuinely influenced the organizational logics, then progress toward experience centricity will be slow.

Getting an Orange Belt in Experience Centricity

The orange belt stage starts with making a deliberate choice to move toward experience centricity and getting buy-in within the organization's leadership. This is a leadership activity that demands alignment for success. Thus, a first logical step is to set up an organizational structure that clearly places customer experience on the map, and then hire the right person to become your experience director. This position will be tasked with creating a shared understanding of your experiential DNA within the leadership, such that you have consensus and authorization to continue with the transformation.

The experiential DNA work will involve the whole leadership group and create your gold-standard experience. As a part of the process, you should apply this gold-standard to some services to check that they are a good fit for your organization. Then you should use the gold-standard to develop some future concept services. These can be used to promote infusion and alignment in the same way that concept cars are used in the automotive industry to influence both the market *and* the organization. When added to the shift from a silo culture and leadership visibility from the previous stages, the spread of the gold-standard experience within the organization will accelerate.

Leadership skills are central here in visibly championing the transformation and the new orientation of the organization. This is particularly true when it comes to having formal organizational structures in place for the transformation, and at the same time supporting the informal organizational behaviors that need to be in place to focus on the experience. Use of success stories, heroes, and internal rituals assist here. Empowerment of frontline employees is central at this stage; it is important to publicly recognize their value by highlighting their hero status and finding success stories.

Getting a Blue Belt in Experience Centricity

The blue belt stage is part of formalizing an organizational structure to deliver on the gold-standard experience you have developed. After you've focused on the informal structures and established an informal experiential culture, it's time to implement new formal structures and strengthen existing ones.. KPIs around the experience should be considered, although this is an area where you'll need to adapt traditional KPIs to fit the current context.

At this stage, your customer understanding should become deeper; you should start looking beyond what the customers say to intuit the meaning they attach to their needs and behaviors. This is the spearhead for innovating new services and developing closer relationships with customers. This will also open up the organization for the next stage, focusing on culture.

Getting a Black Belt in Experience Centricity

The black belt is a deepening and broadening of the previous work wherein you take a more active role in culture. This requires that you focus on and foster interaction between your organization and your customers (as described in Chapter 10) through *trendslation* and the lens of culture. The personality of your services and organization will be the basis for how you engage with culture and meaning. As Claire Dennington discusses in Chapter 10, this can include anything from the more traditional focus on idealistic aspects (Intermarché's "inglorious" fruits and vegetables) to more noticeable political aspects (Nike and Colin Kaepernick), or it may come about though identifying some change in cultural consumption (Apple's "Rip. Mix. Burn." campaign).

Endnotes

1   The value chain concept comes from business management and was described by Michael Porter in his 1985 book, *Competitive Advantage: Creating and Sustaining Superior Performance* (Simon & Schuster). It describes how a firm's operations can be divided into activities in order to increase competitive advantage. The value network describes an alternative to the value chain. In a value network, value is created within a complex network of relations between actors. Customers, and the relationships between them, are a central part of value networks, and the customer is viewed as a co-producer of value.

3

The Structure of the Experience-Centric Organization: The Wheel of Experience Centricity

The key message of this book is that the customer experience is not an afterthought. It is your reason to exist, and an organizational imperative. Everything and everyone in the organization has to focus on it, and support its delivery. That requires an underlying structure that promotes experiential thinking and describes the roles and responsibilities of each part of your organization in its fulfillment. This chapter describes a model for understanding experience centricity called the *wheel of experience centricity*. The wheel allows you to see how the experience a customer gains from a touchpoint connects all the way to the structure and strategy of your organization, and vice versa. Understanding the wheel, and how the parts fit together, is key to unlocking the potential of the experience-centric organization. It integrates and orients the whole organization toward its mission: providing memorable customer experiences.

A Tale of Two Restaurants

Recently, I met with my good friend Søren to discuss this book. Søren is an expert on innovation and we have regularly been discussing experience centricity over a meal and a beer. We met up in our regular hangout, a French crêpe restaurant, but this time we were treated badly by a new French head waitress, who was both grumpy and rude. This ruined the atmosphere for the talk we wanted to have, and we left, disappointed that our experience and expectations had been ruined by a single employee. There were plenty of other restaurants to choose from, so we decided to try a new, small one that I had recently passed. I had registered it because of its name (No. 30), its tiled interior (I think it used to be an old butcher's shop), its size (intimate), and its décor (lots of interesting-looking wine bottles, cozy lighting, nice furniture). I had checked reviews on Yelp and Google and had a good feeling about it, so we decided to give it a try. I booked a table online before we walked over. We were greeted nicely, found a good table for discussion, and had lovely food and wine. Surprising combinations of ingredients, many small and tasty dishes, and a really good choice of wine, all at a fair price. We talked to the chef and to one of the owners, and they explained the concept of the restaurant, their role in the Nordic cuisine movement, and how they had spent time finding the right suppliers of quality food. The dishes were nicely timed so we didn't get too many at the same time, we were well looked after, and when we paid, it was easy to split the bill and each pay our share (a common thing in Scandinavia). We enjoyed it all, and the expectations we had were fulfilled in every way—even exceeded.

Now, you have probably experienced something like this yourself, many times. But let's dig a bit deeper into the restaurant visit, because it reveals the underlying structure of the experience-centric organization.

The Story Revolved Around Expectations, Offerings, and Experiences

The story revolved around our experience that evening, which was a mix of expectations, offerings, and events that unfolded over time. I described the expectations we had of an experience at the crêpe restaurant, based on our earlier visits. Surprisingly for us, it defied our expectations and ended poorly, due to one important aspect. Then I described the offering of a possible new place, No. 30. This offering set great experiential expectations, which were more than exceeded when we experienced the place, finally giving an enjoyable end to the story. As we will see later, offerings, expectations, and experience are difficult to separate, and all relate to experiences in one way or another. But let's move on, now that we've noted that the whole story revolved around these key ingredients.

The Experience Was Fulfilled Through Touchpoints and Interactions Along an Experiential Journey

I also described how the experience was a result of interactions with multiple touchpoints over time. The most notable of these was a human touchpoint, the rude waitress in the first restaurant. I briefly described some of the other touchpoints from our experiential journey through the evening, such as the design of the restaurant, reading reviews on a mobile phone, and so on, but in reality there were a lot more that were not described, such as the menu, sound, sight, interior, and other people. There is a rich mix of elements that are central to any experience, including touchpoints, time, behaviors, and tone of voice. These are all aspects of *experience fulfillment* because, when orchestrated together, they help fulfill our experiential expectation.

The Touchpoints Were Enabled Through Platforms and Processes

I also described reading the online reviews, the online booking of a table, the timing of the meal, and the splitting of the bill. These are examples of the visible (and often invisible) platforms and processes that *enable* the touchpoints to fulfill the experiential expectation. There are many more experience enablers than I mentioned in the story, such as organizational structure (formal and informal), reward mechanisms, accounting, and stock status. For most customers, these are invisible but necessary. Without them, the restaurant would not be able to provide the fantastic experience we had. These factors enable the consistency of the touchpoints, and are key to being able to scale the experience.

Platforms and Processes Are Supported by a Strategic Structure

Moving to a strategic level, I described the business model of the restaurant, specifically its focus on the Nordic food movement and relationship with quality suppliers. Together these components formed the structure that made the restaurant unique and relevant to us as customers, and comprised the restaurant's reason to exist. The structure is the high-level strategy that gives shape to the service, and allows the enablers to support the touchpoints that fulfill the experiential expectation.

How It All Fits Together

What I have described can be structured, and makes sense, as a logical set of roles and relationships. The experience is fulfilled by touchpoints over time, and these touchpoints are enabled by platforms and processes, which in turn reflect the strategic structure of the business. This is summarized in the following table:

STAGE	DESCRIPTION	IN THE RESTAURANT EXAMPLE	CENTRAL QUESTIONS TO ASK
Experiential expectation + the actual experience	The offering supports the customer's expectation of an experience. The experience is what the customer actually experiences through use of the service. Offering, expectation, and experience are tightly linked.	Expectations from previous experiences, and a negative experience in the crêperie. Alternative offering that created experiential expectation. Surprising, novel, and delightful taste combinations. A socially shared happening. Feeling of being part of a food movement.	What experience do we want our customers to have? What experiential offering promises that experience? What is a good fit to our DNA?
Experience fulfillment	The interactions the customer has with the many touchpoints of the service—such as adverts, word of mouth, emails, and employees—along their experiential journey	Waitress, cook, owner, restaurant name, location, web page, social media, reviews, reservations, signage, word of mouth, menu, staff, interior, food, drinks, bill, and more	What touchpoints do we need and how do we design them to be able to provide the offering and experience described above?
Experience enablers	The platforms and processes that are in place to enable the touchpoints	The platforms and processes that are in place to enable the touchpoints	How can we enable the journey, touchpoints, and interactions to provide the desired experience? What platforms and processes help us do this?
Experience structure	The business model and actor ecology	Strategic suppliers, pricing structure, target customer	Who are our strategic partners? What is our pricing strategy? Who do we want to be desirable for?

I hope you can see how the experience relates to the whole, and therefore how the experience depends on the entire organization pulling together. Decisions made at each level have huge implications for the experience and need to be framed in that way, which is why it is important to know the experience you want your customers to have. Every decision, from operational through tactical to strategic, needs to relate to the experience.

From a Linear to a Circular Mode: The Wheel of Experience Centricity

As I developed the content for this book, it struck me that there was something not quite right with the linear, straightforward structure I just described. As a way of understanding, the structure is simple and logical, but two things were missing from it. First is the role of the experiential DNA of the organization. It is central to experience but didn't fit in any one place in my model. The experiential DNA is something that influences every part of the organization and can be perceived as supporting the experience or holding it back, depending on whether and how you have nurtured it. Second, it bugged me that the strategic aspects of the business model and actor relationships were so distant from the offering and experience itself. I kept finding myself saying that strategic decisions define the offering, while at the same time saying that the offering is central to expectation and experience. The only way I could get this to work was to join them together and move from a linear model to a wheel, where the experiential DNA takes its proper place as the hub. Welcome to the *wheel of experience centricity*.

The wheel of experience centricity has five interlocking parts that all rotate around the hub of your experiential DNA (see Figure 3-1). All parts of the wheel are focused on delivering a desirable customer experience, although each has its clearly defined role in supporting this goal. The wheel describes these roles and helps translate experience strategy into operational excellence. If you grasp and use the structure of the wheel, then you are well on your way to developing an experience-centric organization.

The wheel identifies the roles and relationships between the different parts of an organization from an experience perspective and explains how things fit together, both conceptually and functionally. However, the wheel does not present chronological steps for implementation.

It shows the parts that need to work together and how they can integrate their competencies to create the whole—an aligned organization capable of delivering exceptional experiences.

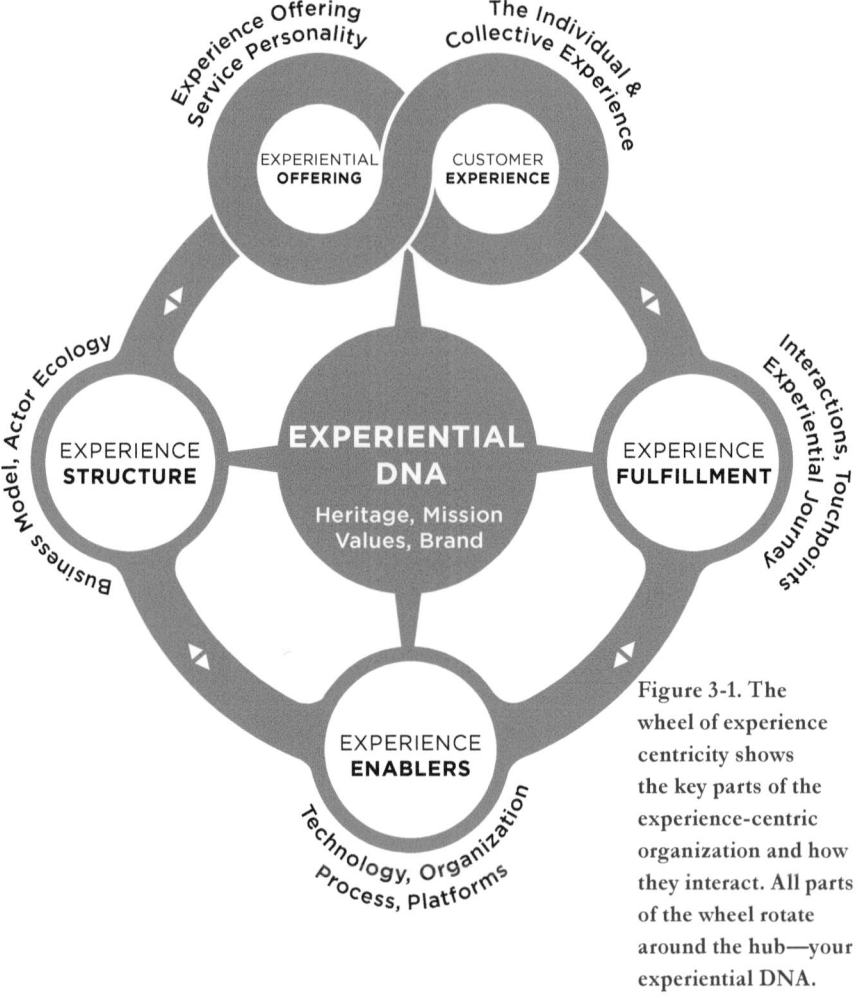

Figure 3-1. The wheel of experience centricity shows the key parts of the experience-centric organization and how they interact. All parts of the wheel rotate around the hub—your experiential DNA.

The Wheel: A Short Trip Around

I will describe the wheel of experience centricity briefly here, and the following chapters will go into each part in more detail. The core idea behind the wheel is that you start with the experience and work around the wheel to deliver that experience. The farther around the wheel you go, the more strategic it becomes, therefore ensuring that you are making strategic decisions from a customer experience perspective.

The wheel can rotate in both directions. In the bottom-up direction, the experience is fulfilled through touchpoints, enabled by platforms within a business model that supports the experiential offering. In the top-down direction, the experience defines the offering, which then dictates the business model (and value network). This process is enabled by technology (and other) platforms, which support experience fulfillment through touchpoints to process the desirable result. Both directions of movement occur at the same time, something we call top-up—that is, the coexistence of bottom-up and top-down processes.

The Experience as the Starting Point

The experience-centric organization not only has a laser-sharp understanding of the experience that customers should have, but also understands that the experience is the perfect expression of its heritage, mission, and values.

In the experience-centric view, everything starts and ends with the experience. You start with a desirable experience—that is, one that you want the customer to have—and then follow the wheel clockwise, working backward through the organization to discover how that desirable experience can be made possible. If you do this, you will be in good company. The two most valuable organizations in the world, Apple and Amazon, both work from the experience backward. It's time for you to join in their success.

You will read a lot more about the experience in Chapter 6, but at this stage, it is important to explain that the experience-centric organization knows its target users so well that it can view the world through the customer's eyes (more on this in Chapter 4). It understands the individual customer, customers as communities (see Chapter 9), and customers as part of culture in its broadest sense (more of this in Chapter 10).

If we zoom in on the customer experience, you will find that it is a combination of customers' expectations prior to using your service (among other things, provided by your offering, word of mouth, reviews, etc.) and the experience they have when using your service. This creates a closed loop between the perceived offering and the experience itself. Both of these are powered by the experiential DNA of your organization, which is an aggregation of your heritage, brand, values, and mission. These three aspects work together to deliver the memorable experience that customers crave, and you must consider all three together when designing for customer experience. This is the *tripod of experience* (see Figure 3-2), and the success of the organization rests on getting it right. It is your triple top line, based on an interplay between your experiential DNA, your experiential offering, and the customer experience itself.

The outcome of the tripod of experience is the experience itself, as experienced by the customer when using your service, but defined and described in advance through their expectation. The offering itself has no value; it is only when the service is used that value is created—what's known as *value in use*. The experience that the customer has is the return on experiential investment.

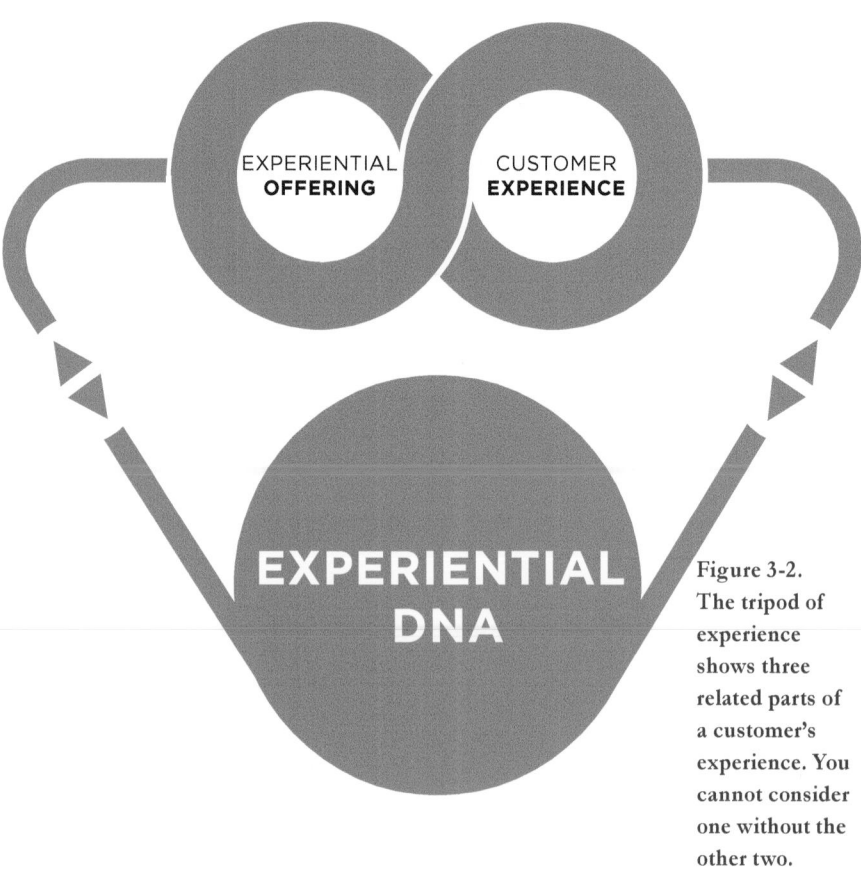

Figure 3-2. The tripod of experience shows three related parts of a customer's experience. You cannot consider one without the other two.

The move from just considering the experience alone toward understanding the tripod of experience is important. Until recently, the customer experience has been viewed simply as a layer on top of everything else, and considered in isolation. By understanding how the elements of the tripod of experience work together to form the customer experience, you can create stronger, more relevant, and more differentiated products and services that bring the customer experience into the heart of the organization.

Noma and the Tripod of Experience

Imagine you are starting a restaurant and you want to give a truly exceptional experience—one that people will praise above all others and travel long distances to have. You would start by defining what people would experience: the tastes, how they would feel when seeing and eating the food, how they would describe the place to others, how the sequence of dishes builds to a climax, and more. Then, you would consider what offering could provide that exceptional experience. How would it be different from other restaurants, and what sets it apart from them? And then, how does this fit with the DNA of the organization, or in this case, as a new restaurant, the mission of the founders? As you do this, you would bounce back and forth between all three—for example, an offering idea might change the experience, and vice versa.

Noma is a restaurant in Copenhagen that managed to do just that. It was recognized as the best restaurant in the world for three consecutive years and people traveled across continents to experience it. The restaurant had a clearly defined experience they wanted to give customers (and succeeded in delivering it). Their experiential offering was emotional and idealistic. It offered fantastic and innovative dishes based on local ingredients, and delivered them with passion and a desire to convince customers through their very experience that local food can be exceptional. Noma went all out to make its customers feel something, and was very clear about the experience it wanted to provide. The experience was a clear articulation of the restaurant's experiential DNA, which combined passion, idealism, and a deep desire to change perceptions. Noma is a great example of an organization that perfected the tripod of experience.

You will find that these are circular questions—that is, they influence each other—and that is how it should be. There are strong dependencies between the three elements, and you should put care, time, and energy into getting them right. As we will see later, crafting the experience has strategic consequences as you move around the wheel, so make sure you have a high degree of confidence in what you choose, and that you prototype it before investing in implementation. Only when you are confident that you have something of strong value should you move on to the next stage: determining how to fulfill the desirable experience you want to provide to your customers.

Experience Fulfillment Through Touchpoints Along an Experiential Journey

How does a customer experience your service? The experience comes through use. Until the moments of truth of using your service, the customer only has expectations, and you have only made promises. The experience comes from interactions with the multiple points of contact (touchpoints) as they progress through using your service or product (the experiential journey).

For example, if you want to take someone out for a meal, there are stages to the experiential journey, such as deciding who to invite, choosing a suitable time and date, choosing a restaurant, inviting people, getting ready, traveling to the restaurant, eating, paying, traveling back, and following up. You can connect these stages to the experience you want your customers to have to design the experiential journey: how can you support the customer as part of the experiential journey, when they are inviting people to join them for a meal?

In this way you can ensure that your touchpoints, interactions, and experiential journey are optimized to deliver on the experiential promise. Gaining a shared understanding and support for the touchpoints and journey that you want to achieve is key. This is a challenge, since the journey will likely hop across internal silos, creating cross-silo challenges. In many organizations silos are not used to working together in this way, and they are usually measured for "within-silo" performance rather than performance across silos.

EXPERIENTIAL OFFERING

CUSTOMER EXPERIENCE

EXPERIENCE STRUCTURE

EXPERIENTIAL DNA
Heritage, Mission Values, Brand

EXPERIENCE FULFILLMENT

EXPERIENCE ENABLERS

In the fantastic visualization on the next page, you can see all of the human touchpoints needed to create a soccer matchday experience. Thousands of touchpoints are all coordinated to create a predefined and desired experience, one that is focused on 22 players on a piece of grass. This coordination is key.

Comb, No, You Don't Need No Comb

Once, when I flew from Scandinavia to the US, my baggage was delayed and I had to stand in line to receive an overnight bag of supplies to keep me going. I was tired and frustrated, and in a looong line of other people, who I assume were also tired and frustrated. When I got to the front of the line, I was met by a customer service agent (my major touchpoint), who was strict, to the point, and seemed totally uninterested in my grumpiness. They sorted the paperwork, then took a night bag out and started to fill it, speaking aloud as they placed items in the bag: "Toothbrush, toothpaste, soap, shampoo, socks, underpants." Then, "Comb," at which point they looked at me and, with a naughty smile that I remember to this day, said, "Comb, no, you don't need no comb," and put it aside.

We both burst out laughing, and I had to agree, as a folically challenged man (balding… OK, very bald), I had no need for a comb.

During that event, we had a shared moment that transformed my experience from awful to enjoyable, changed my mood from grumpy to positive, and gave me an experience I remember to this day—all because the employee went off-script and injected some humor into our interaction. I will never forget it. Empowering your employees to go off-script, and having an organizational culture that supports it (and knows its limits), can create small "wow" moments in a service and turn a customer experience from bad to good.

As a footnote to this, a similar thing happened to me in my local supermarket last week. The checkout person said to me, with a smile, "You do know that I judge people's character by what they buy." After a short conversation, I found that I had passed muster. These kinds of experiences are memorable in a crystal-clear way, because they positively challenge your expectations.

Questions that an organization should ask at this stage are:

- Which experiential journey(s) do we want our customers to follow so that they have the experience we have defined?

The team behind the team

There may only be 11 players a side on the football pitch, but the total number of people actively involved on match days at the Allianz Arena demonstrates just what a sophisticated operation the modern sporting event has become!

In fact, on any given match day, there are total of 74,000 people inside the stadium. In addition to the fans, who are there to support their team, a large number of people provide support to the players and spectators alike, safeguarding their well-being.

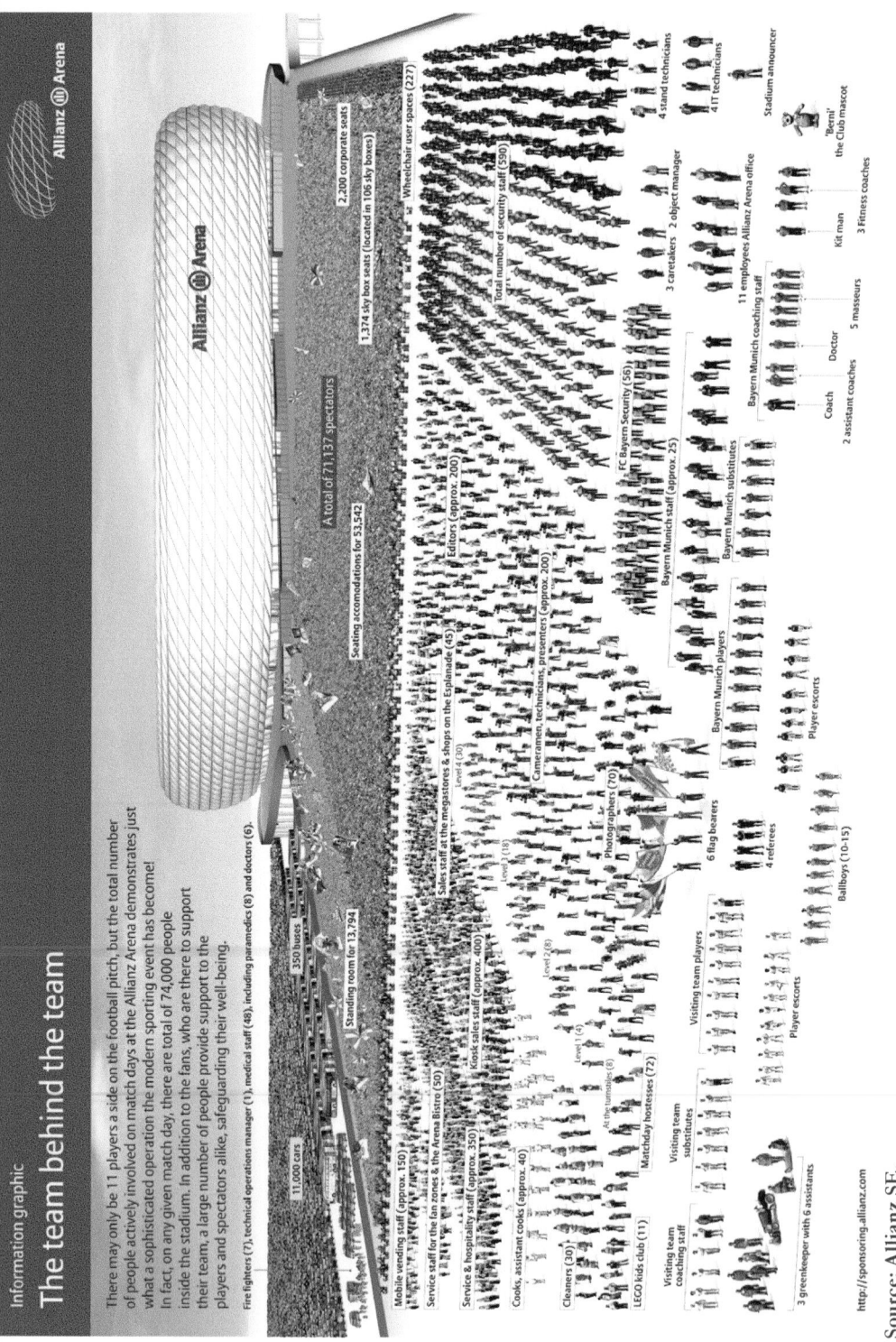

Allianz ⊕ **Arena**

Source: Allianz SE.

http://sponsoring.allianz.com

- Which touchpoints are the right ones to provide the desired experience?
- What are the experiential characteristics of the interactions when the customer uses the touchpoints?
- How is the service personally expressed through the touchpoints?

What is the tone of voice needed to provide the experience? Working with touchpoints is described in more detail in Chapter 6, and aspects of service personality and tone of voice are covered in Chapter 7.

Now, using the meal example again, let's dive down a bit into one of the first stages of your experiential meal journey: choosing a place to eat. Touchpoints here could be friends who recommend a place, an ad, a sign, an expert review online, an app ranking, or simply a return to your favorite place. Booking might involve a telephone, a website, an app, or physically walking into the restaurant. Jump to arriving at the restaurant, and there are multiple touchpoints, from the exterior of the place (you ever judge a place by its exterior? I do), the interior, the person who meets you, their clothing, what they say, how they say it. I could go on, but you get the idea. The customer experience comes from a multitude of interactions with touchpoints along the experiential journey, and you cannot control the order or ways in which they are used.

What is key here is that touchpoints are the only way the customer can experience your product or service, so you should choose and design them to fulfill the experiential promise. This doesn't mean that the touchpoints are the most important part of your organization (though they might be), but it does mean that you have to get them right to be able to give the right experience.

Experience Enablement Through Systems, Processes, Organizational Structures, and Platforms

Touchpoints and their position along the experiential journey cannot exist in isolation. They have to be enabled by IT systems, organizational structures, processes, and platforms. At this stage, the main question to ask is, "How do we enable the touchpoints and the desired experiential journey so the customer consistently has the right experience?" Answering this gives the organization a shared understanding about roles and expectations so they can focus on becoming an efficient and well-oiled machine that enables the touchpoints to fulfill the experiential promise. They then can optimize their platforms, structures, internal processes, reward mechanisms, and supporting functions with an experiential focus. Investments in infrastructure will then always be framed in terms of an experiential value—that is, how will this platform enable the experience we want to give?

In many ways, you could say that these experience enablers *power* the touchpoints. The experience enablers function like an analog watch, in which the different cogs are internal and external actors, working well together to power the touchpoints that provide the customer experience. As an example, take the lovely person who recently met you at a restaurant and showed you to your table. They are part of an organizational structure with a formal and informal culture. The formal covers, for example, the pay structure, degree of hierarchy, working hours, and bonus system. The informal can be how people help each other out when it gets busy, the way they talk to each other, the flexibility between employees to take breaks when needed. All of these have an influence on the dining experience you will have. And this culture goes right down to the formal decision to use a scripted "Good evening sir, how are you tonight?" or the unscripted "Hey, how you doing? You look ready for a great night out." All of these experiences are enabled, in your organization, by the selection of personnel, the training, the choice of scripts (or no scripts), and the design of internal culture.

But it's not just about people. There are technical platforms too. The payment terminal you pay with may be linked to the booking system, the order system, the kitchen task list, and the billing system, and ultimately a waiter who finally presents you with a bill and says, "Thank you for eating here, have a nice evening." Or maybe even, "It was great to see you again, Simon, we hope to see you again soon" (for the regulars).

Experience fulfillment through touchpoints is important because that is where the experience occurs— but to scale your service, the experience enablers are vital. You can only get so far with a creative offering, a great experience, and lots of hard work, if they're held together with ad hoc solutions. Very quickly, you will need platforms and structures that allow you to deliver on the experience you would like your customers to have. It's important, therefore, that these platforms enable the touchpoints instead of constraining them when it comes to experience fulfillment.

Part of a Bigger Structure: The Business Model and Service Ecology

The business model and service ecology form a key structure in two ways. First, they define the actor network and ensure that it is possible to create value from the concept. Without a structure, the offering is only a promising concept; the structure is what defines its viability. Second, they support the experience enablers. The experience structure identifies and develops the value streams and service ecology that build the bridge between a promising experiential offering and the technology and organizational platforms enabling the touchpoint experience fulfillment.

Some key touchpoints might be enabled by a partner organization, and that choice is a strategic or highly tactical one, with the decision being based on your business model for the product or service in question. With the restaurant example, there may be a franchise behind the restaurant that has a particular business model structure and a network of trusted suppliers. Alternatively, there might be a strategic collaboration between a small restaurant and many expert small suppliers, creating a strong but risky dependency. Both of these aspects impact the customer experience, and when taking an experience-centric approach, you should directly develop the alliances and business model based on the experience that you want the customer to have. The choice, therefore, of a franchise solution should rest on whether it fits with the customer experience you want to give.

The actor network is central to value creation, and the ecological way of thinking takes a different approach to the value chain approach that Porter made popular in the 1990s. Experiences are not delivered through a value chain, but instead created through a value network, an ecology of relationships, which has as its center a close experiential relationship between the organization and the customer.

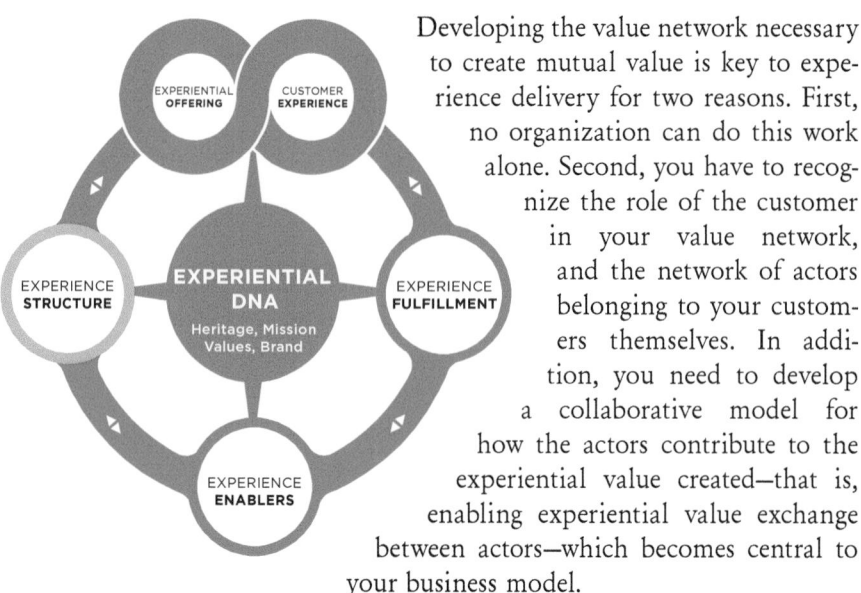

Developing the value network necessary to create mutual value is key to experience delivery for two reasons. First, no organization can do this work alone. Second, you have to recognize the role of the customer in your value network, and the network of actors belonging to your customers themselves. In addition, you need to develop a collaborative model for how the actors contribute to the experiential value created—that is, enabling experiential value exchange between actors—which becomes central to your business model.

At the structural level, the actor network supports an efficient and effective series of platforms to enable the customer experience. The business model defines how value is created and flows within the value network, and how the actor network's powerful web of value exchange creates mutual value for each actor in both the short and long term. At this stage, the customer is a key actor, and the business model is one in which value is co-created between all actors.

There and Back Again: The Offering and the Tripod of Experience

The experiential offering, or *experiential value proposition* (EVP), is the *what* of the service, and can be broken down into two main parts: what you want to offer and what your customers perceive as being offered. The EVP offers a particular and memorable experience to the customer, and creates expectations in customers that are later fulfilled through the interactions they have with touchpoints.

The offering is inextricably linked to the experience itself, since the offering is the promise you make to a customer about what experience they will receive as you go together through the experiential journey. The offering entices the customer to try the service and hopefully build a relationship with you through reuse. We will see later how the offering is key to experience, since people continually create expectations about what is going to happen when we use something. The offering supports that way of thinking by providing expectations for experiences that are so desirable that the customer seeks them out.

On the one hand, the offering is promising something experiential (making an EVP) to customers, and on the other hand, it is the source for developing a business model and service ecology. At the same time, both the offering and the experience have to fit well with your experiential DNA —bringing us back to the tripod of experience (Figure 3-3). To do anything else is either a deliberate strategy to change your organization (something that should be rare), or a mistake. The experiential DNA is the foundation that your customers relate to over time, has a long heritage, and is the core part of your organizational logic. Changing your experiential DNA or not aligning to it is a path fraught with difficulty.

The offering develops from a negotiation between your organization's desired customer experience and your experiential DNA. For the desired customer experience, the organization asks, "What offering do we need to produce to be able to deliver that target experience?" This is an *experience pull* approach. At the same time, your organization needs to translate its experiential DNA into something tangible by asking, "What is the right fit for our organization?" This is a *DNA push* approach. This chicken-and-egg-style negotiation has to continue until both components are optimized, producing an offering that both promises a desirable customer experience and fits with your DNA.

The offering forms the yardstick for customer expectations, and is understood in experiential form even before the customer interacts with a touchpoint. In this way, the experiential offering promises functional, emotional, self-expressive, and idealistic benefits that will later be fulfilled as the customer takes their experiential journey through the service.

If you delve deeper into the offering, you will find that it provides meaning to customers by linking to cultural aspects such as trends or cultural phenomena. The link between meaning and the experience that the offering unlocks (see Chapter 9) is a key part of experiential design and a potential multiplier of experiential value.

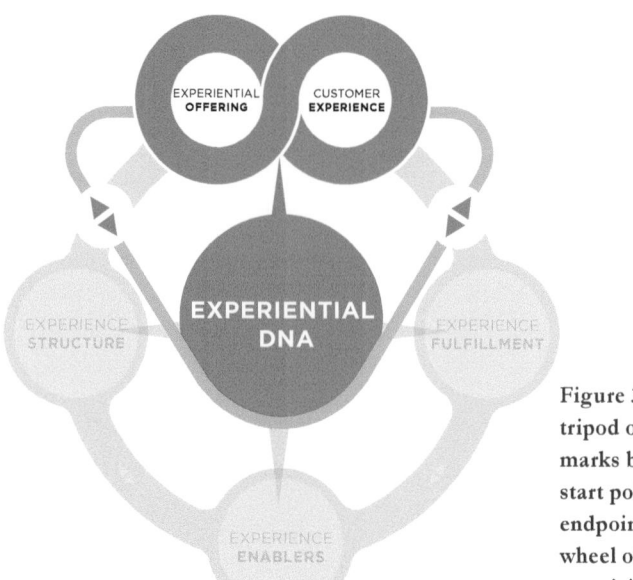

Figure 3-3. The tripod of experience marks both the start point and the endpoint of the wheel of experience centricity.

The experiential offering marks a transition internally in the organization, since it forms the basis for the business model and the actor network needed to realize it. In this way, it evolves from being a concept to a tangible structure. It should be possible to read from the offering (and the experience it promises) which actors will need to be involved in delivery, and what the business model is for the value exchange between actors.

And that closes the circle and brings us back from the offering to the experience itself. We have gone around the circle: the experience is fulfilled by touchpoints; the touchpoints are enabled by (all kinds of) platforms; the platforms are part of a larger business model and service ecology structure; and the structure should be based on the offering.

Experiential DNA as the Hub of the Wheel

We have now taken a quick spin around the wheel, and described how the various parts fit together. But we have one more part to consider: the hub of it all, your experiential DNA (see Figure 3-4). A wheel has a hub and (in this case) spokes that connect that hub to each and every part of the wheel. This hub is your experiential DNA, and it has a key role in the experience-centric organization. You might not have given it too much thought as you have developed as an organization, but it has always been there.

Your experiential DNA, like human DNA, defines what you are and who you can become, and in turn, what experiences your organization will be capable (and not capable) of delivering. Your experiential DNA is the jewel in your crown. As such, it might have been taken care of and regularly polished, or it might be tarnished and faded from neglect. However, it will always be there, defining your uniqueness (good or bad).

At the start-up phase, the organization had a reason to start, and that often is based on some kind of vision from the founders. This is where the DNA starts to form, and as the organization is created, developed, and then scaled, this DNA likewise develops and becomes the organization's way of thinking and doing. It is often left to develop without being given much thought, but that does not mean that it has disappeared; it is just not front of mind. Now, however, in a society that is driven by experiences, it will play a central role in the experience-centric organization.

Your experiential DNA is the foundation for all that rotates around it. It is your raison d'être ("reason to be"). It is a mix of your heritage, mission, vision, values, cultural standing, and brand all

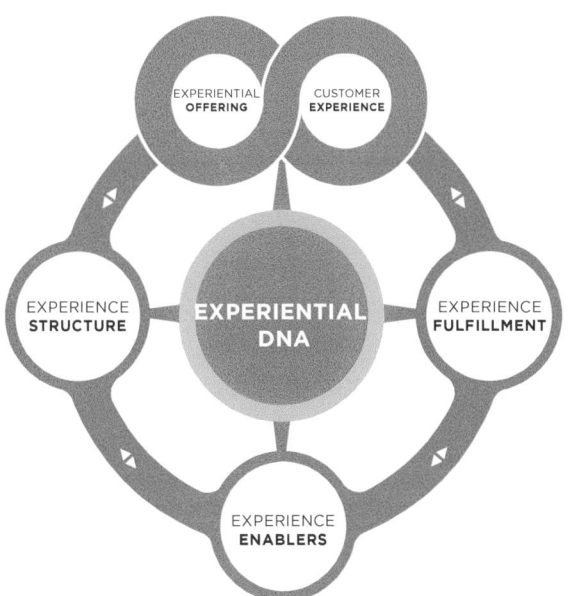

Figure 3-4. Your experiential DNA defines what experience you can or cannot successfully offer. It influences every part of your organization, and is the hub of the wheel of experience centricity.

rolled into one. Only Apple can be Apple. Only Google can be Google. Only you can be you, and the more you understand your DNA, the more you can differentiate yourself from the competition. If you provide experiences that do *not* match your experiential DNA, then you will at best cloud your image with customers, and at worst be seen as irrelevant. From now on, aligning the customer experience, the offering, and your experiential DNA is your main mission.

Your experiential DNA can be defined as the latent potential of your organization and the image it projects to the world. It is a synthesis of external perspective (how you have been perceived), and your internal set of characteristics (how you have been structured and have functioned). Experiential DNA cannot be seen directly, and therefore it is often difficult for people to articulate or discuss it. It needs to be carefully understood through an explorative journey, involving the following stops along the way:

- The historical customer experience: the expectations and experiences that customers have had over time
- Your story: the original dream and how you came to be the company you are today
- Your personality and tone-of-voice heritage: how you have related to customers over time and how customers have perceived this
- Your offering heritage: what you have offered over time and how it has evolved
- What you have become known for and remembered for by your customers
- Your organizational structure and its workings
- Motivators and rewards within the organization
- The information flow within the organization, in terms of how activities are coordinated and how knowledge is transferred
- The mission, vision, and values of your organization: what they are, how they are applied, and how they are communicated

There is no right or wrong way to summarize the experiential DNA. It could be a document, a visualization, or even a mood board. What is important is that you know it very well, like a good friend, and that you adjust your decisions according to it. Good friendships change slowly, and you can influence them, but slowly. It is the same with your experiential DNA. Understand it, nurture it, and make plans for its long-term development.

This means *matching* the customer experience to your DNA, which makes it unique to your organization (see Figure 3-5 for an example). Matching the DNA and the experience might seem like a simple thing to do, but it is surprising how many organizations do not recognize its importance, lacking both the ability and the structures to achieve it. If you don't know the experience you want to give your customers, then you are just guessing, and as we know, guessing has a high probability of failure. How can you expect customers to prefer you as a partner if you don't know what you are offering?

What if you feel you don't have a strong experiential DNA? You might not be aware of it, but you do have one. Every organization does, and if you are a start-up, you have the opportunity to invent one. This is described in more detail in Chapters 9 and 10.

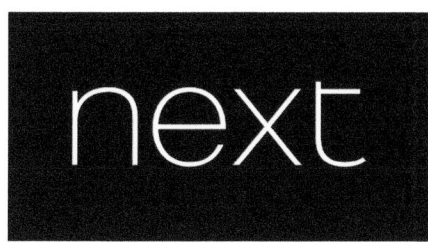

Figure 3-5. The fashion brand Next appeared on the market in 1982, and positioned itself as a fresh new brand among stodgy competitors. By adding "Since 1982," it used irony to forge this identity and its experiential DNA. Now, over 35 years later, it is more mature (and so are its customers) and the firm now wears its age as a badge of pride. The label is now part of the company's experiential DNA. (Source: Next.)

Innovating Your Service Experience Using the Whole Wheel

The focus in the experience-centric organization is on developing and providing desirable experiences to customers, and that requires constant innovation. Surprise and delight can come from many different places, and as we will see later, not every "wow" has to be a big "WOW!" Even though the experience is the ultimate outcome you want to deliver, I don't want to give the impression that you can innovate only in the experience itself. Rather, I want to get you into the mindset of considering the experiential value of all innovations. There is a constant din of possible innovations, and the key is to identify their experiential impact.

Improving Experience and Reducing Costs at the Same Time

A few years ago, a large telco gave me the brief to reduce customer care costs, while improving the customer experience. Sounds impossible, but when we explored the customer experience and listened to customers, we found that it was in fact possible. Customers generally wanted to solve the problems themselves, and the information they needed was already available on the telco site. The problem was linking the two together. Poor site design made this difficult—it required a login that no one could remember, it was hard to find what you needed and navigate the menus, it used technical terms, and so on—even though the final information itself was well designed. This led customers to think, "Well, the information might be there, but I'm never going to find it, so I'll call instead." A combination of solutions based around an online-first approach were suggested, including contextual labels that could be placed on equipment, with short URLs directly linking to relevant pages.

Source: author.

The experience and the offering itself are probably your first thoughts when it comes to innovation in customer experience, but the experience comes from all the parts of the wheel working in alignment. Innovation in any part of the wheel can radically change the customer experience. For example, innovations in touchpoints can give experiential value. Uber is a great example of how a single touchpoint, and its supporting platform, can transform the whole taxi business worldwide. Innovations in supporting platforms, or through organizational design, all have the potential to create better experiences. Employee empowerment is one area of organizational innovation that comes to mind. And of course, innovations in business models and strategic actor collaboration are also strong means of innovating in the customer experience.

There are plenty of painful examples in the past where huge investments have been made, yet they haven't provided the expected experiential benefits (yes, I'm thinking of you, huge CRM investment made 10 years ago). In the experience-centric organization, alignment is always toward improving the experience, and innovations should always be considered in terms of whether they improve the customer experience or detract from it, or if they can provide the same experience at lower cost. Herein also lies a danger—slowly eroding your customer experience by efficiencies of scale that slightly detract from the experience. We have all seen it in restaurants after they make a name for themselves: the portions get smaller, the service more abrupt, the ingredients less exciting, the time you get at the table briefer. Each element erodes the experience a little, until eventually the whole experience collapses and the restaurant becomes empty. In our experience-centric world, these things are quickly noticed and spread, and you can quickly lose your experiential mojo and find yourself removed from the favorite restaurant list. If you find yourself saying, "This has a minimal effect on the customer experience but an impact on our bottom line" too many times, think carefully about

> **"There is a constant din of possible innovations, and the key is to identify their experiential impact."**

what that minimal effect is. Is it really minimal ? Customers are very sensitive to experiential change, and are looking (not always consciously) for excuses to distrust you. Don't give them a reason to start that suspicious train of thought, as it launches a negative spiral that can be devastating. Trust is a fragile thing, and the commitment a customer makes relies on it, so don't stretch it or abuse it.

The Experiential DNA of SAS and Its Current Dilemma

SAS (Scandinavian Airlines) started in 1950 as a shared Scandinavian vision, buoyed by the social democracy movements of the Scandinavian countries, combined with a need for transport over difficult terrain. SAS had style and glamor, and became known for excellent customer service, particularly in business class. It had an internationally known leader in Jan Carlzon, who championed an empowered employee organization, and this gave the company great success. But SAS became too reliant on its business class passengers, started to be complacent, and took its eye off its heritage after

Carlzon left. It was caught out by rapid deregulation and the entry of low-cost airlines exploiting the changing situation. The competition could suddenly offer a better overall experience since they used improved digital self-service touchpoints and, more importantly, new planes. SAS was slow to replace planes and suddenly looked out of touch—and *was* out of touch with its customers. At its worst, SAS treated passengers as if they owned them, and started to behave like the slightly grumpy older relative at a family reunion. Its ownership structure of multiple countries suddenly became a bickering family, reflecting different political directions in the respective countries. This caused problems with reorganization and resulted in huge economic losses.

In its recent attempts to compete with low-cost airlines, SAS has not capitalized on its experiential DNA, instead trying to be something it cannot be: a low-cost airline. The experiential DNA of SAS is unfortunately in total contrast to the customer experience of the airline today, which has suffered greatly. This is evident in a customer quote from a recent online review:

> *This just about summed up our experience and impression of SAS as an airline company, tired, old and lacking in any genuine feeling for service and customer satisfaction.*

> *RIP old girl, you were once a half decent airline company. Luckily there are other new airlines eager to please.*

4

The Core Behaviors of the Experience-Centric Organization

This chapter describes the natural behaviors of the experience-centric organization. You might already exhibit some of these behaviors, in which case the chapter can give you confidence you are on the right track. You might, however, see the need to develop new ones or turn up the volume on some of your weaker ones. If that is the case, read on, as the rest of the book describes more about these behaviors and how you can develop them in your organization.

Both a Roadmap and a Benchmark

The experience-centric organization has core behaviors that characterize it and nurture its development. At some point, the organization's efforts toward experience centricity become energized like a flywheel and start to turn on their own. You can use this chapter to help develop your organization, or as a means of monitoring your progress and seeing how many of these behaviors your organization exhibits. There is no specific order to these points, although arguably the first one—knowing the experience you want to offer—is the most important.

You Know What Experience You Should Offer

The experience-centric organization knows exactly what experience it wants its customers to have. Further, it knows how to make that experience happen through the service personality, tone of voice, and individual touchpoints along the experiential journey. The organization is continually updating and adjusting the experience, and all members of the organization know their role in delivering it. Discussions regarding strategy and tactics regularly center on their relevance to, or consequences for, the desired customer experience.

You See, Hear, and Can Be the Customer

As an experience-centric organization, you listen to what customers want to tell you, rather than seeking answers to what you want to hear. You are also aware that to surprise and delight customers you have to be proactive about customer needs, and intuit needs that customers cannot express. The experience-centric organization knows the desires of its customers and has the agility to react to, and to stimulate, these desires (see Figure 4-1).

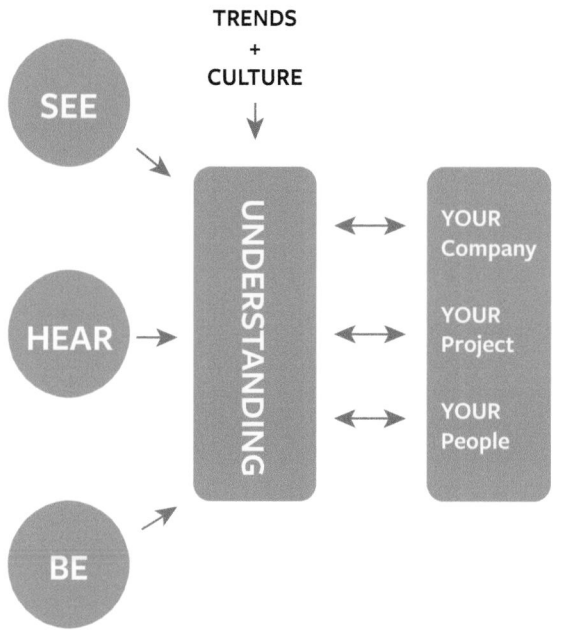

Figure 4-1. Make this the mantra of your organization: See the customer, hear the customer, and be the customer! Understand what this means in the bigger picture, and apply it to your company, your project, and your people.

In this organization, you have built a picture of your customers that comes from an integrated understanding of them—and when you have this, you can have the confidence to sometimes go against what they say. This is because you know that there are other factors in play when it comes to customer desire, and that by going ahead of your customers, you can lead them: they will desire what you are offering. The more you know your customers, the more you can be ahead of them, confident that they will follow you. To paraphrase Atticus Finch, "to really know a man, you have to walk in his shoes."[1]

You Listen to the Customer, and Understand the Meaning Behind What They Say

Even though you are skilled at listening to customers, you have also developed the ability to go beyond what they say and intuit what they mean. You are able to reflect on your customers in context and extract meaning from what they say and do.

Your Customers Believe You Have Their Best Interests at Heart

Because you know your customers so well and deliver on your experiential promise, they consider you benevolent. They believe that you act with their best interests at heart, within the frame of the offering that they have entered into. This builds mutual trust and creates a long-term relationship. It also promotes customer acceptance and tolerance when things don't go as planned or break down.

You Understand the Cultural Zeitgeist and Design for It

The zeitgeist is the spirit of the times. You know what characterizes the zeitgeist, and you follow it as it evolves and changes. You understand how society embraces your offering as part of a cultural movement that utilizes the nature of groups to share, build, and experience together.

The organization continuously engages in trendslation—that is, translating cultural trends into experiences—and has taken a larger role within the culture. This role allows you to be influenced by culture and, to a certain extent, you can influence it in return.

Your Story Resonates with Employees and Customers

You have spent time building a story based on your DNA, supporting that story through the touchpoints of your service, continually rewriting it together with your customers during interactions, and listening to it be told and retold by your customers and employees. The story is not fiction; it is a transformation of your DNA, recounted and experienced in narrative form. And a good story can never be told too many times.

You Are Balanced with Multiple Intelligences

The experience-centric organization balances the analytical with the creative, the practical with the social, and all the while is focused on developing the emotional. You encourage a "multiple intelligences" approach to the organization and the experience it supports. The organization values empathy as a core intelligence—not only customer empathy, but empathy within the organization for the roles and challenges each and every employee takes on to make the experience a success.

You Are Reverse-Engineered from the Experience

The experience-centric organization always works from the experience backward through the wheel of experience centricity. Starting with the frontline employee, it asks, "What does this employee need to be able to give the experience the customer craves?" Then, taking another step back, it asks, "What does this work group need to be able to support the individual frontline employee in delivering the experience?" Finally, it asks, "What does this manager need to be able to support the team and the individual in providing the desired experience?" The same is asked of platforms and infrastructure within the organization: "What enterprise platform will enable the touchpoints to provide the desired experience?" With this view, the term *management* breaks down into a combination of tasking, trusting, and tending to the frontline touchpoints.

You Are Aligned Around the Experience

The organization is aligned around the experience that you wish to give customers. Everyone in the organization understands the wheel of experience centricity and their role in energizing it. There is internal rotation of staff, such that all employees have periods of customer contact and therefore understand the importance of the customer experience, even if they are far from the front line. Everyone in the organization works to support the delivery of a superior customer experience.

You Have Clear Responsibilities and Structures in Place for Experience

Everyone in the experience-centric organization feels a responsibility and a motivation to develop and deliver desirable experiences. Employees are empowered to do it, and they take this responsibility seriously. The CEO is responsible for the customer experience and has a supporting part of the organization, headed up by the chief experience officer (CXO). The CXO in turn is responsible for the orchestration of the experience and is the caretaker and custodian of the experiential DNA.

You Are Symbolic

You know the enhanced significance of certain objects, behaviors, or interactions for customers, and you use them as part of your design. Coupled with this, your awareness of cultural relevance adds to the significance of these symbolic objects, behaviors, and interactions. Customers enjoy a richer experience with you, compared to your competitors, and this gives added meaning in their lives.

Experiential Journeys Are Your Bread and Butter

Experiential journeys have added an emotional layer to your journey structure, and you have found your organization's own way of creating them. You recognize that smileys as a description of the customer experience are a thing of the past. Instead you are specific, describing how the customer should feel at each stage of a journey, and how you can make that happen. You continually craft the emotional curve of your experiential journeys, always looking to improve and tweak it—the odd nudge here, honing the tone of voice there. This extreme attention to detail pays off by fostering employee ownership and a shared desire for perfection.

You Have Authenticity of Purpose

You have an authentic purpose in terms of a transparency between your DNA and the customer experience. This clarity is visible to employees and customers alike, and makes life easier for all. It also encourages forgiveness from customers during service breakdowns, when things don't go as expected. There is a generosity from employees and customers alike that comes from the simplicity that lies in authenticity of purpose.

Brand Has Become Brand Experience

The term *brand* has morphed into *brand experience* as you have focused on translating your experiential DNA into better and better experiences. Branding is now focused on experience fulfillment and interactions with customers, and takes a greater role in innovation projects.

Insights from Lynn Hunsaker

Lynn Hunsaker is a Hall of Fame author at CustomerThink and serves on the Customer Experience Professionals Association's Board of Directors; since the early 1990s she has led customer experience transformation at Fortune 250 companies. She finds that organizations are so caught up in what competitors are doing that they forget to consider what they can and should offer their customers.

If you analyze Disney and others in the forefront of customer experience, you will see that the customer experience permeates the whole organization. They have it in their DNA. The whole idea of customer experience is living up to your brand promise. People are looking for a silver bullet to solve the customer experience. There is no silver bullet.

The CEO is the most critical person in customer experience. If there is no alignment between the CEO and CXO then there will always be a suboptimal transformation.

Transforming silos is the next frontier of customer experience management. As soon as you start working with experience journeys, you will find that silos are causing problems and there is a need to *tame* them. I say tame rather than *bust*, because they need to be there. However, they need to be connected, and a collaborative attitude is necessary. That is a real challenge for an organization that has never really had an experiential focus.

"Transforming silos is the next frontier of customer experience management."

I advocate a three-part methodology called "customer experience DNA." It has three key interlocking elements:

1. Align from the top
2. All hands on deck
3. Value maximization

When companies first start the transformation journey, there is usually too much of a focus on value maximization, and too little on all hands on deck and being aligned from the top. If an organization addresses points one and two, then point three is easier to address.

> **"People are looking for a silver bullet to solve the customer experience. There is no silver bullet."**

It is vital that an organization knows what kind of experience they need to give their customers. The best place to start is to formulate what you want customers to feel. If you can formulate that "we want our customers to feel A and B and C" then you have something to aim toward. If you don't know what outcome the customer is looking for, then you will not be able to develop services that make it happen.

Brand experience, customer experience, and employee experience need to be brought together. Unfortunately, in many cases, [organizations] have divorced themselves from this, and have felt the need to just promise something. This leads to a dramatic fall in trust, and in general trust is going down, down, down because of this. It's ironic that the things on a customer experience manager's mind are often very different to the things that are on a customer's mind.

You Develop Continuously Through Concept Innovation and Experience Prototypes

The development of future concept services is one way that you get involved in the wider societal culture, but the majority of the concept services you develop are used internally to assist with alignment, infusion, and ultimately creating a relevant organizational culture that is infused with the customer experience. You have developed the skills to prototype new experiences based on the innovative offerings that you are always considering. You are confident that your innovation pipeline is an experiential roadmap with a strong fit to your organizational purpose.

You Make "Concept Cars" as Second Nature

The automotive industry has a tradition of developing concept cars (see Figure 4-2), and over time has found that they communicate not only outward to a potential customer base, but also inward, preparing the organization for change. The experience-centric organization

Figure 4-2. The Buick Model Y, built in 1938, was the world's first concept car. Since then, concept cars have become a means of propelling an organization forward, and today, they are developed as much to prepare an organization for change as to draw external customers. The experience-centric organization understands this, and creates concept services as a form of organizational and market development. (Harley Earl and "The Y Job"; source: Flickr.)

knows that developing the equivalent of the concept car within the organization is a means of propelling the organization toward the future—a future that is highly experiential.

You Use Design to Explore and Understand the World and Fail Forward

Studies of designers show that they use design as a way of understanding the problem by trying to solve it. In a kind of trial-and-error process, designers attempt solutions to determine whether they offer promise, and to better understand what might and might not work. This approach, often called "failing fast and forward," is a way of rapidly understanding and learning about a new problem area and a potential solution space. You design with a view to having multiple failures along the way, and you are not precious with your solutions. You expect them to fail during the early stages of a project, because that is how you find out what works.

Exploring Easy and Difficult in People's Homes

When I was working with design company Livework to simplify insurance for customers, I worked to understand what "easy" meant to customers. As part of this work, we visited customers and gave them two cards: one said "easy" and the other said "difficult." We asked them to go around their homes and point out things they were surrounded by that were easy or difficult. The cards helped them focus their minds and pick out individual items in their homes.

The results changed the project's view of simple and difficult and led to a change of direction, toward a new design of insurance policy.

Source: author.

You Are Optimistic, and So Are Your Customers

When the design and delivery of memorable experiences is your core mission, you naturally work to provide better experiences, always with an intent to improve the existing situation. This engenders a culture of directed improvement in the organization that is reflected in the

Insights from Christian Beil

Christian Beil has been successful in introducing the design thinking approach into an extremely large organization. He is a Senior Innovation Design Expert at BASF, Germany, working in the BASF management consulting group Growth & Innovation.

From [BASF's] point of view, there are two major converging aspects pointing to radical change. Firstly, more people are concerned about the environment, and secondly, digitalization and platforms can open [up] radically new solutions. These two are good triggers that can open [up] radically new experiential offerings.

Compared to B2C companies' classical B2B companies are far behind when it comes to customer orientation. With our new corporate strategy, the aspiration is to be the world's leading chemical company for our customers. We want to strengthen our passion for customers throughout the entire organization. We therefore need to go further toward experience centricity. A lot of people at BASF believe this is fine-tuning to the left or right, but in reality it means offering things that are radically different. The awareness is there, and with the new strategy under way, it will play a greater role in BASF.

The core competencies of BASF are good chemists, and research expertise. As an organization we need to find a balance between customer orientation and a technology/products focus. What I see is that the majority of chemists do not know how to generate customer insights. By training they have a different focus, so they need help understanding customers to generate insights, and the group I work for offers this to them."

At the strategic level there is a need for training across the whole company. At the organizational level, more training of middle management is needed toward understanding customers. Focusing on customers gives a focus on your customer base. However, environments have changed and there are opportunities for new ecosystems in which the customer plays a different role. From a customer experience perspective, empathy is vital. The ability to ask the right questions and reflect and then translate [the findings] back into compelling offerings is something we work very hard to develop.

We have done a lot of empathic design, and how to go out and explore needs and pains, including living in relevant contexts and shadowing people getting water, etc. In Mumbai, our team worked with NGOs and lived with families in slums to learn what could be done to understand better. There, we developed a water "ATM" using micropayments, to provide clean drinking water as part of a customer-focused solution. This was well received and is a good example of creating a service offering from what was earlier a product focus.

> **"From a customer experience perspective, empathy is vital. The ability to ask the right questions and reflect and then translate [the findings] back into compelling offerings is something we work very hard to develop."**

New business models based on a service-based customer orientation offer huge potential. As an example in sustainability: the agricultural chemical market uses a large amount of pesticides and fungicides, and use can be error-prone. We worked with potato farmers in Brazil, where we showed that, following BASF expert advice, they could increase yield and quality by applying fewer chemicals. This was developed into a new business model that was service-based with a novel offering. The farmers did not pay for the chemicals, but instead paid a subscription to a service that included advice about when and what to spray, field data, access to the BASF traceability platform, and access to potato buyers, who were interested in purchasing "sustainable" potatoes. Although this would cannibalize BASF sales, the value proposition was seen as so compelling that it would offer long-term advantage for BASF. In other words, instead of selling a product, BASF was offering more yield, better quality, and market access.

market. This optimism and faith is something that your customers share and take part in. They feel it through the interactions they have with your organization, and are therefore willing to accept that sometimes things won't go as expected. Optimism and faith translate into fault tolerance and loyalty and a positive circle of improvement in the customer experience.

You Continually Monitor the Multiple Experiences Your Customers Have

As an organization you are aware of the difference between the lived experience, gained directly from interactions with touchpoints, the remembered experience afterward, and the shared experience as told to others. You know these well, and monitor each continuously. At the same time, you do not have a tyranny of metrics within the organization, since you balance measurement with your own insights at all levels of the organization.

You Know That the Devil and God Both Are in the Details

You are successful at matching the overall offering with the detail in the customer interactions, so that together they are an experiential fit for your experiential DNA. This creates an experience that is more than its individual parts or the sum of those parts.

The organization knows that customers understand the offering as a holistic promise providing experiential benefits, delivered through interactions with many touchpoints. You understand this, and also know that it can be hard work to be obsessed with the details. At the same time, you know the pleasure customers gain when you get it right.

You Have a Sensory Orientation

You actively and wisely use all five senses in the touchpoints of your service to support the experience you want to give customers. You know that the visual sense is very strong in most interactions, but you diligently use the four other senses too.

You Are Known as Much for What You Don't Do as for What You Do

Choosing the right investments in infrastructure, the right organizational changes, and the right innovation projects to move forward is more about saying "no" to options than saying "yes." There are countless possibilities to invest in projects, but the experience-centric organization invests only in projects that improve alignment around the customer experience. This means saying "no" more than "yes" and continually questioning how an investment will improve the customer experience.

Design Thinking Is a Core Competence in Your Organization

You constantly strive to improve existing situations, always looking for a creative leap. You understand that design thinking adds something to your existing skill set,[2] and make it a core competency in your organization. Design thinking is found in the leadership of all experience-centric organizations, as an approach to continual innovation in changing situations.

Abductive Thinking

Recent design research has discovered that designers use a little-known but important kind of thinking called *abductive logic*. Traditionally we think of inductive and deductive logic, but abductive logic is an important third way of reasoning. Abductive thinking is thinking about how things might be, rather than how they are or have been. This is a logic that is used in all disciplines, but designers are trained in it. They look past what is and explore what can be. It is a fundamental way of thinking, of generating new hypotheses, and it is central to innovation. When combined with the ability to visualize what can be, and to make prototypes of it, abductive thinking is a core innovation capability.

You Do the Right Thing, and Do the Thing Right

The experience-centric organization knows the importance of getting the right fit between the service offering and its experiential DNA. At the same time, it has an attention to detail that ensures that the experiential vision also imbues the touchpoints and interactions. This is a combination of doing the right thing, and doing the thing right. The two are inseparable, and this ambidextrous way of working is key in the experience-centric organization. Doing the right thing focuses on zooming out and asking the big questions about what it is you offer as an organization. What does banking mean in a mobile and socially connected world? How should healthcare be provided when the patient has spent two days Googling their illness and knows more (in some cases) than the doctor? The continual questioning of what can be at this level is proactive, looking for radical innovations and continually exploring experiential futures. It's always striving to improve the service offering. At the same time, the experience-centric organization also has its eye on doing the thing right. It zooms in, right down to last detail, recognizing that it has a promise to deliver on. This ability to move between a macro view and a micro view is a core competency in the experience-centric organization (see Figure 4-3).

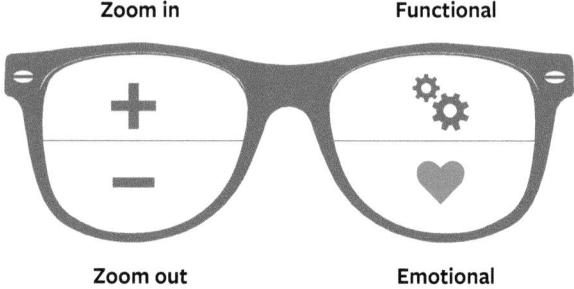

Figure 4-3. Zooming out and zooming in, focusing on functional and emotional, is a typical approach to experience-centric innovation. During this process the organization zooms out in terms of developing new offerings and zooms in on the detail, the individual touchpoint experience. At the same time, it focuses on combining functional value and emotional value.

Doing the Right Thing—It Pays to Get It Right

If you had an hour to save the world, what would you do? This question was supposedly asked of Albert Einstein many years ago, to which he replied, "I would spend 55 minutes defining the problem, then 5 minutes solving." Whether true or not, this statement summarizes the importance of fully understanding the broader context of a project as part of its resolution. At a project's start, an organization knows little about what the problem actually is but makes big decisions regarding its solution, so it's crucial to develop a rapid and broad understanding, particularly around user aspects. This is a cheap way to reduce risk further down the line.

Studies of the innovation process show that the first stages of an innovation project have the greatest potential to influence the final outcome and cost of the project. However, teams often hop over them to start developing something quickly. The front end of a project generally constitutes about 8%

of the project life cycle, but it involves decisions that determine 80% of the project costs. This is because decisions made early are decisions of direction, rather than detail. Getting this right at the start is a way of improving how the remaining 92% of the project life cycle is used and reduces the risk of failure. Once you realize this, it makes sense to be thorough at the start of a project.

As Visual Groupies, You Co-Design

Co-design is your normal way of working, because you know that any innovation will impact the whole wheel of experience centricity in some way or another. By having representatives for each part of the wheel working together, you speed up development and implementation and reduce problems along the way.

The organization works visually, sketching during discussions to illustrate and clarify ideas and reduce the risk of misunderstandings. In other words, through this visualization, the organization shows it has listened, understood, and imagined how a solution might work if implemented, and communicated that idea so that all can understand it. You encourage visualization in all cross-functional discussions (including leadership meetings).

You Encourage "Coolhunting" for Experiences

You encourage people to bring home and share new and exciting experiences with others, be they innovative offerings, touchpoints, platforms, or structures. This promotes a culture of looking for and discussing new and valuable solutions. This is *coolhunting* in its best form, an organizational interest in exciting new innovations with a goal to share them and learn from them. Coolhunting is part of the formal and informal structure of your organization—formal in terms of providing a means to facilitate and reward sharing, and informal in terms of being infused in and a natural part of the organizational function.

Coolhunting ZOZO

One of my colleagues discovered ZOZO.com and immediately spread the news to others at work. ZOZO is innovative in both its offering and its touchpoints and detailed interactions. It is experientially a step change in clothes shopping for the large number of people who don't fit standard off-the-rack sizes. This got us all interested not only in trying out the offering, but also in discussing the potential that lies in its clever use of a smartphone as a 3D scanner. Within the design community, there is often a lot of sharing of new experiences and experiential offerings, and this leads to new ideas and inspirations in projects and in the everyday. Maybe the same should be true of your organization!

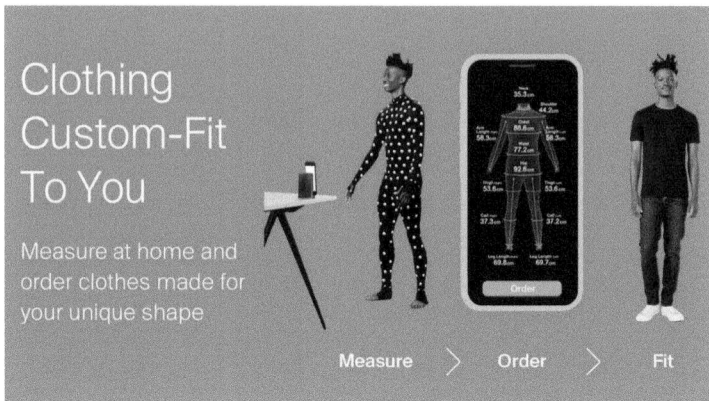

Source: ZOZO.com.

You Emulate the World of Film in Your Own Way

You understand the flow experience of film and want to emulate it, but in your own way. *Flow* is a term that was first used in 1975 by the psychologist Mihaly Csikszentmihalyi to describe a situation of complete absorption in a task, resulting in loss of one's sense of space and time. You know that films are characterized by exactly the same things that characterize services: a strong experiential message, a large team of disparate specialists that need to collaborate to deliver that experience, a high degree of complexity, technical constraints, budgetary constraints, and (not least) aspects such as the peculiarities of individual stars.

Changing the Mindset of Customer Contact

Picture this scene: the main offices of a global telco in Stockholm (one with a customer-centric goal). A customer walks in with a complaint, and everyone in the office suddenly is busy, or tries to look busy. Nobody wants the discomfort of having to deal with "the problem."

This was the reality when we started a service design academy in Sweden as part of an initiative to develop competencies in the organization of listening to customers. During a carefully crafted course, we wanted to shift the focus from "What's the matter (with you)?" to "What matters to you?" to teach listening skills and imbue a real love of customer contact.

The course and workshops were a success, and some months afterward we heard how things had changed. Now, when a customer comes to the office, there is competition to talk to them. The reason? Changing the mindset to one of listening, combined with the empowerment to act on the situation and make it better. A customer listening culture makes things happen.

In addition, you recognize that films have cultural relevance and have the ability to fit with the culture of the moment. Your services continually evolve to do the same.

Do Job Promotions Take You Away from Your Customers?

Generally I have found that the higher one's position in an organization, the more distanced they become from their customers (they don't necessarily dislike customers, it seems, just contact with them), and the more out of touch they become. Regular customer contact is replaced by cold numbers, surrogates for real customer insights, and lack of feelings. I'm not sure why this is; perhaps they get out of the practice of customer contact, they feel they are too busy, or they're just glad that they don't have to talk to those "pesky customers" anymore. In her book *Divining Desire: Focus Groups and the Culture of Consultation* (OR Books), Liza Featherstone explains how everyone hates the focus group. Participants feel awkward, the facilitators feel awkward, and the people behind the two-way mirror really don't want to hear what the participants say. In addition, feedback from a focus group needs to be taken with a large pinch of salt because you can't always trust what people say in such a setting. Why is there such a fundamental disconnect between companies and customers? Well, I think it is because organizations are not good listeners. It is alien for them, and for an organization that is active and hectic, it is difficult to sit back and really listen.

You Avoid the Trap of Number Comforting

You understand that the customer experience cannot adequately be described through measures and quantities alone. You have a pragmatic approach to the use of quantitative data and use it critically. You do not go in for "number comforting" as a means of distancing yourself from customers, but instead use customer data in a way that brings them inside the organization.

You Are Not Afraid to Go Against Customer Wishes

You have the confidence and experience to look beyond what your customers are saying. You know that they most often can talk well about what they know, about something that exists, and you respect that they have limited abilities to look into the future like you can. You know that sometimes you need to talk to customers in a different way, and get to know more about what their lives are like and less about what they want.

You Know That Meaning Is the New Money

You reflect on broader cultural issues and are not afraid to ask yourself what these customer and cultural inputs really mean at a deeper level. You understand that people are looking for meaning in their lives, and strive to develop meaningful experiences for your customers. You do this because you know that meaning is the new currency; it translates into devoted and loyal customers and long-term relationships.

How Designer Christopher Bailey Transformed Burberry Through an Experiential Vision

Christopher Bailey transformed Burberry in both aesthetic and financial terms. In 2001, Burberry was a heritage rainwear brand that had become the butt of tabloid jokes. Bailey built a new identity, and the Burberry trench coat was transformed into a sought-after and highly lucrative trophy piece. It also served as a crucial plot device in the story Bailey was telling the world about Burberry, which framed the brand as a glossy, romantic, modern version of Britishness.

But Bailey was more than a clothing designer. He was the experience director of Burberry. In 2009, when Burberry moved into its new state-of-the-art center at Horseferry House, Bailey remastered every modern detail—right down to the mineral-water bottles he designed for the canteen. He hired people from gaming companies, and he walked the floors to sit with coders. He oversaw the photographic and video studios installed in the basement, where product could be shot and uploaded to Burberry.com in minutes. Bailey became the first-ever designer at a publicly traded fashion company to be named both CEO and chief creative officer.

In 2008, Burberry became the first brand to live-stream its catwalk show, something that is now commonplace for most designer labels. It was one of the first brands to utilize social media and certainly the first luxury fashion label to see the value in Snapchat. It was the first fashion brand to have a channel on Apple Music. In 2014, it was the first brand to use in-tweet purchases. Famously, in 2016, Bailey changed the face of the fashion calendar format forever by introducing a see-now, buy-now concept that enabled consumers to buy the collections straight off the catwalk rather than waiting for six months.

Bailey's transformation of Burberry was experience-led, powered by desirable products. It shows how clarity of experiential vision can demand and initiate innovation in multiple areas, thereby creating great commercial value.

Source: Flickr user atomtesuwan and Creative Commons.

Endnotes

1   Atticus Finch served as a moral hero for many readers in the book, *To Kill a Mockingbird* by Harper Lee, published in 1960

2   *Design thinking* is a term used to describe how designers approach and carry out their work. It has its roots back in the 1950s with the emergence of industrial design as a separate discipline, but was introduced as a term by Tim Brown from IDEO in 2008 in the *Harvard Business Review* article, "Design Thinking," 86 no. 6 (2008), 84.

5

Organizing for Experience Centricity

Great experiences are provided by the whole organization, where everyone has a part. This chapter describes how you can structure the organization around a carefully crafted combination of formal and informal organizational culture. It integrates design and design thinking into organizational change, showing how you can design your organizational logics to align with the experience you want to provide. It introduces the idea of organizational prototyping, which applies design thinking principles so you can approach organizational change in the same way you approach innovation, by design.

Innovation in service has been described as the unique application of organizational competencies and ways of working and thinking to create value in use. This chapter introduces the new competencies, ways of working, and ways of thinking that an organization must develop on its path to experience centricity. It uses design thinking as the basis for what I term *experience thinking* and *experience doing*, which can be characterized as having the customer experience at heart, being customer-centric, visual, culturally aware, and collaborative, and simultaneously retaining the powers of being effective and efficient at service delivery. Developing experience-centric organizations is a team sport, where everyone has their part.

When you watch the credits of a film, you see how many people worked together to provide the experience you had during the previous couple of hours. The credits also include people who are indirectly involved—people in accounting and finance, for example—because there is a recognition that a film is a huge collective effort. The same mindset should apply to your organization: everyone is involved, and everyone is necessary. This includes the customer (it is strange how much organizational design ignores the customer; it's as if they do not exist). This approach makes all employees stakeholders, and recognizes that the customer is a stakeholder too. Indeed, the experience-centric organization is a co-designed and co-produced organization.

The customer experience is a reflection of the organization that delivers it, and the experience-centric organization requires an experiential way of thinking and doing as its cornerstone. The organization as a whole needs to be structured to support and play a part in the experience that is provided to customers, because the whole organization is involved in its production. Everybody contributes to the customer experience, and everybody has to *feel* that they contribute. This means both a sense of part-ownership, along with the pride that goes with it, and an understanding of their role in making it happen.

To achieve experience centricity, you'll need to design new or updated organizational logics that are aligned around the customer experience. That is the theme of this chapter: what you'll need to transform your existing organizational logics into experience-centric ones.

Doing What You Love, and Loving What You Do

The great motivation researcher, Teresa Amabile had a mantra: people are most creative when they are doing what they love, and loving what they are doing.[1] This idea is mirrored by the famous researcher in flow Mihaly Csikszentmihalyi, who describes flow as complete absorption in what one does, resulting in a loss of one's sense of space and time.[2] Both explanations are relevant to the experience-centric organization, because great experiences come from motivated and focused employees.

To enable the necessary aspects of alignment, infusion, and orchestration, it is important that people feel that they are a part of something greater, and have a sense of co-ownership of the customer experience. This requires two things:

- An intrinsic motivation in the organization's employees to be a part of the grand scheme of the experience (that is, every individual identifies with the experiential mission of the organization)
- A way of working and a structure of work such that individuals feel that they are enabled by the organization to contribute in the best way they can

This is why the authenticity of purpose of the organization should be clear. The clearer it is, the easier it is to recruit people to the organization, motivate them, and develop structures to assist them. Further, authenticity of purpose creates a self-selection of employees, as people who do not align with the organization will leave. If people do what they love in work, and are enabled to love what they are doing, you will have a well-functioning organization.

Who Owns the Customer Experience

A discussion about who owns the customer experience within the organization is central and needs to be clarified early on. The customer owns the experience in the sense that they have the experience and their perception of experiential value is key. At the same time, everyone in the organization should feel that they contribute to the experience and, in that way, have some ownership of it.

From the organizational perspective there needs to be clear understanding about who is responsible for ensuring a great experience and who is responsible for designing for this experience. These are two different things. The CEO is responsible for ensuring that the experience can be delivered and obtaining organizational alignment around it. The CXO is responsible for its design. The CXO is analogous to the director of a film, and therefore should have creative responsibility for developing the experience vision and designing for it. This is not the same as artistic vision, since the CXO has to balance feasibility, viability, and desirability: feasibility in terms of being able to deliver the experience, viability in terms of it creating mutual value, and desirability in terms of customers loving it. This is a critical position and the CXO needs to be chosen carefully, since it is an interpretive role. The experience director interprets the DNA of the company and the zeitgeist of the market to develop an experiential vision. The CEO is a key partner in this, and has the role of translating the vision into action together with the rest of the leadership.

The interplay between the CEO and CXO is important, as is the relationship between the CXO and the rest of the leadership. The CXO has to be a team player while also being welcomed as such by the others in the team. The dynamic of this new role and the interactions between the different team members are key to the success of the transformation you are embarking on.

Designing Organizational Logics

The term *organizational logics* describes how an organization works—that is, the ways of thinking, believing, and doing in the organization.[3] Organizational logics are unique to the organization, and while it may mot be easy to describe them, they are always there. When someone says, "That's not how things are done around here," they are referring to a logic that the organization uses, but perhaps has never explicitly defined. Your organization has multiple logics, and most likely they are not experience-centric, so this means you will have to transform them.

Organizational logics are systemic, structural, and cultural. They're systemic because an organization is based on systems, each designed and put together in a particular way to achieve something (i.e., some logic was applied to define what these systems should achieve and do). They're structural because organizations are made up of governing structures and rules. However, organizational logics are also highly cultural, since they are based on beliefs, expectations, and values. Cultural logics relate to motivation and the organization's reason to be, and are therefore central to the organization's identity. In this way, they form a central part of your experiential DNA and are therefore important to identify and change.

This combination of systemic, structural, and cultural logics defines how the organization thinks and works, and its development over time has made your organization what it is today. These logics make a particular kind of sense within the organization and are not really thought about, as they have always been there. They're something you get to know when you start to work in an organization and something you need to transform as the world changes around you. As you shift toward becoming an experience-centric organization, you will have to design new organizational logics, recognize the logics you have now, and plan a transition. During this transformation, you will have to focus more on cultural aspects, since the customer experience is often a reflection of the internal culture of an organization. The structural side, therefore, should be seen as a support for the culture you want the organization to have, and for the experience you wish to provide.

We talked earlier about enabling the organization to deliver the right experience, about alignment in the organization, shared ownership of the experience, and the infusion of experiential thinking throughout the organization. All of these are central parts of the organizational logics you need to have in place.

The Importance of a Symbolic Focus

Since experience relates to emotions, meaning, and feelings, the symbolic aspects of your organizational logics have particular importance. This is why I emphasize the importance of leadership, and particularly leadership actions. As you'll see in Chapters 9 and 10, the experience-centric organization reacts to cultural meaning, but it is also a part of it and even forms it. Every action by the organization will be viewed through a cultural lens, and many will be given symbolic meaning. If a leader places their office among the call center staff, it says something about their role and importance in the organization. If the CEO of Harley Davidson goes to a hog rally, it speaks as much to Harley staff as it does to hog owners about the importance of customers and motorcycle culture. If the story about an employee who goes the extra mile for a customer is retold and becomes a legend in the organization, it says something about their focus on customer experience. It both influences the organization and reveals something about it.

When we hear that Sony CEO Akio Morita had a special jacket made to enable him to carry new Sony products in development, that says something about his focus on innovation. When the CEO of Ryanair (a low-cost Irish carrier) says he is considering charging customers for going to the toilet on flights, that says something about his attitude toward economy flights and customers. When a customer goes to the effort of writing a song about his guitar being broken by an airline's baggage handler,[4] it becomes a symbol of customer relations within that airline. Myths and stories form an important part of the symbolic fabric of your organization, so when transforming the organization, you must understand the deeper meaning of actions and design those symbols into the transformation. Which stories do you want to be told within your organization? Which ones are told now?

Interview with Olof Schybergson

As CEO of Fjord, Olof Schybergson knows a lot about digital transformation. Fjord is a part of Accenture Interactive, and now has over a thousand designers spread over 27 offices. This makes them one of the largest design and innovation consultancies in the world. Olof believes strongly in design as a strategic resource and argues here for its role in the transformation of whole industries.

Q: Talk about transformation toward experience centricity.

A: I think one of the meta-challenges of many CEOs is about how to reorient the business to be more experience-centric and how to move from the industrial calcified model to a flexible and fluid agile living business.

It's pretty much impossible to take the old model and replace it with the new model overnight. So it's not just about staying in the old and ignoring the new or also jumping to the new. It's rather a careful or wise pivot. The pivot is to a living business that is adaptable, scalable, and fluid. It is needed because the everyday way of generating value is being challenged and needs to be reinvented. The wise pivot is where you maximize efficiency to free up capacity to invest in the new, which you build gradually. Then you move the old core into the new. It's not a wholesale shift it's a gradual increased investment and focus on the new.

> "Triggers vary, but often the important questions are quite existential, like 'How can I create an experience that is best of class?' 'Who are my customers tomorrow?' 'What business am I in?' and 'What business should I be in?'"

Q: What are the tripwires along the transformation journey?

A: It is a great challenge to free up mindshare and organizational leadership capability to be able to focus on the new. This is especially true when the new is very small. There is a key calibration question about how much you can invest in the new before it becomes a meaningful business.

Tradition can be a problem. Organizations that have worked in one way are often ill-equipped to build new ways of working, especially ones that might cannibalize their existing business. So this can lead to a kind of organ rejection. You have to be prepared to face some headwinds and to challenge your own way of thinking, your traditional talent model, and so on. If you pull the plug on your new business too quickly, you will lose out. If you are not prepared to meet headwinds, then you are in danger.

Transformation toward experience centricity is a C-level responsibility. Lack of C-level and CEO-level sponsorship is a major tripwire. Transformations such as these are a major changes in the way that an organization thinks and acts, and should not be placed down in the organization. They have to be led from the top.

Q: How do you see the role of design in this transformation?

A: We are increasingly seeing design being used to create a strategic compass for the company. Triggers vary, but often the important questions are quite existential, like "How can I create an experience that is best of class?" "Who are my customers tomorrow?" "What business am I in?" and "What business should I be in?" Design helps ask, explore, and answer these questions.

Design is essential to make sense of the [qualitative] and [quantitative] data to make things meaningful and actionable. The fusion of data and design is important.

There can be an inability to mobilize around design—an inability to know where to start and how to get off the ground when going across different business units. Many realize that it is important. It is less about resistance and more about activation.

Creating Alignment and Empowerment Within the Organization: The Top-Up Approach

The top-up approach mixes a top-down leadership message with a bottom-up empowerment model. Leadership is important, and it is vital that leaders take a lead in the experience-centric organization. They are better placed than others to transmit ideas because they command attention within the organization. Those ideas can be transformative because they easily become symbolic, and can be backed up through structural actions. Leadership views have to be seen in the organization as guiding lights toward experience centricity.

At the same time, the experience-centric organization recognizes that the customer experience occurs in the interactions between the customer and the employees (or other touchpoints). This requires enabling and empowering the front line to be able to deliver on experiential expectations. The top-down approach needs to be supported by a bottom-up one, and starting with the interactions is a great way of achieving this.

One of the benefits of focusing on the experience is that everyone can relate to it, and it has the effect of aligning dissenting views or approaches within the organization. The customer experience is something that everyone can understand and relate to personally. It creates a clarity of purpose within the organization, and has a logic that few can argue against. Therefore, taking an experiential focus can relieve internal tensions in the organization and create high-level agreement. When this focus is coupled to the adoption of the wheel of experience centricity, it creates structures and roles that the entire organization can embrace. Add to this the interaction-out approach, described in the following section, and you'll gain the alignment you need.

The Interaction-Out Approach: Working from the Experience Outward

The experience-centric organization knows what experience it wants its customers to have. This is the starting point for designing and discussing how the experience can be fulfilled through the touchpoints of the service.

The interaction-out approach, illustrated in Figure 5-1, can be used by a cross-functional development team. It starts with the experience and the question: "If we want to give experience X, then what should we do as an organization to empower the employee (or technology) to co-produce this experience together with the customer?" That will give you a focus on the employee experience (or touchpoint design) and how to enable it. Then it is possible to work backward, and discuss how to enable the frontline employer through the team or group working together. Here the focus can be on formal and informal organization. Further back again, we can ask, "What should the team leader do to enable the team to deliver the experience?" This can continue further and further out into the organization to create a structure, a way of thinking, and a way of working.

All the time, you can use the wheel of experience centricity to discuss experience fulfillment, enabling, and structure. What platforms do we need such that the touchpoint potential can be fulfilled? What structure do we need to have a viable business model? This inverts the traditional *push* hierarchical view to being one of experience *pull*, where the moment of truth—the customer experience—is in focus.

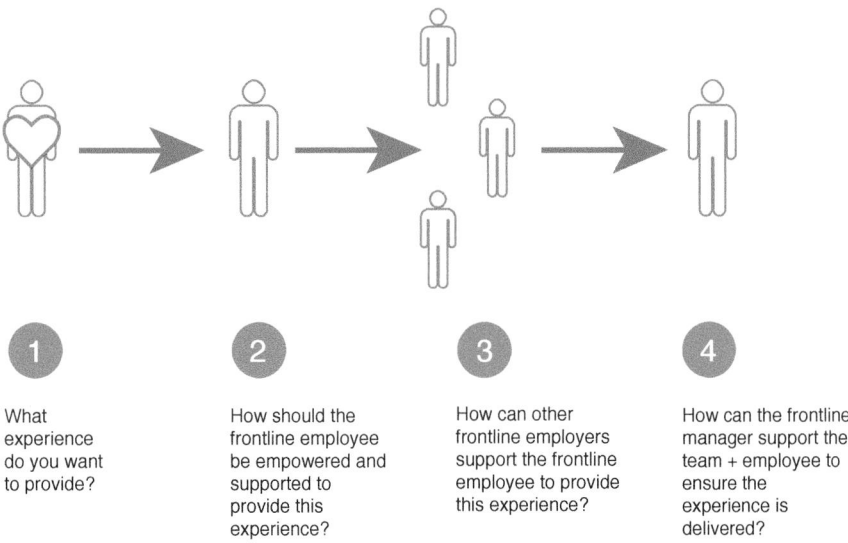

1	2	3	4
What experience do you want to provide?	How should the frontline employee be empowered and supported to provide this experience?	How can other frontline employers support the frontline employee to provide this experience?	How can the frontline manager support the team + employee to ensure the experience is delivered?

Figure 5-1. The interaction-out approach forces you to start with the experience and then ensure that the touchpoints (in this case frontline employees) are enabled to provide this experience. In this way, you work from the experience outward, and can define the role of other employees and managers.

Rotating Jobs to Develop Experiential Empathy

Earlier chapters have stressed the importance of "experiencing the experience" during design and development, but this also applies to others in the organization who may be far away from the customer experience. To get on board, they have to experience the experience the organization provides from a customer's point of view. When a janitor at NASA famously said in the 1960s that he was not cleaning offices but helping put a man on the moon, he was demonstrating employee alignment with the overarching mission of the organization. Likewise, in the experience-centric organization there is alignment among employees, and job rotation—hosting people from other departments—can be a means of understanding what the intended experience is, how difficult it is to provide it, how important it is to customers, and how essential it is that everyone contribute to the mission. The closer you are to the customer, the easier it is to understand this, but as mentioned, not all functions in the company are close to the customer. Therefore, job rotation is a good way to imprint on all members of the organization what it means to provide a fantastic experience. The CEO and CXO need to be a part of this exercise as well, both for the symbolic effect, which cannot be underestimated, and for the practical learning they will bring back to the leadership team.

Infusion as Part of a Design Strategy

I have used the term *infusion* a lot in this book, because it is a strong means of creating change within the organization. As explained before, infusion can be likened to placing a tea bag in water and watching the color spread. So, we could say that infusion works by dripping important aspects into the organization at the right places, and supporting their spread. These drips usually are a mix of light-bulb moments, symbolic acts, and some formal process changes.

Remember that for organizational change to happen, the organizational logics need to transform. Infusion is a powerful way to accomplish this transformation. Infusing an organization successfully requires a carefully designed infusion strategy. Although infusion might appear to be a spontaneous set of occurrences, it is important to plan them and have a structure for them. Sometimes they happen by themselves, due to natural communication from leaders and managers, but they always have to be supported by planned actions. These can be courses, social media, formal process changes, myths, stories, news articles, and even concept services (for more about concept cars and concept services, see Chapter 4). So, create an infusion plan and make sure it contains plenty of emotional and symbolic aspects. These are, after all, the changes you want to see in the organization.

Empowerment

The symbolic story of the Nordstrøm employee handbook has created a myth inside and outside of the organization that encapsulates the customer service culture at Nordstrøm. The handbook, which all new employees receive, is simply a postcard that says:

> *Our number one goal is to provide outstanding customer service. Our employee handbook is very simple. We have only one rule: use good judgement in all situations.*

It is symbolic because it says a lot more to employees than the literal words convey, and it is mythical because, although true, it is only part of the story. Nordstrøm actually has a detailed employee handbook with guidelines for many aspects of behavior, such as its social media policy.

Empowerment refers to both the transfer of authority downwards in the organization and the recognition of someone's ability to act, and to act in the right way, as a situation requires. This recognition increases an employee's responsibility and can be a strong motivator for them. Implicit in empowerment is trust in the employee to do the right thing for the good of the customer and company, and a symbolic message of shared responsibility.

At some point in your transformational journey, you will encounter situations where you have to decide between scripting the experience and empowering your frontline employees to do the right thing. This is not an either/or option, and a combination of scripting and empowerment can work well. McDonald's is a highly scripted organization that delivers a consistent experience around the world, and the experience it offers maintains its established market position. However, the strict focus on scripting leaves employees vulnerable and often reduces the quality of the experiential delivery, because unexpected situations occur all the time and require people to go off-script. If the employees are strictly taught to follow a script, and have tightly defined roles, then their freedom to be spontaneous is seriously limited—and the experience will suffer for it.

Empowering Production Workers at a Manufacturing Plant

When working with a large manufacturing company, I was involved in the implementation of a just-in-time production system. The goal for this work was to reduce stocks and streamline production. However, there quickly arose a point of contention about how empowered the production employees should be. The logic of the organization at the time was top-down production scheduling, resulting in clearly defined "production scripts" that had to be followed, no matter the status of the production system.

After talking to the employees and working several shifts there myself, it became clear to me that there were two fundamental problems:

1. What they were being asked to produce was very often not what was needed, leading to huge stockpiles of unnecessary materials. The employees could see this, but were powerless to do anything about it, and felt frustrated.

2. The knowledge, education, and abilities of the employees in relation to the task were in sharp contrast to the beliefs and attitudes expressed by management toward them.

It was clear to me that the employees could form self-organizing teams to manage production, and that they could be brought closer to the sales department and given responsibility for receiving repeat orders from customers. To do this, a clear information system needed to be designed, so that everyone could see the performance and stock situation. We suggested a huge (analog) status board that showed, in real time, the status in the store, and a self-managing team empowered to take repeat orders and deliver on these orders. When presented, the status board idea was given the green light, but there was a huge difference in opinion between management and the project team about empowering the employees. Managers just did not consider the employees capable enough to take on the responsibility, and fought hard against it. We suggested some organizational prototyping to try it out, and a prototype status board was created and a trial initiated for the self-organizing team.

The prototype exceeded expectations: employee motivation increased, turnover decreased, stocks were radically reduced, and customers were thrilled that they could finally receive assurances about delivery from people involved in production. The prototype became fully operational, and the system was rolled out to many more departments during the following two years. If we hadn't given the employees the trust and authority that they were ready for, the system would not have worked so well, the employees would have remained frustrated, and the customers would have lost out on a positive experience. This just goes to show how empowerment fits well with both functional benefits, the emotional and the symbolic. This is why empowerment is central to delivering an exceptional customer experience.

There is a difference between American and Scandinavian approaches: the American approach tends to be more tightly scripted and hierarchical, while the Scandinavian approach is less scripted and has a flatter organization. There are multiple reasons for this, and I advocate a combination—a script and the empowerment to deliver on the desired experience. If the employees know and understand the experience that customers should receive, they will be joining the company because of it, they will be naturally able to deliver it, and they will be better able to make the multiple small adaptations to the experiential journey that are needed to make it successful.

Removing Silos

In a recent survey from the American Management Association, 83% of executives said that silos existed in their companies and 97% thought they have a negative effect.[5]

Silos breed mini-fiefdoms within the organization, making people less likely to collaborate, share information, and work together as a cohesive team. Indeed, silos encourage competition and division (interestingly, they are often called *divisions*) instead of collaboration. Silos are a consequence of value chain thinking, rather than value network thinking, and they force the customer to navigate their way across your organization, rather than you helping them along their journey. Further, KPIs for silos usually encourage within-silo results, rather than cross-silo collaboration. It is rare to see a KPI based on the latter.

Channel silos have historically popped up to cope with a new technology (e.g., internet, social media). But customers usually want to freely move between channels, and this can cause problems. Managing the experience across touchpoints then becomes a challenge since you are also managing across silos, again bringing in all of the disadvantages of silos, and few of the advantages.

Not surprisingly, this leads to poor decision making, poor collaboration, and low morale, and it impacts the company's efficiency and profitability. Often silos are developed based on a function that has its own field of knowledge (marketing, sales, etc.), and this can lead to rivalry and power struggles between groups. Customer don't care about your silos, but they are often forced to navigate between them—so make it easier on the customers and remove them.

Mind the Gap: Using a Gap Analysis to Map Your Position

Determining the degree of change needed in your organization and choosing a transformation strategy to get there both require careful planning. A *gap analysis* is a valuable tool to help you identify how much change is necessary and plan the transition. Knowing the current situation and your desired future situation will make you better able to plan the transition. Chapter 4 is a good starting point for a gap analysis of how far you are from the key aspects and behaviors of an experience-centric organization. Go through the list, and honestly ask yourself if you exhibit these behaviors partly, mostly, or totally. Then combine your results with your position on the five-step experience-centric organization trajectory (Chapter 2), and you will have a good starting point for your organizational journey. This journey may start with a short sprint, but parts will always be a marathon, and you need to be prepared for this.

Your change strategy will depend on your starting point and the gap you have to bridge. As with all organizational change, it is wise to plan, to not rush into radical change, and to pace your transformation. However, each organization is unique, so there is no universal approach here.

Measuring Progress: What Can't Be Measured Can Be Managed

Although metrics can be important management tools, there is a danger of overreliance on them, to the detriment of good judgment. Research contains many examples of incentives that reduce effort or motivation, much of which goes back to the idea of the rational human being (see Chapter 6) with a focus on a quantitative approach to leadership. In *The Tyranny of Metrics* (Princeton University Press) author and historian Jerry Muller explains how we became reliant on measures, and he highlights examples of overreliance on data. Muller's main finding is that what can and does get measured is not always worth measuring, may not be what we really want to know, and may take focus away from the things we really care about. The main message in his book is that "measurement is not an alternative to judgment: measurement demands judgment." In other words: data isn't always better, but thoughtful reflection always is.

The focus on design thinking in organizations has led to several requests to develop KPIs in that area. In one project, we conducted a thorough analysis of design thinking research and identified 17 core traits of design thinking. We then set about developing KPIs for these, all the while being aware of how KPIs can be used at the enterprise level, for business units, for individual departments, and at the employee level. What we found is that design thinking is not easily quantified in itself, and that many aspects of it do not lend themselves to outcome-related measures. For example, design thinking is visual in nature, and although it is possible to measure visual production, the measure would have little value. Another example is that design thinking is reflective and involves reframing a question—to look at it from a broader perspective and really understand the problem—before trying to solve it. Again, this is very difficult to quantify, but is something that you can gauge from subjective monitoring. This does not make these aspects unimportant, but rather a part of your organizational logics requiring subjective evaluation.

We also discovered that some aspects of design thinking can be measured as outcomes, some can be measured in terms of completed stages of development, and some can be measured in terms of process conformance. Others cannot be measured at all, at least not in any directly meaningful way, such as customer empathy at organizational level. Although not measurable, this is an important organizational behavioral trait.

KPIs can be critical for goal setting and performance management, for benchmarking, and for increasing motivation to achieve specific targets, but they have to be balanced with reflection and subjective views; you should be able to reflectively *feel* how things are going, rather than looking at numbers to determine this. The contact with customers, the reviews online, and the cultural comments about your organization will all contribute to this. Rather than taking the rational economic approach, we encourage listening, analysis, and reflection as key skills for the experience-centric organization. No, don't throw away numbers, but do allow for qualitative values and reflective analysis.

Prototyping the Organization

One of the core behaviors of design is to prototype, and there is often a misunderstanding about why designers prototype. Many people believe that a design prototype is a nearly finished version of a product or service as a final sign-off before production. While this is one type of prototype, the goal of prototyping is to gain a better understanding of the problem. When you try something in a quick-and-dirty way, it is highly likely to fail, but that failure gives you insight into why it failed and can produce a breakthrough in understanding the problem. As mentioned in Chapter 4, this is termed *failing forward and fast*—that is, failing with intent to understand.

The same approach should be applied to an organizational design process. It is rare to get an organizational design right the first time around, and it can take some time to fine-tune one when it is in place. Is it possible to prototype an organization? Can you evaluate the value of an organizational change, before implementing it? Answering these questions is not straightforward, and introduces some maybes into the conversation. Since all service innovations have an element of organization in them, some degree of organizational prototyping will be needed. However, large-scale organizational change is difficult to prototype, and I haven't seen examples of this being carried out (other than through small-scale trials of something that might be scaled). The area of organizational prototyping, while important, is one that is still new and needs further development.

Integrating Design Thinking and Design Doing into Your Organization

One central message of this book, is that design is key to your development. But when I say design, I don't mean just any kind of design. I want you to hire designers, because this will give you the competencies necessary for your transformation. But you need to be critical about what kinds of designers you use, because in my experience all kinds of people use the term *design thinking*, but they don't always have the right skill set to help your transition in an experiential way. All people who design want to make things better, but the types of designers I want you to connect with are usually (but not always) those who have been to design school. They are visual, have user empathy, and have a history of combining aesthetics, function, and materials (including technology). My experience is that a new brand of designer, the service designer, with a background in a creative design discipline is good at this, but you will find fantastic industrial designers, graphic designers, and interaction designers who can help you.

Be Less the Rock Star, More the Facilitator of Co-Design Processes

Design has changed during the past few decades, moving away from the image of the rock star product designer who took a brief, then went into their black box only to finally pull a rabbit out of a top hat with some amazing designs. Today, designers are trained to be facilitators and collaborative co-designers, working with other disciplines (and customers) to develop solutions together. This approach is necessary to be able to design for experiences that have consequences all the way around the wheel of experience centricity. But design is about much more than facilitating processes. It is also a highly experiential discipline, both taking inspiration from other experiences and being able to create them. Being able to both think and do experientially is a critical design skill.

Finding the right design match for your organization requires knowing your experiential DNA well. This is why I suggest that your first contact with designers is through an external design consultancy as part of the five-step path to experience centricity. Bring designers in at the journey phase, and get a feel for the right designers for your organization. Designers need to have a personality that fits your organizational DNA and the ability to co-design with others.

Develop DesignOps Within Your Organization

One of the key aspects of design that is not always understood is that design is preoccupied with method. *DesignOps*, short for Design Operations, is the organizational unit that plans, defines, and manages the design process within an organization. You should develop a DesignOps team in your organization that is cross-disciplinary and reports to the CXO.

While the term DesignOps is recent, a similar role has existed for a while. It is an evolution of process management, with the recognition of the experiential aspect that design brings. DesignOps has become a popular term now, because design teams are growing and there is an increasing need to focus on unifying the design approaches within an organization. The DesignOps manager is not necessarily a designer, and the team will most likely comprise different disciplines. What is common to all members of DesignOps is their focus on using methods to support the organization's experiential vision. Thus, they have an operational role but an evangelical role too, and can be central in the infusion of customer experience within the organization.

Endnotes

1. Teresa M. Amabile, "Motivating Creativity in Organizations: On Doing What You Love and Loving What You Do," *California Management Review*, 40, no. 1 (1997).

2. *Flow* is a concept that describes the feeling of being immersed in a task to the extent that time and place disappear. It is described well in Mihaly Csikszentmihalyi's book *Flow: The Psychology of Optimal Experience* (New York: Harper Perennial Modern Classics, 1990).

3. The concept of *organizational logics* is derived from institutional logics, which describe how an institution develops belief structures that influence its behaviors and decision making. See Patricia H. Thornton and William Ocasio, "Institutional Logics," in *Handbook of Organizational Institutionalism*, ed. Royston Greenwood et al. (Thousand Oaks, CA: Sage, 2008).

4. "United Breaks Guitars" was a song and an early viral video hit by the musician Dave Carroll, written after an experience where his guitar was broken by a baggage handler on a United Airlines flight in 2008. It is often used as an early example of customer empowerment through social media.

5. "America Management Association Critical Skills Survey," amanet.org. The survey was published in 2016, but is no longer available online.

PART II

The How

6

Starting with the Experience

In this chapter you will learn about how customers experience products and services, and how you can use this knowledge to design for better experiences. It shows how we act like scenario machines, always being prepared for different scenarios to play out, and how experiences have deep evolutionary roots related to our survival. In this way experiences are impossible to separate from expectations. We have thousands of experiences every day, most of which we do not even notice, but this chapter will show you how to design for experiences that your customers will remember, and share with others.

The customer experience is a co-productive, value-creating act. Without customer action, there is no experience, only an offering. A service creates value only when that offering is experienced by the customer through use. Because of its importance, it's time to learn more about the customer experience, and how we can innovate to account for it.

Moving from Function to Experience

When I first moved to Scandinavia I did some work for a world-leading toothbrush manufacturer, Jordan. At the time, their claim to fame was the ergonomics of their toothbrushes and the effectiveness of the bristle head. Their ads were all about function, not emotion. Today they have a design approach focusing on experience. One particularly successful product stands out because the whole design is based upon how Jordan wants you to feel (see Figure 6-1). I love these toothbrushes, and so do others; they are incredibly popular in Scandinavia and are desirable to a lot of people.

There are two interesting things about this approach. One is price sensitivity. People do not consider how much these toothbrushes cost; they just want them. When I do executive teaching, I often have a group of about 40 people, and of these, maybe 30 have these toothbrushes. When I ask what they cost, people make wild guesses, usually way over (even double) the actual price. The second is the experience that the toothbrush gives. It breaks with expectations that a toothbrush is purely functional. It is affective—people get pleasure from it when they use it. Why? Because it has an emotional connection that is regularly triggered, each and every time it's used.

Breaking this down even further, the brand's success has to do with the fact that there are multiple variants of the toothbrush design, and the customer gets to choose something that appeals to them emotionally. The toothbrushes are very well designed, down to the most minute details, and they are different from almost all other toothbrushes on the market. I appreciate this, and feel a high degree of benevolence toward the company (the feeling that someone has my best interests at heart). I genuinely feel that people have thought of me and my needs when designing the toothbrush I use. Taken together, these factors transform a chore into something pleasant, and I appreciate that someone has done this for me.

Figure 6-1. The Jordan toothbrush has multiple designs, allowing you to choose the one you most like. It is a great example of the move from function to experience. (Source: Jordan.)

I feel that someone has seen me, understood me, designed something beautiful for me, given me a choice, and allowed me to enjoy what previously was a chore. I am thankful to Jordan (the company) and Geir Øxseth (the designer) for giving me something of great value in the little daily rituals of life.

This story highlights the importance of the move from a functionally focused world to an experiential one. Jordan toothbrush ads today don't talk about the ergonomic grip, or the cleaning efficiency. Instead, they appeal to our emotions and appreciation of beauty. As a consequence of this, customers do not have a buyer/seller, transactional view of buying these toothbrushes. The emotional connection has made this a relationship, a part of everyday life. The toothbrush is a small example that shows how we have left the logical and functional world behind. As we will see in this chapter, our desire and need for good experiences are central to who we are as human beings. The more I research and study customer experience, the more I am aware of how experiences are an existential part of our being.

What Is an Experience?

Brian: "You're all individuals."
Crowd (in unison): "We are all individuals."
Individual: "I'm not."
   —MONTY PYTHON: THE LIFE OF BRIAN

First, what *is* an experience? Answering this can take you deep into psychology and philosophy, but let's start with the following definition, before delving more deeply into these disciplines: *An experience is a happening that leaves an impression on someone.* I like this definition because it links what you work with, the "happening," to the customer, the "someone." What you need to achieve as an organization is to leave an impression, hopefully a positive one. So, to summarize the key points of this definition:

Happening
   Your offering and how it is delivered through touchpoints

Impression
   A specific, relevant, and memorable customer experience

Someone
   Your customers and your employees

We Are Emotional—Not Rational—Beings

Who was it that introduced the misguided notion that we are rational economic beings? This has been the driving logic in our understanding of behavior for far too long, even though it has never really been a model that sat well with psychology or sociology. It's difficult to understand how it happened, but we seem to have gone through a dark period of considering people as rational and logical, with strong functional needs, despite seeing evidence of the opposite around us. It's as if we were trying to imagine ourselves as and mold ourselves in the image of Spock from *Star Trek*.

Death of the Rational Human Being, 21st October 2015

It is difficult to pinpoint when the idea of the rational human being was born, but the national Danish newspaper *Politiken* marked the date of its death (in Denmark) on the 21st of October 2015.[1]

The paper proclaimed this due to the publication of a landmark government document describing how people do not always act in their best economic interests, are not always rational, and have identifiable behavioral biases that are irrational. The government acknowledged that people use gut feeling and are spontaneous, intuitive, and biased by social norms in their decisions, and argued that this should have consequences for government economic policy.

This is most likely not news to you, but it is important, given that government policy has been based on the idea of the rational human being for many

years, that governments are finally beginning to design it to take into account the biases that we exhibit, either alone or in groups.

In many ways, this government document was an admission that earlier policies had not been designed for people, but for an idealized economic being—a design that made life easier for economists, but harder for the government's customers (its citizens). It is significant that now government policy will, to a greater extent, be citizen-centric, in terms not only of needs but of behavior as well.

This model of rationality has deep roots in the Reformation, several hundred years ago. In the past the focus was on the scientific method, and our capacity for logical reasoning—what distinguished us from other animals in the animal kingdom. It is true that we are different from other animals, yet recent research shows that this is because we are *emotional*. We are irrational, but according to renowned psychologist and behavioral economist Dan Ariely and many others, we are "predictably irrational;"[2] we have inbuilt biases that we have developed over many years. Lisa Feldman Barrett, a leading researcher in and professor of psychology, argues that humans are unique in the way we develop and use our emotions as part of our everyday experience.[3] In her book *How Emotions Are Made*, Barrett summarizes how we have unique emotional responses to the world around us that lead us to view it and respond in highly irrational ways. (Yes, that includes when we're filing our tax returns.) So, look at the world around you, and notice how emotional it is (and has always been). Embrace it, breathe it in, and consider it the "new" normal.

Interactions Are Central to Who We Are

In one of my very first psychology classes, I remember discussing the classic study by Held and Hein from 1963,[4] which aimed to discover how perception developed. They used kittens in their experiment, and had a carousel-like contraption to harness them in pairs. One kitten was allowed to walk around and experience the world in a normal way, through action and exploration. The other was in a raised basket and connected to the first kitten. It moved, but it was steered by the movement of the first kitten. Thus, the second kitten could only observe the experience in a passive way. After a period, the two kittens were tested. The one that had actively experienced the world had developed perception, while the other had not developed adequate perception. This shows that active experience is central to our ability to function in the world. It has existential importance.

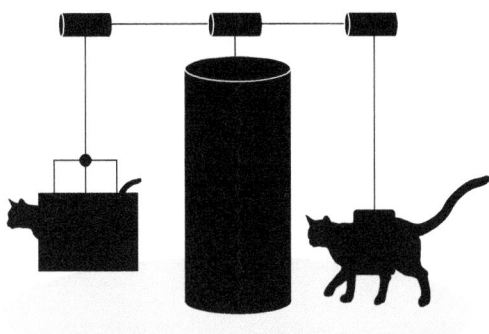

Experiences Do Not Mean Disneyfication

I encounter many leaders that believe a good customer experience is somehow a Disneyfied version of what they do today. By this, I mean they think that adding an entertainment layer on top of their service will make it into a fantastic experience. In this chapter I show how this is wrong, and describe how to create memorable ordinary experiences that are not entertainment-based services. It is a widespread myth that experiences have to be entertaining to be memorable (or valuable), and this has unfortunately created a sense of superficiality around customer experience (not that I think Disney is superficial; it is, however, in the entertainment business for a certain user group). As we will see, experiences need to be authentic to your organization and the expectations that you set for your service, and they can also be highly functional. Services such as Uber and Airbnb that offer great user experiences do not offer Disney-like experiences, so why should you?

What Would Your Service Smell Like (If It Had a Smell)?

If this is something that you have discussed in your leadership, then you're already on your way to having a black belt in experience centricity. If you think this is a stupid or weird question, then please suspend judgment and read on.

When we work with organizations, we find that many leaders find it hard to describe the experience that the customer will have. This is understandable, since as humans we have trouble describing absolute states, and particularly absolute states in the emotional sphere. However, one of the great advantages of being human is our fantastic ability to consider things in relative terms. We can, for example, only distinguish between roughly seven visual stimuli when we see them individually, but we can see thousands when we compare them with others. We also have strong metaphorical abilities—that is, comparing something to something else. So, we often ask leader teams questions such as: If your service were a car, what make would it be? If your service were a supermarket, which one would it be? These questions help to define the experience that is right for an organization to provide, because if you decide that your service should be comparable to an Audi, you already have something strong to develop from. This works all the way down to "If your service had a smell, what would it smell like?" Go on, give it a try. Are you fresh and citrus-based, spicy, or slightly leathery and traditional? See, it works! You are already on your way to describing the experience of your service.

Experience Is a Means of Survival

To explain the existential importance of experience, let's go back to evolution and childhood. We understand the world through our experiences with it, and we become who we are through the experiences we have as we grow up. This might sound obvious, and it is. However, one thing we know is that things that relate to survival are prioritized by our brains, our bodies, and society. Experiences are central in our lives. They are the basis of our existence. We don't crave products or services—we crave the experiences they give us. In this way, all is experience. We are designed to experience as a way of surviving, and we carry this instinct with us throughout our lives. It is not surprising, therefore, that the customer experience is an extension of this existential requirement. It is, after all, how we have learned to become who we are.

As a company, you should pay attention to this, because tapping into an existentially important aspect of your customers' lives gives you access to them at an unprecedented scale. However, in discussions with companies, I repeatedly hear that the customer experience is important, but that the organization does not know how to improve it, and has difficulty understanding exactly what experience they should be delivering. Because of this, initiatives never get off the ground, or become uncoordinated. If this sounds familiar, then read on.

> **Experiences are central in our lives. They are the basis of our existence. We don't crave products or services—we crave the experiences they give us. In this way, all is experience.**

Humans Are Emotional Scenario Machines

It is important to realize that we always evaluate experiences in relation to expectations. Neurocognition teaches us that we are scenario machines, always expecting multiple potential outcomes, predicting what will happen next. Recent research suggests that we are continually creating scenarios about what is likely to happen next in our lives. These scenarios are developed in real time, and continually adapt, based on a complex mix of previous experience (how it was last time we did this), memory of recent events (what has just happened), and cues from the context we are in (what do these touchpoints expect from me?).

These multiple scenarios are not something that we are aware of, but they help us prepare for situations that might occur. In evolutionary terms, they might have been scenarios like an animal rushing out of the bushes, or a fish swimming close to our net. This is something that researchers believe is unique to human beings—continually trying to predict multiple futures so as to be prepared to act on them. And it makes sense, particularly because our ability to respond to events is limited if we are not prepared for them. We simply don't have the bandwidth or processing power to be totally spontaneous (even though we think we are), so to make it easier on ourselves, we predict what is going to happen and use that as a starting point for our preparedness and actions.

Lisa Feldman Barrett expresses this clearly:

> *We usually think of predictions as statements about the future, like "It's going to rain tomorrow" or "The Red Sox will win the World Series." But here, I'm focusing on predictions at a microscopic scale as millions of neurons talk to one another. These neural conversations try to anticipate every fragment of sight, sound, smell, taste, and touch that you will experience, and every action that you will take. These predictions are your brain's best guesses of what's going on in the world around you, and how to deal with it to keep you alive and well. [...]*
>
> *Through prediction, your brain constructs the world you experience. It combines bits and pieces of your past and estimates how likely each bit applies in your current situation. [...] Right now, with each word that you read, your brain is predicting what the next word will be, based on probabilities from your lifetime of reading experience. In short, your experience right now was predicted by your brain a moment ago. Prediction is such a fundamental activity of the human brain that some scientists consider it the brain's primary mode of operation.*[5]

Kindness Is Contagious

Why are we generous? We give blood, post reviews online, tip service providers, and donate to charity, even though there is nothing in it for us. Well, kindness rewards the giver by releasing endorphins and oxytocin, and it creates new neural connections. The implications for such plasticity of the brain are that altruism and kindness become self-reinforcing habits requiring less and less effort to exercise. Even the act of imagining compassion and kindness activates the soothing and affiliation component of the emotional regulation system of the brain. So that explains its effect on us, but what about its effect on others? There is evidence that kindness can be contagious. This can be explained by the accepted reciprocal behaviors, for example, showing praise, giving gifts, and returning a favor. A recent anthropological study of generosity shows that we reciprocate generosity, and that we adjust our generosity to the norms within a group.[6] This group-wise behavior has strong implications for the design of a service, because it basically says people will treat you as you treat them. Because we perceive services as having human traits, we will reciprocate the personality, behavior, and tone of voice of a service encounter. Treat a customer well, and they not only will see the giver (your staff, for example) in a positive light but also will treat you well in return. This can lead to a positive cycle of customer relationships. Knowing how customers will respond to you is yet another reason for designing your personality, behaviors, and tone of voice with experience-centric intention.

Expectations for Service Are Based on the Scenarios We Construct

If we place this view of scenario making in the context of services, we can see that we as customers are continually running through scenarios or stories that set expectations about what is likely to happen when we encounter a service (the offering) and what will actually occur in the details (interactions with touchpoints). We have all experienced this, particularly in situations where things are new. Newness challenges the mind to run through multiple scenarios and develop the right one for what to expect and what to do. The scenarios help us quickly make sense of a system and determine the right behavioral responses. As a designer you can immediately start to see how to design to make the experience better, reduce stress, and prevent confusion by explaining the concept, creating clarity so that people can immediately understand which of the many scenarios is correct. Prepare the customer beforehand through a carefully crafted experiential offering, and deliver on it through the interactions that are designed to fulfill that promise. The goal is not just to meet expectations, but to exceed them, because that is what makes experiences memorable. Human beings don't have the capacity to remember each and every experience we have, and to be honest, our memories would be very gray and uninteresting if we did. It is when expectations are exceeded that we take note, because it is a natural way to influence our scenario production for the next time we encounter the service.

We Are Evolutionarily Hardwired to Get Pleasure from Beauty

A beautiful image, a beautiful person, a stunning landscape. Why do we get pleasure from them, and is it something learned, or innate from birth? Neuroscience breakthroughs in recent years are increasingly painting a picture that the brain is hardwired to promote aesthetics, and that this gives us an evolutionary advantage. In his book *The Aesthetic Brain* (Oxford University Press), Anjan Chatterjee shows that aesthetics are an instinct—that is, inherited rather than learned (although they're added to through learning). The core message of this interesting book is twofold. First, positive experiences are a key part of our evolutionary survival, and therefore something we fundamentally seek in our lives. Second, beauty is linked in some way to evolutionary advantage. We are simply hardwired to get pleasure from beautiful things. Beauty in an image, a landscape, a person we know, a shared cultural happening, or even a mathematical equation triggers our brains in a positive way. This is not culturally dependent, and it is inborn. So, not only do we have an economic argument for beautiful design,, we also have an evolutionary one. We are hardwired to enjoy beauty.

Experiences Require Interactions with Things over Time

Customer experiences come through interactions with your service—specifically interactions with touchpoints along a journey. This means that when you are considering the experience that you want your customers to have, you also need to have in the back of your mind how the customer receives this experience, and how you can design the interactions to give desired and desirable experiences. Experiences are how we learn and understand, and the basis for all knowing. They are how we predict and discover. This means that customer experiences are linked to expectations and historical interactions, so to understand these, you need to deeply understand how a customer will relate to your offering, including in a cultural context. This is the domain of the designer, designing for interactions that fit with the customer's understanding of the world.

Interactions are central to our understanding of the world, and create our expectations of the experience before we have it. There is always a tension when designing services between doing exactly as people expect (consistency) and doing things differently, but better, than expected (innovation). This is the difference between following and leading and is always a decision you face when designing for experience: the comfortable and safe route, or the challenging novel route. The CD Baby cover letter is a great example of doing something different, but in a way that's consistent with our learned expectations and with the company's DNA.

Insights from Lynn Hunsaker

Lynn Hunsaker is a Hall of Fame author at CustomerThink and serves on the Customer Experience Professionals Association's Board of Directors; since the early 1990s she has led customer experience transformation at Fortune 250 companies. She finds that organizations are so caught up in what competitors are doing that they forget to consider what they can and should offer their customers.

Unfortunately, organizations buy technology based on jumping on bandwagons rather than considering what they want to achieve. A classic example of this is the wave of [customer relationship management and enterprise feedback management] investments, which offered great opportunities to build relationships with customers. However, the investments were often made for self-centered purposes such as upselling and cross-selling, and value was stymied for lack of a proper focus on building relationships.

Nobody owns or even "has" customers. You really have to strengthen relationships and get to the point where the customer feels that you get them. People don't look for loyalty programs, rather they want to feel that the company gets them. I think we have taken the human part out of business and need to put it back.

When organizations try to understand their customers, they rely way too much on quantitative measures and predetermined questions. By doing this they lose a lot of information about customers. That is a real pity, since customers who have used your product or service will easily tell you what their goal was, the reality of the experience they had, and the consequences of this. Just getting a score of seven tells you very little.

"People don't look for loyalty programs, rather they want to feel that the company gets them."

We are putting way too much pressure on quantitative data and everyone would be a lot happier if we increased the qualitative. Everyone is spending so much money on dashboards, but dashboards don't really help you understand your customer base. It's ironic that the things on a customer experience manager's mind are often very different from the things that are on a customer's mind, and that is not only very sad, but also a way to rapidly lose market share.

How to Surprise and Delight: The CD Baby Letter

"Your CDs have been gently taken from our CD Baby shelves with steril-ized contamination-free gloves and placed onto a satin pillow. A team of 50 employees inspected your CDs and polished them to make sure they were in the best possible condition before mailing.

"Our packing specialist from Japan lit a candle and a hush fell over the crowd as he put your CDs into the finest gold-lined box that money can buy.

"We all had a wonderful celebration afterward and the whole party marched down the street to the post office where the entire town of Portland waved 'Bon Voyage!' to your package, on its way to you, in our private CD Baby jet on this day, Sunday, November 18th.

"I hope you had a wonderful time shopping at CD Baby. We sure did.

"Your picture is on our wall as 'Customer of the Year.' We're all exhausted but can't wait for you to come back to CDBABY.COM!! Thank you, thank you, thank you! Sigh..."

—Derek Sivers, president, CD Baby, "the little store with the best new independent music"[7]

Brands Are Postboxes in Our Minds

I'm not sure that Lisa Feldman Barrett would totally agree with Al Ries and his daughter and coauthor, Laura, when they use the met-aphor of postboxes for branding, but I think she would see the rele-vance.[8] The Rieses liken our understanding of branding to having a series of post-sorting boxes in our heads, each labeled with a different category. They claim that we only have space for a limited number of postboxes, and that each postbox category has limited capacity. Very often these postboxes are full, because there is hypercompeti-tion for almost everything these days. As a new entrant, we can only gain access to these postboxes by ousting something that is already in there, or more radically, by creating a new postbox and being the first in that category. Apple and Nintendo are very good at creating new postboxes in our minds and being the first to fill them. We recognize them for this, and appreciate their boldness. And Virgin, for example, is a master at identifying postboxes that are ripe for change, and goes in and aggressively challenges those within the postbox to oust one or more of the incumbents and take a lead role, primarily by improv-ing the customer experience. If you compare the experience of Virgin Atlantic with British Airways, you see how Virgin has a very different and appealing (to many) experiential value proposition, precisely as a means of cleaning out a dusty postbox and placing themselves inside.

So, How Do We Create Memorable Experiences?

If experiences are the same as expected, then there is a good chance that people won't remember them, even though it might reinforce the consistency of their scenario. People experience thousands of things a day, but very few make it into their memory as something worth telling others about. That does not mean that they have not noticed the experiences, but it does mean that the goal of creating desirable and memorable experiences has not been met. If you want to become memorable, then you need to differentiate your organization from expectations and innovate the experience. Ironically, in many areas, the existing customer experience is so poor, and so removed from expectation, that just being consistent may be enough to become memorable. Customers would say, "It was great, everything just worked." However, the number of these comments is decreasing, as many service providers are striving to provide reasonable consistency. Innovation, therefore, requires differentiation from the norm. You have to innovate on what people have as expectations and find ways to do things differently, in a positive way. This means innovating so that people create new concepts in their minds, constructing new under-standings of what an offering is and how it is experienced.

Size Matters

When you think back on your summer holiday, a meal at a restaurant, or even a meeting, it is often specific incidents that you recall. In fact, we seem to remember things as snapshots rather than long videos. There are two key factors that imprint experiences on our memories.

First, the intensity of the experience matters—that is, how much it arouses your emotions. Second, the direction of the arousal seems to play a role, with negative arousal being more memorable than posi-tive. This is why particularly bad service is remembered so well, but it applies to surprisingly good service too. The peak intensity of the emotion and its timing are also important. Consider the following quote from a customer about a memorable holiday experience:

> *When on holiday in Scotland, we missed the ferry back from our trip to an isolated Scottish island. This was a crisis, as it connected with the last bus back to town. Dreading the thought of a very long walk in the rain during our journey on the next ferry, we were amazed to see a bus waiting for the ferry when it docked. The bus driver said*

that he had remembered us from the morning and that he hadn't seen us return during the day. So, he drove out specially, just to pick us up. We will never forget that. Never.

Beauty and Love Are Closely Linked

The mOFC is neither a football club nor a political organization, but instead a part of our brains (the medial orbito-frontal cortex), and a significant part when it comes to emotions. The mOFC seems to light up when we perceive beauty, and studies show that beauty, at least beauty through form, also stimulates the part of the brain linked to love. Studies also show that beauty, at least beauty through form, stimulates the part of the brain linked to love.[9] Interestingly, it appears that beautiful music and beautiful images stimulate the mOFC equally, but music does not stimulate the part connected to love. Sorry, Ozzy, I don't love you after all.

It seems, therefore, that beautiful form has more potential in terms of eliciting love-like experiences than beautiful music. The key to all of these studies is that of *perceived* beauty, since the research only studied music and images that the subjects themselves had categorized as beautiful beforehand. This is why people's perceptions of good design can elicit love-like responses in the brain, and why as a society we are becoming design-aware. However, the question of whether a universal beauty exists, one that everyone agrees on (and falls in love with), remains unanswered—beauty is still in the eye of the beholder, at least until further work is carried out. An interesting additional study showed that beauty in mathematical equations had the same effect, for those who understood them, as beauty in music or in form.[10] Thus, beauty in mathematics may be closely related to beauty in the wider world. The authors cannot explain why, but suggest that it has to do with some realization that beauty is related to something making sense to us. This potentially takes the perception of beauty into other areas, such as biology, chemistry, or anything that is considered well designed. And by well designed, I mean more than visual form, which I've already described as central, including a process or a construction if it makes sense to us.

How We Remember Experiences Is Key for Design

Given the choice between two medical procedures—a painful procedure that lasts 8 minutes or a painful procedure that lasts 25 minutes—which would you choose? Sounds like a simple choice, doesn't it? You'd pick the short painful procedure rather than the long one, of course. Nobel Prize winner Daniel Kahneman and Donald Redelmeier asked this question, however, and found a startling result.[11] When asked about their experience afterward, patients who had undergone a longer procedure rated the experience as less uncomfortable than patients who had the shorter procedure. How come? Well, the patients' experiences ended differently. The longer procedure ended with a period of low pain, rather than intense pain, while the shorter experience ended at a painful high point. Changing the ending, Kahneman and Redelmeier found, causes us to remember the whole experience differently. As they put it, what we experience in the moment and what we remember about the experience are very different. Their key findings were that the peak and the end were the most important when patients recollected their experiences.

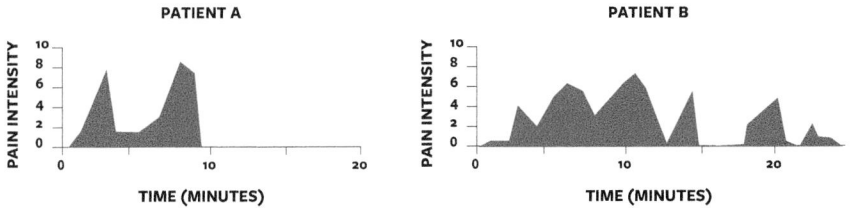

Figure 6-2. The classic study by Daniel Kahneman and Donald Redelmeier showed that we remember experiences through their peaks and end states. This has become known as the peak-end rule.

Desirability and Passion Are Part of Our Culture

We burn and are aflame with desire; we are pierced by or riddled with desire, we are sick or ache with desire; we are tormented, and racked by desire; we are possessed, seized, ravished, and overcome by desire; we are mad, crazy, insane, giddy, blinded, or delirious with desire. Our desire is fierce, hot, intense, passionate, incandescent, and irresistible; and we pine, languish, waste away, or die of unfulfilled desire.

"THE FIRE OF DESIRE: A MULTISITED INQUIRY INTO CONSUMER PASSION"[12]

Desire has an interesting relevance to the customer experience: it drives much of our behavior, due to extremely high expectations of an expected future payoff. Desirability creates a strong scenario in our minds about how we will feel when we actually achieve the target of our desire. It is especially interesting in this context, since it drives us to action.

Desire has many definitions; however, the definition that comes closest to describing consumer behavior is the following from *Webster's*:

> *The natural longing that is excited by the enjoyment or the thought of any good, and impels to action or effort its continuance or possession; an eager wish to obtain or enjoy.*

From this definition, three elements of desirability can be identified:

- A longing for something
- A motivation that is embodied through action or effort
- The strong need to obtain or possess

Individual desire and collective desire are nothing new. For example, in the 1600s there was such a desire for tulips (yes, tulip bulbs and flowers), that one type of tulip, the Admiral Liejken, was priced equivalent to 180 tons of cheese. In the same period, nutmeg was such a rare and desired spice that people made their fortunes from shipping it. Indeed in 1667, the Dutch valued it so highly that they swapped the whole of Manhattan with the British to gain a tiny, tiny island called Run, where it grew. At this time, desire was often linked to scarcity, so in many situations desire was never fulfilled, except by the wealthy.

Although desirability has always existed, it has now become a global phenomenon and part of our collective culture. We see desire in terms of mass-produced objects, which in today's globalized market become not only desirable, but also attainable. There is sometimes, but not always, a degree of scarcity connected to objects, and desire is now predominantly symbolic. That is, it is the symbolic value that makes things desirable, particularly in terms of supporting personal identity construction. Beats headphones are an example of desirability in a symbolic sense. To buy them is to say something about yourself. The Apple iPhone is a good but well-used example that we all recognize. At times, the PlayStation and the Nintendo gaming consoles were also desirable, creating a socially fired enthusiasm to obtain them. The *Harry Potter* books, Marvel films, and every now and again, various musicians have all been seen as desirable, and this has become a part of our culture as we look for the "next big thing." The mechanisms for this seem unclear, but desirability feeds off a customer experience base, while also being spread by media and word of mouth to create blockbuster successes. But how does this play out in services? In the services world, the examples are not as frequent, since until recently we have not been able to use the self-identity aspects of services to promote ourselves. However, this has changed due to social media, so we can now broadcast our service use; services are now becoming desirable. Starbucks, for example, Virgin Atlantic, the Body Shop, the early Google search page, and even Uber have all had traits of desirability in which people actively expended energy to find and use them. More recently, Facebook, Snapchat, and Instagram have all been desirable to the extent that people put considerable effort into getting and using them.

Your goal as an organization is to understand what could make your service or product desirable, and design that into your solution. It usually involves a degree of innovation, some highly emotional return on investment, coupled with high symbolic value. As we will see in Chapter 9, it is often the underlying meaning that we find desirable, and understanding meaning and designing for it is vital to creating desirable experiences.

Design for Experience, and Why You Cannot Design Experiences

Now that you understand more about experience, this section describes how you can design for what defines an experience. Since this is a book about organizational structure, and not a book about designing experiences, the section is brief. However, I describe some key aspects of translating knowledge about experience into service offerings such as staging, orchestrating experiences, and storytelling. If this gives you an appetite for more, check out the Further Reading section in the Conclusion.

Only the Customer Can Tell You About Their Experiences

Experiences are personal and unique to each customer and experienced through mind and body. This sounds obvious, but it is a key point. Only by listening to customers can you understand their experiences. You cannot design experiences, but you can design *for* experiences. You might consider this a trivial difference, but from a design point of view, it is significant. Experiences are personal and lie within the customer. They may be collective and shared, but you can only design the context for where they happen and how they happen; you cannot design the experience itself. This has important implications for your innovation projects. First, you have to have some means to understand the experience from the customer perspective, which means having contact with customers. Second, you have to have an understanding of customer behavior, why customers do what they do, and why they experience what they experience. Finally, you have to be able to translate these pieces of knowledge for the customer's context through design.

Customers Are Primed Through a Precise and Relevant Offering

Earlier in this chapter, one of the main themes was that humans act like scenario machines, producing multiple scenarios all the time about what might happen. In other words, we create expectations of the experiences we will have when we use a service. This allows us to assess the potential value of the service, and to be prepared for an expected experience when we come to use it. When designing services, you need to develop a precise and relevant offering to assist people with this scenario production—precise in terms of giving them experiential cues about how the service will feel, and relevant in terms of having a good fit with what they need and what they know about your organization (for example, from earlier interactions with you). Your offering therefore needs to be designed to help customers imagine scenarios regarding the experiential value that they should expect. It also should be designed so that during use, as they experience your service (through its touchpoints over time), they feel that they already know the service, thanks to this priming. Designing for the experience, then, means being able to clearly prime a customer and to precisely deliver on this priming through use.

We Tell Others Stories About Our Service Experiences

Since services are not tangible, we cannot show someone the service experience we've had. It is not like a car, a chair, a cup, or another physical product that we can present to people to admire its form, materials, and construction. There are plenty of magazines about furnishing a home, full of lovely photos, but few about services—because what would you be able to illustrate visually? It is difficult to *show* how uncomfortable my last flight was with Ryanair or how nice my trip was on the 14 bus in Copenhagen. But I can tell others about it as a story, in which I accentuate the emotions, the people, and what stood out (good or bad). So, when designing your service, you need to look for aspects that will make a good story: a dramaturgic curve, a cast, and carefully designed events that stick in the memory. If you design your service as prompts for a story, you will find that people use these cues to tell a story about it, and you then create a positive circle of experiences.

Pine and Gilmore use the phrase *staging of experiences* in their book *The Experience Economy* (Harvard Business Review Press), and I think this is a good metaphor for designing for experience. Think about it in a theatrical sense and you can design a stage for experiences, employ relevant actors, set the scene, and influence expectations—but it is only at the moment of truth, the service delivery, that it is experienced by the customers.

Using Storytelling as Part of Experience Design

In the book *This is Service Design Doing*, by Marc Stickdorn et al. (O'Reilly), theatrical methods and the dramatic curve are described as design tools for experience design.

One company that subscribes to this idea is workplayexperience, which uses theatrical knowledge as a design tool. Formed by theatre personnel, it works to help develop storytelling as an approach to designing for memorable service experiences.

Source: *This is Service Design Doing.*

Giving Your Service Needs a Personality

Jennifer Aaker, daughter of brand guru David Aaker, has followed in her father's footsteps and become a branding expert in her own right. She has spent a lot of time researching brand personality, and shown that services can be described as having a personality.[13] We create meaning by giving human traits to services, and this helps us understand them.

In fact, services always have a personality, whether intended or not, and we often describe a service encounter using personality terms. As an organization you need to choose that personality beforehand, and implement it through the offering and the touchpoints.

Discussing the personality of a service is not common; many organizations just let it appear on its own, risking brand dilution and customer confusion. Take a few moments now and think about the personality of your service, and then consider whether your customers would agree with your description. If you don't know how your customers view your personality, then go out and ask them. You will probably be surprised.

A personality makes it easier for a customer to adjust their expectations to the service, since it allows them to make connections to concepts and personalities they have encountered during their lives, which helps them navigate and use the service. It also helps members of a project team design service interactions, and it helps frontline employees understand how they should relate to customers. Chapter 7 goes into more detail about how the experience value proposition and your DNA can be translated into personality traits, personality, behavior, and tone of voice. These are key aspects that you can communicate in your offering and follow up on by designing for experience. A service personality allows us to create expectations, makes it easier and more comfortable for us to interact (since we already "know" part of the service), and makes it easier to communicate about the service afterward.

Give a Nudge and a Wink

When you are designing for experience, you need to combine the elements of nudging and winking. *Nudging* can be described as using behavioral insights to develop the way you present your offering through touchpoints.[14] *Winking*, however, can be applied to the offering itself, in terms of developing an offering, personality, and tone of voice that together seduce the customer with experiences that they find desirable. This can be achieved through radical improvements in usability, utility, or pleasurability.

Both nudging and winking can and should be incorporated in the design of an offering, and they offer contrasting ways to provide memorable experiences. I will not go into great detail about nudging here, since there are many people better skilled than me who have written about it. What is important is that during the design phase, your team is aware of the potential of nudging to improve the customer experience.

Design for the Now and Then

When designing services, you need to design for the experience as it is being delivered and, at the same time, for how the service will be remembered afterward. The healthcare example modeled in Figure 6-3, shows how they are related, yet different. As you can see, the experience that the patient recounts during the journey is different from the ones later remembered. This is only natural, since during a medical procedure there is a high degree of uncertainty about the outcome, while afterward that uncertainty is generally resolved.

How we view the experience of withdrawing cash from an automatic teller machine will be different from the experience we recall afterward. Experiences during the journey can often relate to ease and pleasure of use, whereas before use, they relate to the desirability or attractiveness of the service offering, and afterward reflect the sum of experiences in relation to expectation. It is as if after an experience we do some form of emotional accounting about the service in which expectation, use, and result are integrated and stored away for later use (this, by the way, is why the Net Promoter Score is quite a useful measure, even though it has many weaknesses).

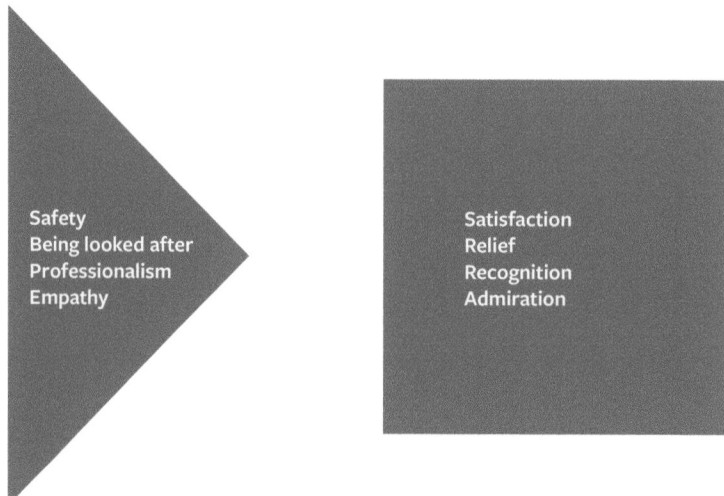

Experience **during** the journey   Experience **resulting** from the journey

Safety
Being looked after
Professionalism
Empathy

Satisfaction
Relief
Recognition
Admiration

Figure 6-3. The experience we have during service use (in this case a medical procedure) is different from the experience we have afterward. You need to design for both.

Mix Yourself to Some Desirability

Desire, as we have discussed, turns marketing on its head, since people seek you out, they talk about you, and they follow you. Designing for a desirable customer experience requires a unique mix of:

- Utility—what the service does
- Usability—how easy it is to do it
- Pleasurability—how it feels before, during, and after use

Desirability is the combination of these three basic ingredients that fits the unique characteristics of your organization—that is, your experiential DNA (see Figure 6-4). All products and services are a combination of these three aspects, and designing an offering demands an understanding of each. Utility focuses on the functional value that your service can give a customer. Usability focuses on ease of use. Pleasurability focuses on the feelings customers have before, during, and after they use a product or service.

Desirability

Figure 6-4. Each experience is a mix of utility, usability, and pleasurability. During a project it is key to discuss this mix and find the right fit for the project and the provider organization.

Again, each project requires a unique combination of all three components, and it is necessary during the design process to discuss the mix that fits the project and your organization's experiential DNA. This is fundamental to the project and should be settled at the start to avoid drift.

Look and Feel Are Important

Earlier I mentioned a book by Anjan Chatterjee called *The Aesthetic Brain*. It describes how getting pleasure from beauty is a universal trait we have from birth, and therefore the importance of beautiful design to experience should not be underestimated. Good design translates to memorable experiences, through the integration of utility, usability, and pleasurability. It primes us beforehand in terms of expectations, it helps us during use, and it weaves a red thread of beauty through everything we experience.

Strive for the Extraordinary Ordinary Experience

Good experiences deliver on an experiential promise. They do not have a superficial top layer, and they fit with the brand and the heritage of the organization. A memorable experience does not always mean entertainment. Let me introduce the "extraordinary ordinary" experience (Figure 6-5).

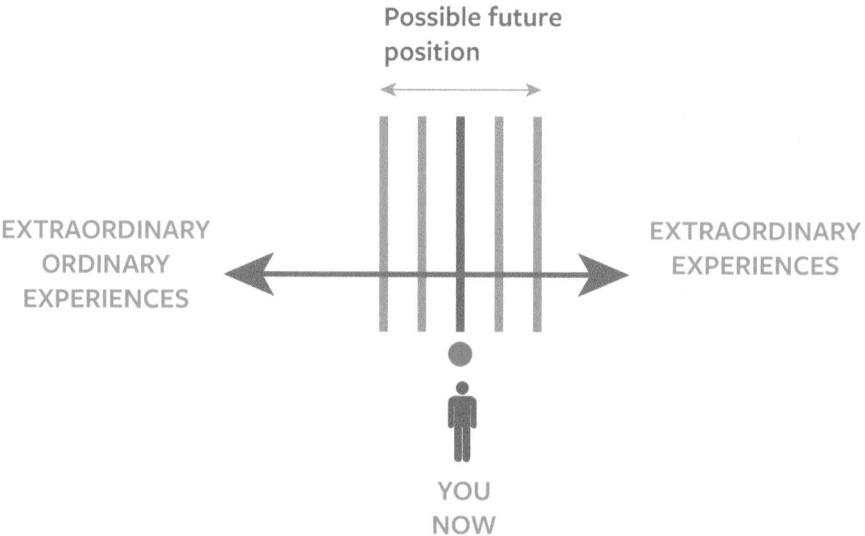

Figure 6-5. There is a continuum between the extraordinary ordinary experience and the extraordinary experience. The extraordinary ordinary experience is memorable because it just does its job well, while the extraordinary experience is memorable because of its richness of experiential detail.

In their breakthrough book *The Experience Economy*, Pine and Gilmore discuss the entertainment value of experiences and how entertaining experiences contribute to a new kind of economic offering. Readers of the book unfortunately assumes that all experiences have to have entertainment value. While they were right to focus on the importance of experiences for the market, they were wrong to imply that experiences had to have entertainment value. This led to a huge surge in attempts to add some entertainment icing atop an ordinary service cake, rather than increasing efforts to understand what was the right experience for the service in question. Entertainment add-ons initiated a wave of advertising, often using text such as "enjoy the (product name) experience." Common to all these services was an implied unique and memorable entertaining experience, and an inability to deliver on them. When you used these services, you were usually disappointed to find some uncoordinated design on top of a very average product.

This was the period of "premium mediocre experiences," where a little icing on a very mediocre cake was sold as a premium or exciting experience. Customers saw through the hype, promises, and let downs. This resulted in customers questioning the very term *experiential* and realizing that delivery, not promise, is the key to value. So, do not ever, ever, ever consider adding entertainment as a top layer to your offering unless it fits well with your DNA. It doesn't work, and it damages your reputation for longer than the short-term benefit it can give.

Researcher Mauricy Filho and I coined the term *extraordinary ordinary experience* to describe service experiences that have a high functional value but not necessarily entertainment value. Have you ever been to a garage to get your car repaired, and it all went so smoothly that you told others about it? Well, that's an example of the extraordinary ordinary experience. These experiences just work, and work so well that they exceed your expectations. They deliver a little more, a little better, or a little more consistently because of their design. The little more is not entertainment, but perhaps functional benefits and ease of use. You remember such experiences because *they just work really well*.

The extraordinary ordinary experience is a memorable experience for an everyday product or service. We can plot experiences on a scale from the extraordinary ordinary experience to the extraordinary experience, which is a "wham bam wow" experience, highly experiential and emotional. But both types differentiate themselves by doing things exceptionally well.

Your job as an organization is to know yourself and your experiential DNA well enough to be able to place yourself on that continuum with confidence. Then, consider in which direction it is right for you to move along the scale. Should you add more richness to the experience, or should you pare it down to be more functional? This positioning is key for your future development and success, and does not always mean moving up the scale. As we have shown, many companies have great success from the extraordinary ordinary experience.

The Art of War/Love by Sun Tzu

Bear with me on this one: it's one of those thoughts that take a bit of time to follow. When I was studying for my MBA, *The Art of War* was a text that many leaders related to. This was a time of hard business, after all, and the applicability of Sun Tzu's wisdom was clear. One particular quote has stuck with me since then, because I have always been surprised by how many companies do not know themselves very well and it struck a chord with me:

If you know others and know yourself, you will not be imperiled in a hundred battles; if you do not know others but know yourself, you win one and lose one; if you do not know others and do not know yourself, you will be imperiled in every single battle.

This morning, I was writing that hate and love are actually very close to each other, and how easy it can be for bad customer experiences to turn a customer against you. This made we wonder whether Sun Tzu's wisdom could apply to something other than war, namely experience design. If, by extension, we can say war and love are closely connected, maybe his work could give insights into the art of love (because we know good experiences stimulate the same parts of the brain as love) If so, then he would probably have formulated that thought this way:

If you know the experience you want to give, and know yourself as an organization, you will never be imperiled from customers' interactions; if you do not know the experience you want to give, but know yourself, you win some customers and lose some; if you do not know the experience you want to give, and do not know yourself, you will be imperiled in every single interaction with a customer.

This makes sense to me, and it embodies the core elements of the wheel of experience centricity: knowing yourself (your experiential DNA) and the experience you want to give. Hopefully it makes sense to you too, and I can only hope that Sun Tzu is not turning in his grave at my attempt at making love, not war.

Avoid the Trap of the "Mediocre Premium" and "Premium Mediocre" Experience

We have all experienced these kinds of services, and they both underperform on experience. Premium mediocre services promise something over and above the mediocre, but do not deliver. Mediocre premium services deliberately position themselves in a premium category, charge a premium, and may superficially look like an exclusive service, but they basically just charge more and do not deliver on that promise. Both of these inhabit an unhappy valley of experience in which the promise does not add up to a better experience: one talks up a mediocre service, and the other positions a mediocre service in a category it does not belong in. What you get is really just a bad service with a few experiential aspects added. You might be tempted to do a quick makeover of a poorly functioning service to "add a bit of experience," but don't do it. Not only are you eroding your brand, but you are also creating unhappy customers. And, as I have already mentioned, unhappy customers leave you and tell many others about their disappointment. You are destroying value for what looks like a quick win, and it will take you a long time to come back from it.

Support Off-Script Experiences

If after reading about how we experience the world as scenarios, you thought about scripting your experiences as a way to create consistently good experiences, you're thinking correctly, but you might still be on the wrong track if you script too tightly. Scripting the interaction with a customer is more common in the US than it is in the rest of the world, and as we discussed earlier, McDonald's is probably the best example. There, the dialogue is carefully scripted, including the upsell to extra fries and the like. The advantages of this approach are that you gain strong consistency and the expectation/experience loop is carefully honed and steady. The disadvantage is that life is not a play, and many situations occur that require going off-script. When such occasions arise, following a script can detract from the experience.

But, as in many situations, a strength is also a weakness, since such a high degree of consistency does not make the experience memorable or delightful for the customer (Figure 6-6). To remain memorable organizations must continually update their offerings, so, over time, sticking to scripted consistency makes you vulnerable to other, more experiential opponents.

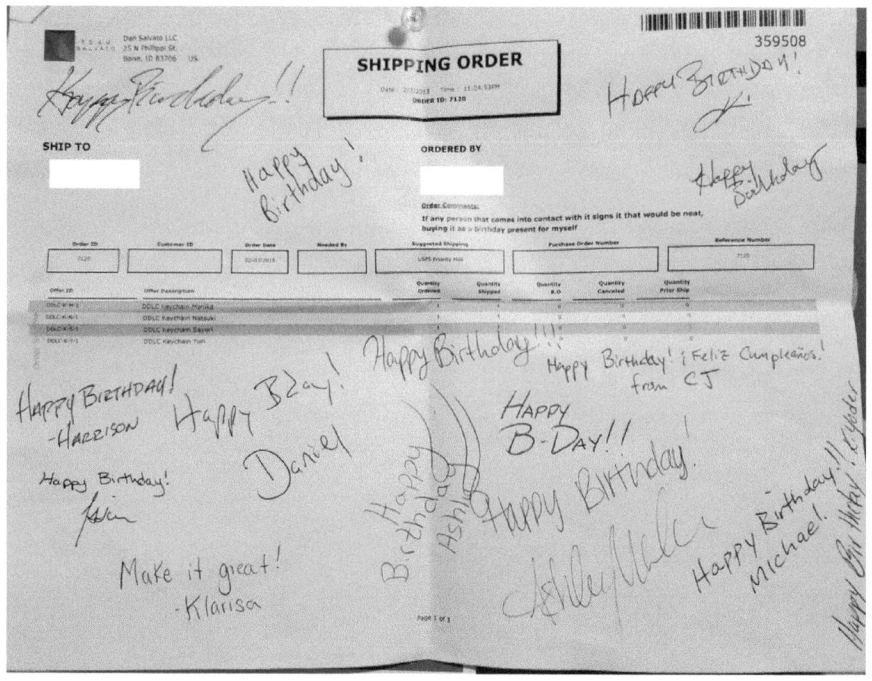

Figure 6-6. Off-script behavior can surprise and delight a customer. This customer who ordered a birthday present for himself asked for the order to be signed, and was so overwhelmed with the response that he posted his shipping order on Reddit and got thousands of upvotes. This kind of thing cannot be scripted and is a great expression of organizational culture. (Source: Reddit, 2018.)

Succeeding with the Extraordinary Ordinary Experience

Two companies have achieved great success by designing, sticking to, and refining their extraordinary ordinary experiences: Amazon and easyJet. They just work, thanks to a conscious organizational effort to provide exactly the experience they do. We all know Amazon, and you would not judge their offering as high design or entertaining, but it works and it works well—each and every time.

easyJet is a large European budget airline that often competes with the lowest-price airline, Ryanair. But they compete using experience, and have worked relentlessly for years to fine-tune their extraordinary ordinary experience. Everything from easyJet's advertising, through the email confirmation, to the pilot announcements supports the company's experiential value proposition: youthful, free, and easy travel. Again, it works, and it works well. And the results show that it is paying off. Ryanair, their major competitor, issued two profit warnings in autumn 2017, and admitted last year that customers wanted not only low fares, but a decent flying experience as well. Ryanair's outspoken chief executive Michael O'Leary admitted in November 2017 that easyJet "wiped the floor with us on the customer service front."[15] O'Leary doesn't realize how much work he has ahead of him.

Source: easyJet.

Endnotes

1   "Death of the Rational Economic Human" was a piece in the Danish newspaper *Politiken* (October 21, 2015) describing how the Danish government had based earlier economic models on citizens acting in a rational economic manner, and now were applying new knowledge about human behavior to their policies.

2   Dan Ariely, *Predictably Irrational* (New York: HarperCollins, 2008). The book summarizes published literature about our irrational decision-making behavior and is a good starting point to understand our various biases when making decisions.

3   Lisa Feldman Barrett, *How Emotions Are Made: The Secret Life of the Brain* (Boston: Mariner, 2018). Barrett is professor of psychology at Northeastern University and the book summarizes recent research into neuropsychology.

4   Richard Held and Alan Hein, "Movement-Produced Stimulation in the Development of Visually Guided Behavior," Journal of Comparative and Physiological Psychology 56, no. 5 (1963): 872–6.

5   Barrett, *How Emotions Are Made*.

6   Kristopher Smith et al., "Hunter-Gatherers Maintain Assortativity in Cooperation Despite High Levels of Residential Change and Mixing," *Current Biology* 28, no. 19 (2018): 3152–7.

7   The CD Baby letter is not sent out anymore, but has been referred to multiple times online. See, for example, *https://selnd.com/2WdQlM9*.

8   Al Ries and Laura Ries, *The 22 Immutable Laws of Branding* (London: Profile Books, 2000).

9   Tomohiro Ishizu and Semir Zeki, "Toward a Brain-Based Theory of Beauty," *Plos ONE* 6, no. 7 (2011): e21852.

10 Semir Zeki et al., "The Experience of Mathematical Beauty and Its Neural Correlates," *Frontiers in Human Neuroscience* 8 (2014): 68.

11 Donald A. Redelmeier and Daniel Kahneman, "Patients' Memories of Painful Medical Treatments: Real-Time and Retrospective Evaluations of Two Minimally Invasive Procedures," *Pain* 66, no. 1 (1996): 3–8.

12 Russell W. Belk, Güliz Ger, and Søren Askegaard, "The Fire of Desire: A Multisited Inquiry into Consumer Passion," *Journal of Consumer Research*, 30, no. 3 (2003): 326–51.

13 Jennifer Aaker writes about brand personality in several articles. This one sums up the concept well: Jennifer L. Aaker, "Dimensions of Brand Personality," *Journal of Marketing Research* 34, no. 3 (1997): 347–56.

14 Richard H. Thaler and Cass R. Sunstein, *Nudge: Improving Decisions about Health, Wealth, and Happiness* (New Haven, CT: Yale University Press, 2008).

15 Nathalie Thomas, "Ryanair's Michael O'Leary: easyJet 'Wiped the Floor with Us,'" *Daily Telegraph*, November 21, 2013, *http://bit.ly/2Wdvwk3*.

7

Experiential Translation: From Experiential DNA to Customer Experience

Your experiential DNA is your prime asset, and this chapter explains how you can translate it into the right experience for the customer. It shows that a successful translation will not only develop your unique experiential position, it will also make it hard for competitors to copy you.

Recently I moved to Denmark, and enrolled with a new doctor. I had moved within Scandinavia, so the general welfare model was the same. However, I became acutely aware of how I was learning about the doctor's practice, partly because I had this book in mind (but mostly because I am a nerd). I was reflecting on every point of contact, and using these small experiential moments to piece together like a jigsaw a coherent idea of the personality of the service they offered. I don't mean just the personality of the doctor (although that was a major part of it), but the personality of the whole service, constructed from all of the small interactions I had. From booking an appointment to arranging a blood test, receiving results, going to consultations, waiting in the waiting room, and talking with the doctor, I was putting together a coherent story based on multiple small snapshots of experience. This went right down to details like the furniture in the waiting room, the pictures on the wall, and even the pens—everything. I built up a cohesive story about the doctor's practice based on all of these touchpoints, constructing a personality, behaviors, tone of voice, and style of interactions.

And then I asked myself, why was I doing this? If you have read Chapter 6, you will understand that I was gathering information to create scenarios in my head, to prepare myself for future trips to the doctor's practice. I was learning how that particular place worked in an experiential way, so that in the future, I could make my life easier. I would know how to talk to the doctor, what information I needed when booking an appointment, how to behave when entering the waiting room, and so on—a whole load of experiential scenario clues that would make my life easier. Looking more closely, and using the terms in this book, I was decoding the offering, based on my interactions with the different touchpoints and the experiential journeys I had with them. Not only this, but I summarized this offering and experiential story about the doctor's practice for myself, so that it wouldn't take much space in my memory.

In other words, I was working through the tripod of experience (see Chapter 3) backward, creating an experiential image in my mind, based on my interactions over time, piecing all of the touchpoint interactions together and then storing them in the simplest possible way in my memory as an offering/experience/DNA combination.

Experiential translation does the same, but as part of a deliberate design process. Translation is a means of ensuring that the experience you want the customer to have from all of their interactions with your touchpoints is a transparent representation of the experiential DNA of the organization. To enable this, you need to have a way of summarizing your experiential DNA, so that it can be used as part of a design process. This is the *experiential platform*, a transparent representation of your experiential DNA, but described in such a way that it can be used for design purposes. I doubt that the doctor I went to had given thought to this at all as he designed his practice, and it showed clearly. He was also paying the price, as I could see that there was a rapid churn of patients.

Designing for experience is all about multiple translation processes. You translate from customer insights into a desirable experience and offering, you translate that to touchpoints and a journey, and you translate *that* to organizational structure and culture. And all the time, you translate your experiential DNA, to use it in each and every decision you make.

Why Do You Need to Translate?

If you don't have a target, what can you aim for? As an organization, if you do not know what kind of experience you want your customers to have, then how can you make it happen? Good experiences don't happen by magic or by accident, but through direction, understanding, and guidance.

The most important reason for translating, and for involving the leadership in it, is to decide on a direction and agree to focus on a personality and desired experience for your organization. This shows both intent and direction and ensures alignment.

Second, as you start to develop services that implement this personality, you will need to communicate that target personality and customer experience to design teams.

This chapter is about the translation between the experiential DNA of your organization and the experience the customer has when using your service. It describes how you as an organization can create an experience platform that can be used throughout the organization as a means of both identifying the experience you want to give customers and designing the details of your projects. In this way, the experience platform forms a standard within the organization for everything you do. This translation process can be summarized by the following formula:

Experiential DNA × Translation = Experience platform

If you are an existing organization and already have a strong grip on your brand, then you are well on the way to doing this work. You may already have developed a personality for your service or organization. In my experience, most organizations translate their brand into values and a visual identity, but rarely define the personality of the organization or the experience they wish to provide. The experience-centric organization needs to be clear about the experience it wants to give, and that means moving beyond visual identity.

The experience platform is a reference point and should be considered one of the basic building blocks of the experience-centric organization. It builds on and summarizes the experiential DNA of the organization, describing it in an experiential way so that it can be used in the design process. Each and every organization has experiential DNA that defines and delineates what it can and cannot offer and what experiences it can provide for the customer. However, the experiential DNA is a complex mix of your brand, your heritage, your organization, and your position in the market and needs to be translated in a cohesive way to aid design for experience. By converting your DNA into a reference platform, you create something that everyone in the organization can consult when defining what you want the customer to see and feel when they experience your service. It becomes a statement of intent, a target, and a design reference tool, all in one.

Moving from a Visual-Identity Brand to an Experiential Organization

Brand experts will recognize the need for this translation, and it could be argued that this is just good branding. In theory I would agree, but in practice, "brand" has become synonymous with visual identity. It is surprising how many organizations end up developing visual identity handbooks, instead of experience handbooks, as an expression of their brand. It is perhaps a carryover from product thinking, in which the product is the main point of focus and branding is needed to identify the sender, through a logo, web presence, and packaging. As we have seen from Chapter 3, however, the customer experience is enabled by touchpoints, behaviors, personality, and tone of voice, all of which lie outside the traditional brand handbook.

We have consistently used the terms *experience* and *experiential DNA* in this book, because the term *branding* has become misused and misunderstood. The experience-centric organization is about more than the brand as the term is generally used today, so we needed new terms that have a specific experiential focus. Branding has often been discussed in terms of a promise—that is, used as a means of *promising* something through advertising. The experience-centric organization is instead all about *delivering* experiences that are co-created with customers, and this is the focus we'll use from now on. The brand as it is presented in the organization, while important, is only one part of the experiential DNA.

Translation is all about connecting the customer experience to the experiential DNA of your organization, and in doing so developing a personality, behavior, and tone of voice that complement your visual identity. This does not deny the importance of the visual identity, but rather places it in a context where it is one of many contributors to a customer experience. Now's the time where we focus on the others.

Experience First: The Mantra of Experience Centricity

While it goes against the accepted structured, analytical approach, it seems logical to start by crafting a desirable experience and work backward. The customer experience is where value is created, so it makes a lot of sense to start there, doesn't it? Crafting desirable experiences draws customers to you, and draws more attention through word of mouth than advertising. Experiences find their market because they get you noticed and shared, recommended, reviewed, and boosted by customers. To achieve this, experience fit is key; you have to start with the experience, one that cements the offering into place through use and that fits your organization and your heritage. The right experience gives meaning to customers, and also gives you meaning as an organization. Without that burning desire to offer something experiential, something that makes you proud to deliver, your customers will see through you and dismiss you as fake.

The Two-Way Street of Experience Fit: Making a DNA Match

There is a close relationship among the three elements in the tripod of experience: your experiential DNA, the experiential offering, and the experience itself (see Figure 7-1). They are powered and structured by the wheel of experience centricity, such that the whole organization stands behind them.

Starting with the experience and using the tripod of experience requires you to work backward to describe the offering that is needed to provide that experience. If you are a start-up, you can use this approach to define your experiential DNA. However, if you are an existing organization, you also need to work the other way around the tripod, to ensure a DNA fit. In this approach, you start with your experience platform, and discuss the customer experience you are able to provide.

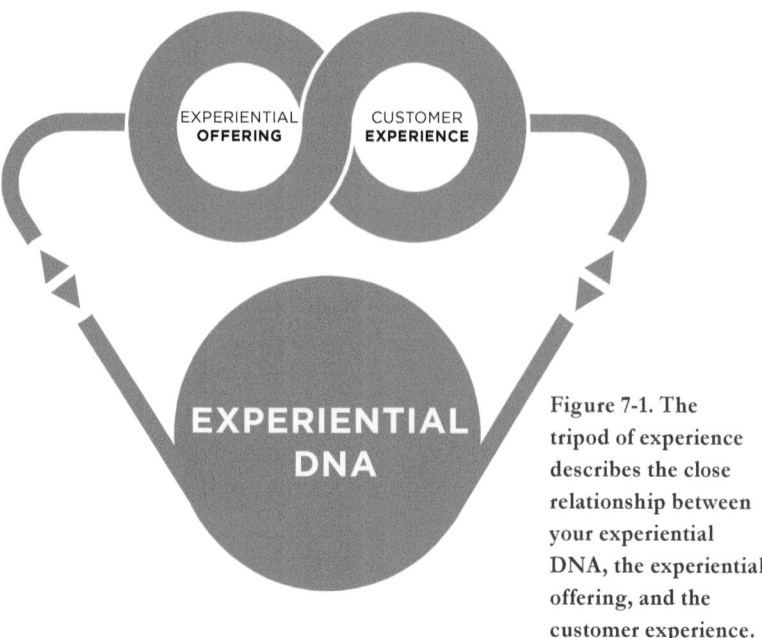

Figure 7-1. The tripod of experience describes the close relationship between your experiential DNA, the experiential offering, and the customer experience.

In reality, when innovating you will find that you continually switch between starting with the experience, starting with your experiential DNA, and starting with the offering, but always with a focus on the final customer experience. You might have conversations like:

- What kind of experience do our customers desire?
- What if we offered X? How would the customer experience be then?
- What experience can we offer that is a natural consequence of our DNA?

Each of these approaches is a natural way to work with the tripod of experience, and innovation can come from any of the three components. What is key is that finally all three elements fit harmoniously together so that the customer perceives a clear line from the experience, through the offering, to the DNA of the organization. This is a design thinking approach, focusing on "what can be" as the basis for experimentation. This approach also requires that you know your organization and your customers equally well, so that what you deliver is something that customers desire.

Fit or Stretch

The customer experience must be a good fit to your DNA, because the whole organization is a part of its delivery. A mismatch opens you up to high risk of failure. But as in strategy, you can develop a perfect fit to what is, or you can stretch the organization in a new direction. This is an approach where you deliberately aim to change your experiential DNA, which would entail organizational transformation. The degree of stretch depends on your organization—you have to know your organization really well to make sure that it can develop the new competencies and stretch to fit the new experience chosen. Experiential DNA is not totally static, but it changes slowly. The term *fit* here does include a little wiggle room to stretch your organization toward the experience, and in this way you can consciously move your organization each time you innovate.

Creating an Experience Platform

The translation process comprises three steps, resulting in an experience platform that can support design decisions, which in turn will always be infused with the organization's experiential DNA.

The three steps of translation are:

1. Identify your experiential DNA.
2. Translate it into a service personality and exemplify its behaviors and tone of voice.
3. Build out your personality to develop an experiential platform for use within the organization.

You can then start to create principles for design, iterate, and use the platform you've created for design.

Identify Your Experiential DNA

In the same way that your own DNA, as a reader of this book, is the code for your life as a person, the experiential DNA is the code, laid out for your organization, that defines what experiences you can and cannot deliver. Your experiential DNA is a mix of who you are, who

Interview with Nicholas Ind

Nicholas Ind is a branding guru with several books to his name. He has worked with and advised a broad range of commercial organizations such as Adidas and Patagonia, as well as nonprofit organizations such as Greenpeace and UNICEF. As he explains, it is important to him that an experience focus is part of the culture of an organization.

The experience is the core of what the brand is about, and the challenge facing organizations today is how to establish and maintain their experiential position. Brand is not a promise, because if you are to make a promise then it implies you can control its outcome. Brand makes an offer and has influence over the experience but does not control it. Where the brand fits in, it frames the experience. It creates an expectation and positively acts to satisfy that expectation. Controlling the outcome is not possible, since the experience is defined beforehand. Someone outside the control of the brand might influence this. Take Trip Advisor as an example—it can have a huge influence on a trip that you have booked elsewhere.

An organization has to be clear what its brand stands for. For example, LEGO went back to what they stood for. They opened up and let others co-create. But to do that they had to redefine the brand. [If] you are to give freedom, you also need clarity and order. Brand clarity is important and requires a deep understanding of the brand. In LEGO, this meant taking it back to its roots and an understanding of its past. That gave it authenticity both internally and externally.

I think experiential DNA and brand DNA are pretty much the same thing and both relate to your roots. To uncover your DNA requires an understanding of where you come from. We often get fixated on the future and miss where the brand has come from. Adidas has been good [at understanding] where they come from, and they bring key things in from their past. Authenticity is key here.

"We often get fixated on the future and miss where the brand has come from." This relates also to an understanding of how you are seen externally. Majken Schultz from Copenhagen Business School talks about how image influences identity. How others see you needs to be understood, as well as how you see yourself. Then you need to consider whether this is reflected in actions you take.

Q: Are organizations good at understanding the culture that is around them?

A: Understanding and reacting to culture is very important. Some companies are good at it and are attuned to the world around them. But many organizations become blinkered and see things from their own point of view for too long. You can easily lose attunement to the broader sense of what is happening around you.

We are in a period where culture is changing very quickly. For example, the retail experience of Apple shows how culture quickly absorbs newness. When they ventured in, it was a new and exciting concept, but over time it lost its specialness and that created a need for renewal. Knowing when to change is key, and this requires you to continually reinterpret who you are.

you have been, and who you want to be, and it balances the customer perspective and the organizational perspective. Thus, internal culture and the customer view both play an important part in your DNA.

Your experiential DNA is a mix of:

- Your mission, vision, and values
- Your brand strategy and history
- How you view yourselves
- How you are viewed by your customers
- Your heritage (as viewed by yourselves and as viewed by customers)

Many organizations think they know these things, but in reality their understanding is based on fragments of information and not articulated in detail. Identifying the experiential DNA is often the first time that they develop a balanced internal and external experiential view of the organization. Taking this step, and then acting upon the DNA identified, is a major milestone along the path to experience centricity. Once you have carried out this work, you will wonder why you didn't do it sooner.

If Your Service Were a Car Brand

I remember getting into a passionate discussion with a leadership group in a service organization by asking them to compare themselves to a car brand. After some discussion, they argued for an hour about how they wanted to be

similar to Saab, with its Nordic sensibilities and strong but subtle design, and Audi, with its driving experience and German efficiency. In the end they settled on a combination that was clearly defined.

This nuanced and passionate discussion was in stark contrast to how the leadership group otherwise discussed emotional aspects of their organization. By using analogies (e.g., supermarkets, people, airlines) we were able to have the detailed discussions that were needed to be able to obtain an experience fit. The company went on to match their newly identified experiential DNA with the basis for their offering, touchpoints, and approach to service.

If you are working at a start-up, you have the luxury of creating your experiential DNA. This will normally emerge through an interplay between understanding customers, the mission of the start-up partners, and the development of the offering.

The outcome of this process is a DNA description that has a long-term influence on the organization, and should only be updated gradually and organically as the market context changes.

Warts and All ...

Being able to influence people's emotions requires great insight into your organization and the people you want to influence. Consider a comparison from music: it is not uncommon that musicians create their best music at some personal cost, which is part of the reason it carries such emotional resonance across the years. For example, Joni Mitchell once said that her audience connected with the honesty of a great song because "it strikes against the very nerves of their life." She then added, "To do that, you have to first strike against your own."[1]

It can be painful exploring your own DNA and accepting some harsh truths on the way. But this process is important, and the insights you gain allow you to embrace your organization, warts and all, safe in the knowledge that you will build something fantastic from it. This is not me getting all New Age on you, but influencing emotions requires that you yourself understand them.

I recommend experiential DNA be identified together with external specialists as part of a long-term collaboration. This is because your own internal view can often skew your results, so you most likely need an independent opinion. I specify *long-term* collaboration, because knowing your DNA is just the first step. You have to then be able to apply it, and you most likely will need support for this later. However, you will need to be closely involved, because the internal view requires discussion and is key to creating organizational alignment. You may also find that the results of the experiential DNA challenge and update your brand. In almost all projects where I have worked with experiential DNA, the brand has been updated as part of the work.

Translate Your DNA into a Service Personality and Exemplify It

The second stage is to take the experiential DNA and describe it in detail, as if it were a person creating your service personality. In this way you give your DNA a human face and describe the experiential behavior and tone of voice expected of your organization when a customer (or employee) interacts with it. A successful transformation will result in a personality that can be used for design and evaluation and, when implemented through touchpoints and customer journeys, will shine through and be recognizable to customers.

In the same way that an author describes the personality of someone in a novel so well that you feel you know them, you should describe your service personality so fully that you feel you know the service deeply. When the personality is correctly chosen, it instills confidence within the organization, since employees recognize it as a reflection of the organizational DNA. Several times I have heard people say, "Wow, that's us!"

Service Personality

Service personality is a recent construct, based on brand personality but specifically tailored to the characteristics of services.[2] Brand personality has been considered an important concept in branding for some time, although primarily for product-based organizations. The term originated in the 1950s within advertising, and evolved during the late 1970s to describe the non-functional characteristics of a product. It became used as a common, practical term for assessing non-product-based, nonfunctional dimensions of the brand.

The term became widely debated and discussed in the 1990s, due to the work of Jennifer Aaker. She defined brand personality as "the set of human characteristics associated with a brand" and presented quantitative research that identified five key personality dimensions.[3] Her 1997 article on the subject became important for marketing and strongly influenced the view of branding at that time. Aaker's five core personality dimensions were criticized as being limited, and although there was agreement that brand personality was relevant in conceptual terms, critics disagreed about its core factors, components, and cross-culturality. This is due, in large part, to a desire for reliable and independent quantifiable factors for use in quantitative research.

Brand personality is commonly used in destination tourism, and is central to the destination branding model proposed by Ekinci (2003).[4] Further, Murphy et al. (2007)[5] show that tourists are able to identify and express the brand personality of tourism destinations. Brand personality has also been studied in terms of the design of a particular touchpoint—a wine label, for instance—to show how it can be used to evaluate the brand personality of a store. Azoulay and Kapferer link brand personality to behaviors, which has particular relevance to the branding of services. They note that:

Indeed, the personality of individuals is perceived through their behavior, and, in exactly the same way, consumers can attribute a personality to a brand according to its perceived communication and "behaviors."[6]

The term *brand personality* thus has a wide range of application and relevance in branding, particularly services branding, and is suited to a "multiple touchpoint" view of services. I have further developed this definition in my own work to establish the term service personality.[7]

We use a mix of words, images, audio, and video to describe the service personality, and using analogies to other existing brands and personalities is an effective means of doing this—not because you should copy them, but because they have elements that we all understand and can relate to.

The Hot and Cold Approach

In Scandinavia, the UK, and the US, kids play a game known as "Hot and Cold" each Easter to find hidden Easter eggs. While the kids search, observers give them tips such as "You're getting warmer," "You're getting colder," "You're getting hot," and "You're burning up!" as they approach an egg. The same approach can be used to hunt for the personality that fits your organization, and this is a technique I have used with companies several times.

Armed with a good actor, writer, printer, and video camera, we have explored alternative service personalities to find the one that fits. After choosing initial experiential words and discussing the experiential DNA, we script a customer encounter based on each of the keywords and a few outliers (which act as a slight but positive provocation). The script is played out with the leadership, and we evaluate their responses in terms "warmer" (that is more like us) or "colder" (that is less us). We deliberately use these terms first, as the team is often unable to say exactly why a personality doesn't work. Sometimes people will say, "That's a bit closer to us, but it lacks some X," and can be specific, but sometimes not. After a broad first run of the hot-and-cold exercise, the scripts are rewritten to account for the feedback, acted and filmed again, and repeated. After a few iterations we end up with a really precise experiential representation of the organization that has been defined, refined, and agreed on.

As I have mentioned, the only way to experience an experience is to experience it, and this applies to your service personality as well. The best way to discuss and identify your personality is by experiencing it through example. This is because we are generally poor at describing a personality but good at recognizing one. Authors and actors are better at describing personality, but you are best at recognizing whether it fits. Therefore, it is useful to collaborate with, for example, a good actor to try out alternative personalities to find the one you are happy with.

At this stage, you and your leadership group have the agreed-on perfect representation of your organization. It is then possible to work backward, to describe this endpoint in words and images in order to capture the service personality and the experience it delivers.

Build Out Your Personality to Develop an Experiential Platform

As part of the translation process it is important that you develop terminology within the organization to discuss, negotiate, and form the experience you wish to have, so when you find it, you are able to explain it to others. But experience shows that we are quite poor at describing these things, and it takes time to learn the terminology. Thus, it is wise to have some design help along the way. If you are moving along the experience-centric maturity scale, you have most likely employed a designer to act as CXO, or you may still be using outside help. At this stage, it is important that there is commitment and buy-in from the whole leadership group, because they will have to support and represent the outcome in their work. Not only this, but the leadership group represents a large part of the organization and therefore the experiential DNA. Working cross-functionally is central to success.

My experience is that the journey to explore, develop, and describe the experiential platform is as important as the outcome, since it forces leaders to dive into and understand experience. This is not something that can be outsourced and then conjured out of a designer's hat, but rather something that should be facilitated and co-developed within the whole leadership team.

Your experiential platform is a description of the personality and experience that you want your customers to have. It comprises both a video description of the personality, and examples of how that personality is expected to behave. It includes examples of generic touchpoints where the personality is applied. This allows it to be communicated such that people are able to experience the experience. Essentially, the platform describes an experiential target, exemplified by different touchpoints and experiential journeys. Similar to other standards, the experiential target should be carefully designed and then rarely updated.

Mauricy Filho, who carried out his PhD on service branding, describes the experiential platform as a form of brand experience handbook. I have to admit struggling with this term, since *handbook* conjures images of three-ring binders filled with pages, images, and specifications, rather than a tool to allow people to experience the experience itself. Still, your experiential platform requires interactions, time, and touchpoints, so examples are a necessary part of your deliverable. Those examples will form the basis of your principles for design.

That's AMAZING!!!

Recently, I called the customer service hotline for my daughter's mobile subscription. She is subscribed to a young, trendy mobile operator and the customer service representatives were young and obviously had two principles they had to follow in their conversation. One was to be enthusiastic, and the other was to find something positive that they could compliment the customer about. I met an extreme version of this, someone who was so enthusiastic I felt unnerved as she gushed about the fact that I could speak Danish, English, and Norwegian: "Wow, that is so cool. You can speak all of those languages. That's amazing!" In reality, it isn't; my Danish sounds Norwegian and my Norwegian sounds Danish. It made me laugh, because it was so obvious that being complimentary was part of her training. I only wish it had been something worth the compliment, or maybe not expressed so gushingly. Sincerity is key, and if she had been genuine, I would have felt flattered. As it was, it felt tacky.

Create Principles for Design

When you have settled on the personality that fits your organization, and have examples of it for different touchpoints that you are happy with, the next stage is to create principles for design based on them. You develop the principles *after* you have created the specific examples of touchpoints, because making them will give you some insights into why, say, a particular tone of voice was chosen (see Figure 7-2).

There are many kinds of design principles, from the high-level versions that guide a whole process (for example, "start with the customer"), down to detailed versions for interactions (e.g., font and color requirements). The principles in the experiential platform lie somewhere in

NIKE + RUN CLUB   19m ago

Someone busier than you is running right now. Get out there.

Figure 7-2. The Nike tone of voice is designed to motivate as part of a winning mentality, telling you that you really have no excuses to not run. But some people might find this tone of voice provocative or insulting. Knowing your target audience is critical when working with tone of voice, and you need to take a position to get noticed.

between. They are not principles for how to approach innovation, nor are they detailed design requirements, but they can be used to inform a service and its interactions. Depending on the experiential DNA and your personality, they might include guidelines such as being conversational with customers (one used by Airbnb) or recognizing their history with the company (reminding them in a positive way of their loyalty), giving surprising treats (Pret A Manger employees are allowed to give away items to customers), or using humor (a principle from a telco I worked with aimed at younger people). The principles you choose will be dictated by your experiential DNA and personality, and you can start to explore them by asking, "How would our personality behave (and what would it say) if X happened?" The answer will help you define your organization's principles for design.

Review the (Almost) Finished Platform

The platform is never totally finished and should go through regular cycles of improvement. This is particularly true in terms of keeping abreast of societal changes and trends (see Chapter 10). At this stage your platform should contain the following:

- A summary of your experiential DNA
- A description of your service personality, behaviors, and tone of voice
- Examples of the personality applied to different touchpoints
- Principles for design

Together, these components offer a strong basis for designing new services and improving existing ones. They also have been part of a valuable journey to develop your existential approach, and undoubtedly will have helped foster a strong experiential focus within the organization. Now, the platform is ready for use as a means of evaluation.

The Gold Standard Experience

The image below is of the ISO international standards for length and weight. They are stored in atmospheric and temperature-controlled conditions to always be exactly correct.

You should have the same focus on the experience you want to deliver to your customers and create your own standards as a target for the organization. These standards become something that you can always refer to and relate to, and when adhered to, they can help the organization maintain experiential alignment and consistency.

Your standard experience will not be a physical object—it will take the form of an image, text, or enactment—and it cannot be as precisely defined as weight or length. However, the experience platform you have developed within the organization will convey the desired and desirable experience.

Source: National Institute of Standards and Technology.

Using the Platform for Design

The final part of the translation cycle is to deliver on the experiences that you have designed for as part of the platform. This entails using the "gold standard" personality as a target for design work in the organization. This step in itself might seem trivial, but it is not. It requires dedicated functions to implement throughout the organization, and it can require quite a lot of legacy work to update existing touchpoints and journeys. It is therefore worthwhile to evaluate the platform

Insights from Mauricy Filho

Mauricy Filho earned a PhD in service design by studying the process of translating brand into customer experience. He has extensively researched the changing world of branding and how it relates to the customer and employee experience. As Mauricy explains here, it is key that an organization knows what experience it wants to provide.

Today, the things that define the brand for people happen through use—use of a service, or use of a product. This is important because organizations should be concerned about "What experience do you want the customer to have and how can you deliver it?" If you do not know the experience that you want the customer to have, then you will not be able to differentiate yourself in the market. This is where branding should now have its focus.

In many ways, we are seeing a new era of branding. Branding made mistakes in the past because it was associated with advertisements and manipulating people. Consumer maturity saw through this around the year 2000 and there was a backlash against brands. Probably, the most visible expression was Naomi Klein's book *No Logo* and the sociocultural context it built upon. Today, this has changed and has moved toward a focus upon the customer experience.

To be relevant in an experience-centric society, you have to know who you are, what you can do, and what experience you want to provide. Some organizations might try to just follow trends without knowing this, but by doing that you quickly lose who you are.

You have to make experience strategic—make it a strategic lighthouse or North Star. Then, through design, devise your processes, systems, interfaces, and resources to enable these experiences to emerge. If you work strategically and know the experience you want to provide, then you can develop an experience proposition that is aligned with the brand and your business strategy. Then you can design the service and its enablers, making that experience happen. Internal branding is important in this context. In order to externalize an experience, you also need to be able to internalize it. This is important, because there is no experience until the settings that enable it are in place and working. Until then, it is still only an idea.

This gives other advantages. Once you know who you are, you are also able to reinterpret it—you can extend the frame of where you see yourself. For example, when Porsche extends into off-road cars, it must rethink what Porsche means—high-performance vehicles, and luxury. Whatever you do, you must not lose the thread to your core, and that means that you really have to know who you are.

> **"You have to make experience strategic—make it a strategic lighthouse or North Star. Then, through design, devise your processes, systems, interfaces, and resources to enable these experiences to emerge."**

From an organizational perspective, it is about mindset. There is a need for the organization to shift focus to the customer experience as something that can be managed strategically, in a way that is aligned to the brand. For an organization addressing this, it requires strategic focus. Experience innovation does not necessarily require new technologies, but new arrangements of resources in a way that can enable better experiences for the customers.

Organizations should focus upon the position of the customer experience within the organization. It's time to stop splitting between those who promise and those who deliver (e.g., marketing and UX [user experience]). Once you combine the two, you have a new C-level position with responsibility for customer experience.

Finally, looking to the future, you have to embrace cultural aspects. There are clusters of people spread around the world that need similar things. These could almost be described as consumer tribes, or a kind of postmodern segmentation. These niches will become more relevant in the future, and customer experiences aimed toward niche clusters will emerge. Culturally relevant offerings are appearing more and more across geographical boundaries and this is, to me, one of the future growth areas of customer experience.

before rolling it out, to ensure that it works and gives the desired results. To evaluate the platform, you should do some design work on several customer journeys, making sure that the project design team uses the platform as a basis for their work. You can take this testing as far as implementation to be able to evaluate the final customer experience, or alternatively (depending on the degree of change), you can put the platform through experience prototyping after the design stage. Either way, you have to have a strong conviction that the platform is correct, since it will influence the whole wheel of experience centricity, including major systems and structures.

Rolling Out the Platform

The journey you have embarked on thus far will have given you plenty of insights into the experience that best fits your organization. The platform hasn't defined the offerings or the customer experience, but through the personality it has given the service some basic direction. The use of the platform can, depending on the degree of change, have a major impact on the customer experience, so its roll-out merits consideration. Customers are particularly sensitive to changes in personality and tone of voice in a service. I have used a Scandinavian bank for many years, and they, like many other banks, are transforming their personality and customer experience. Unfortunately they are struggling, as transforming from a stodgy and reliable but autocratic and hierarchical bank to one that is customer-oriented is quite a change, and they haven't updated all of their touchpoints yet. That means I may encounter several touchpoints that speak directly to me with a nicely composed mix of visual design and tone of voice and then the odd, autocratic one, with an old-fashioned visual design and terrible tone of voice. This stands out and brings back my old prejudices, preventing me from accepting their new personality and making me think it is superficial. Since touchpoints usually cross different silos within the organization during a customer journey, there is a real risk that there will be some legacy problems that could destroy all the work you've done along the way if you do not do a careful roll-out of the platform.

The platform roll-out should be coordinated with other experiential changes in the organization. As a planning measure, carry out a gap analysis to evaluate the distance between the existing customer experience and the expected new one. Based on this analysis, the roll-out should be part of a systematic change plan. The platform is an important part of the infusion process, and should be complemented by a successful service innovation (a quick win), quick and visible changes, and several future concept services. Together, these should form a wave of change within the organization that is part of a virtual circle, gaining acceptance and positive development along the way.

The Importance of Belief

Finally, you need to believe in your experience platform. *Belief* may be a strange term to introduce into a hard business context, but it is essential when you are innovating through experience. If you do not have a strong belief in the experience platform now, then you should question why and then do something about it. The platform is a key transformation tool, and will influence customer experience and your bottom line over time. Further, the platform starts a substantial change process by redesigning the touchpoints, enablers, systems, and structures throughout the organization. As the platform is rolled out, belief will aid the transformation process and contribute to experiential fit, becoming a core competency of your organization.

Endnotes

1   Malka Marom, *In Her Own Words* (London: Omnibus Press, 2014).

2   Jennifer L. Aaker, "Dimensions of Brand Personality," *Journal of Marketing Research* 34, no. 3 (1997): 347-56.

3   Aaker, "Dimensions of Brand Personality," 347.

4   Yuksel Ekinci and Sameer Hosany, "Destination Personality: An Application of Brand Personality to Tourism Destinations," *Journal of Travel Research* 45, no. 2 (2006): 127-39.

5   Laurie Murphy, Gianna Moscardo, and Pierre Benckendorff, "Using Brand Personality to Differentiate Regional Tourism Destinations," *Journal of Travel Research* 46, no. 1 (2007): 5-14.

6   Audrey Azoulay and Jean-Noël Kapferer, "Do Brand Personality Scales Really Measure Brand Personality?" *Brand Management* 11, no. 2 (2003): 143-55.

7   Simon Clatworthy, "Bridging the Gap Between Brand Strategy and Customer Experience," *Managing Service Quality* 22, no. 2 (2012): 108-27.

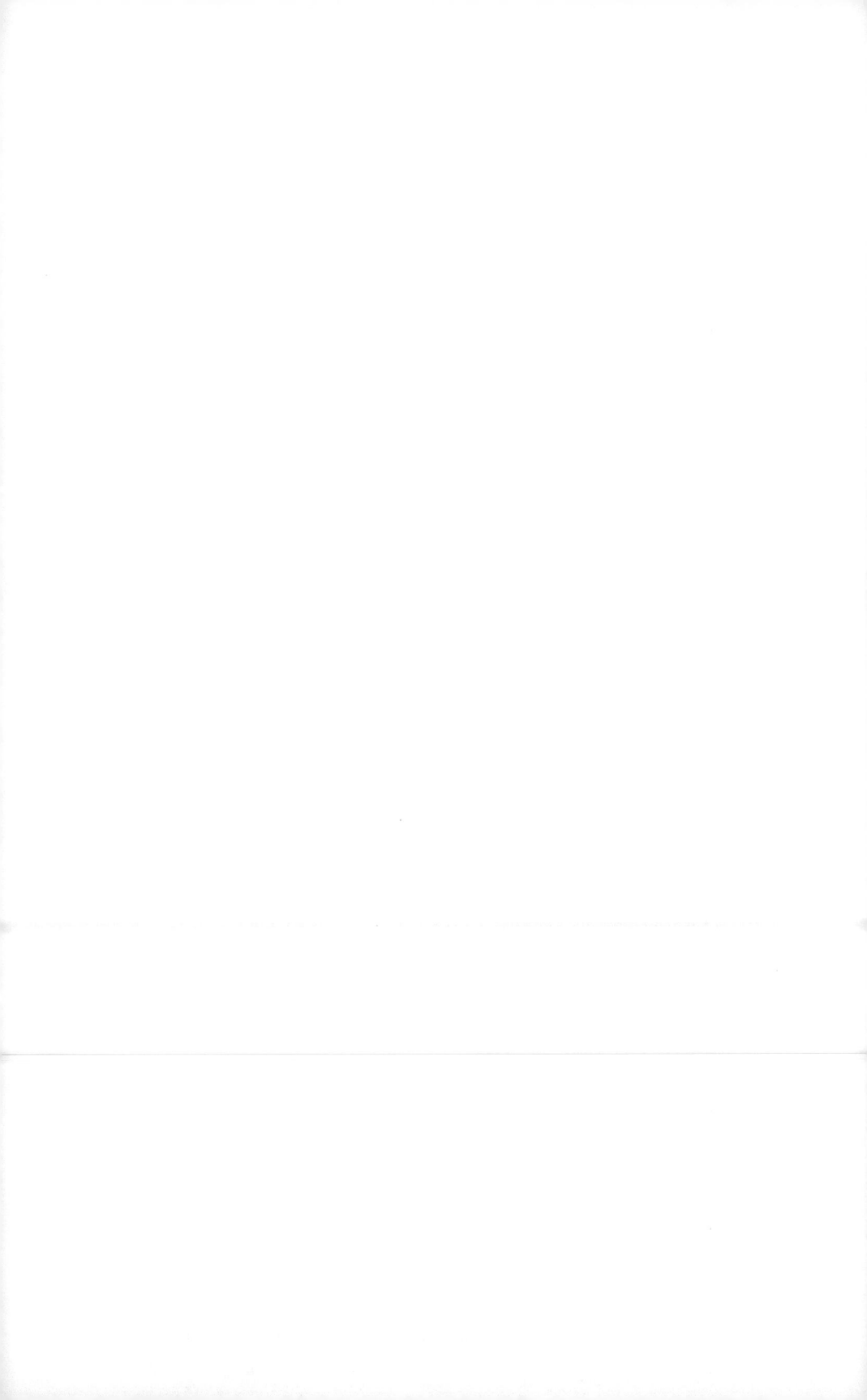

8

Experience Fulfillment: Designing the Experiential Journey

In this chapter you will dive down into experience fulfillment and get an understanding of how customers experience your products and services as a journey that comprises touchpoints and interactions along the way. You will learn how to orchestrate these touchpoints, and how experience prototyping can give you insight into the customer experience at a very early stage of the innovation process.

A recent *Consumer Reports* survey asked people to rate everyday annoyances on a scale from 1 to 10, with a score of 10 being "annoys you tremendously."[1] Respondents rated the failure to get a human being on a customer service line an 8.6, second only to hidden fees (8.9) and more irritating than spam email (7.5) and inaccurate meteorologists (4.3). This means the second most irritating situation in people's everyday lives is a service touchpoint.

The Whole Made from the Parts

What experience do customers have when using your services? Most likely, it's very different from how the company experiences itself. Studies show that many organizations believe that their customers are having great experiences, but the customers themselves do not agree. There is a huge mismatch between what you think you're offering and what customers perceive. This is because your customers view you and your services through the multiple touchpoints that they meet along their customer journey, and your organization is not designed for this experiential way of interacting. Silos are the main culprit, as customers navigate from silo to silo, encountering different people, ways of working, terminology, and interaction styles. Advertising, word of mouth, and reviews are touchpoints they encounter before using your service. Then they use touchpoints for onboarding during first use, followed by the multiple touchpoints they encounter as they begin using the service regularly and you build a relationship. If they are unlucky, then they might encounter errors too, and customer service touchpoints to help them recover from those errors.

What Are Touchpoints?

Touchpoints are the points of contact between the service provider and the customer. The majority of touchpoints are tangible, and many are interactive. The collective experience of all touchpoints forms the customer's view of the service. Different touchpoints are in focus at each stage of the service journey, and some are more critical to the customer experience than others.

Notice that we use the term *touchpoints* rather than *channels*. There are several reasons for this. First, channels are a company-centric way of looking at interactions with customers. The term *touchpoints* includes the customer from their own perspective. Second, channels implies broadcast: a one-way, one-to-all communication. The experience-centric organization is more interested in interactions and relationships than broadcasting a message, so the channel metaphor doesn't work. Third, channels implies a limited number of prescribed communication means without overlap, in the same way you click from channel to channel on the TV. In reality, there are multiple touchpoints, even down to the smell of freshly baked bread in a supermarket. Finally, customers jump from one touchpoint to the other without even thinking about it. Thinking of channels gives a linear impression and colors the design process. Thinking of touchpoints , however, pushes you to see the service through the customer's eyes, which can often be quite messy.

If you view your company in this way, you will see it in fragments, glimpsed through multiple touchpoints along a journey, and you will maybe react with, "This isn't us; we are much more than this!" But this is how customers see your company—through multiple small windows (your touchpoints)—and they piece the whole picture together themselves based on those glimpses (along with word of mouth, cultural understanding, etc.). It's necessary to view your company and your offering through your touchpoints, then, simply because that's how your customers see you.

Touchpoints are the points of contact between a service provider and customers and one of the major pain points for many of today's services.

Each time a person relates to or interacts with a touchpoint, they have a service encounter. This delivers an experience (good or bad) and adds something to the person's relationship with the service and the service provider. The sum of all experiences from touchpoint interactions colors their opinion of the service, and of you as a company.

Customers don't think of how these touchpoints are coordinated, and they don't care; they just expect them to work and give value. They hop from one touchpoint to another without considering which department was responsible for designing and maintaining it. Customers expect a positive and consistent experience no matter how they access your service, and all of your incredible branding work has primed them with expectations of a particular kind of experience. If your touchpoints aren't up to the job, you will create a mismatch between expectation and experience, and that means disappointed customers (and as we know, disappointed customers tell others about their disappointment).

> Touchpoints are a window into your very soul—your experiential DNA.

If you are serious about delighting your customers, then you can't avoid spending some time working on the orchestration of your touchpoints (see Figure 7-1). That means looking at your service as a whole, and creating multiple touchpoints that work together along the customer journey. It's no good having one exceptional touchpoint if you have neglected the others—you have to provide consistent and excellent service delivery through them all. This reinforces your brand and

Figure 8-1. Touchpoint cards help teams consider which touchpoints may be relevant to a project, and are available on the companion website (www. experience-centric.com).

ensures consistently high levels of satisfaction, efficiency, and loyalty. It will result in a positive cycle, where customers tell other customers, and the brand and experience are aligned.

You can evoke specific feelings in a person during a service encounter by thoughtfully designing and coordinating your touchpoints. By taking a holistic view, you can define total experiences and map these to individual service encounters. This is the zooming in and zooming out approach described in Chapter 4: designing both the sum of the parts and the individual parts themselves.

Improving Your Touchpoints

In this section, we will look at how you can innovate your touchpoints to improve service offerings, user experiences, and customer value.

Start with the Experience and Work Backward

The overriding question you have to ask yourself as an experience-centric organization is, "Which touchpoint combination do we need to fulfill the experiential promise given by the offering and the brand?" There are multiple different touchpoints that all have to align to the experience you want to give. When you focus on them in the design process, you will find that there are many more touchpoints to your service than you initially thought.

View Experiential Journeys as a Customer Experience Approach

In Chapter 6, we talked about how customers view and develop scenarios before and during their experiences. Scenarios in this context are short journeys played out in preparation for service encounters , so they're a good way to think and describe how the customer experience unfolds. They incorporate time very well, and they allow for a great visualization of the entire service, so that you can see the whole and the parts together.

The customer journey has become a common way of describing a service over time, and the experiential journey improves on it to focus on the experience that the customer has (see Figure 8-2). In his book *Mapping Experiences* (O'Reilly), Jim Kalbach presents many examples of experiential journey maps, each with a different focus.

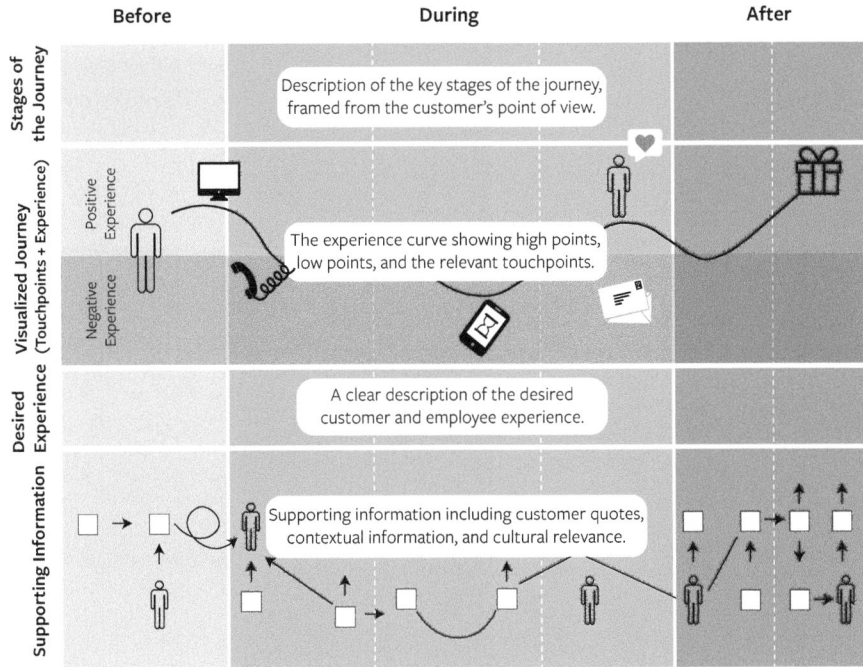

	Before	During	After
Stages of the Journey		Description of the key stages of the journey, framed from the customer's point of view.	
Visualized Journey (Touchpoints + Experience)	Positive Experience / Negative Experience	The experience curve showing high points, low points, and the relevant touchpoints.	
Desired Experience		A clear description of the desired customer and employee experience.	
Supporting Information		Supporting information including customer quotes, contextual information, and cultural relevance.	

Figure 8-2. The typical contents of an experiential journey map.

The experiential journey map illustrates how the customer travels through your service, which touchpoints they meet along the way, and how they experience the journey, both as a whole, and at each point. It has a timeline base and an experiential structure, and a journey is typically divided into three main parts: before use, during use, and after use. This timeline can be at a macro level (e.g., a lifelong relationship with a bank) or a shorter time scale (e.g., a customer requesting a loan), and you should nest the micro-journey into the macro one to find out how they support each other. Common to all experiential journey maps is the separation of the before, during, and after phases, since innovations in the before and after stages can be especially important.

The main focus of the timeline is to visualize the experiential journey, noting the expected touchpoints. This allows you to show the dramatic curve of the journey and to identify significant points along the way. These can be points of peak experience and the build-up to them, or potential pain points that will need attention. In addition to the visualization of the experiential journey, the map identifies and describes the stages of the journey, specifies the desired experience for each stage, and provides supporting information.

Avoiding the Two Traps of Journey Design

I was working with a doctor on developing a better customer journey, when he proudly stated that he had done it already and had the perfect solution worked out. When I asked him to show me the journeys, it was obvious that he had fallen into the two traps of journey design:

- The journey was really his journey, not the customer's (patient's) journey. He had described what he did in relation to the customer, not how the customer viewed the journey.
- The journey started when the customer came into his office and it ignored everything that had happened beforehand, such as the customer visiting their own doctor before getting the referral, receiving information about the appointment, finding their way, and so on. We know that a high percentage of patients never show up to their appointments, and this failure to understand the early stages of their experiential journey might explain why.

Avoid the two main traps of journey design. Journeys always begin before your involvement, and are always described from the customer's perspective.

The journey should always be viewed through the customer's eyes, and needs to take into account all stages of their journey, including those before your organization enters the picture. This can include a customer researching service offerings before engaging with your service (and how you can influence that), discussing the service with friends, or being exposed to your advertising message. The pre-use phase is important because it makes you aware of how the customer starts the experience with you. The post-use phase is important too, because this is where there is huge potential for positive follow-up. We know, for example, that after using a service, customers like to review the experience in their heads, and can often have a kind of buyer's remorse, or at least reflection (was it the right choice, what was it like, etc.). Studies show that people will often look at reviews of products and services after buying or using them, as a way to reassure themselves about their choices. It might in fact be our nature to try to add closure to the scenarios we have created and the experiences we have had, and the post-use phase offers you a great opportunity to influence that closure in a positive way.

I often find that organizations say they have already worked a lot with customer journeys, only to find out that they have really been working with process flow charts. Process flows view the world through the company's eyes, are process-centric, and often assume a certain behavior from the customer. Process flow charts are important, but only as a means of translating an experiential journey into a blueprint for implementation. They should not be viewed as the same thing as an experiential journey.

Likewise, an experiential journey is not a blueprint for design. It is a design target, detailing the desired experience for customers as they use your service, and a means of describing a service concept from the customer's point of view. It details the offering and allows you to check for cohesion with your experiential DNA. Further, it allows you to see the downstream implications the experience may have for experience fulfillment, enabling, and structure. The experiential journey needs further development to be a blueprint for implementation, in which the organization presents more detail, particularly around these downstream effects.

Consider Direct, Indirect, and Partner-Controlled Touchpoints

Touchpoints are often direct and "owned" by you, such as a website, a brochure, or a letter. During the past few years, however, indirect touchpoints have come into focus, since they are important influencers of customer expectations and experiences. Indirect touchpoints are not directly developed, controlled, or presented by the service provider, and can include things such as transport to an airport, or airport security. They can also be friends, family, or word of mouth, online reviews or blog/tweet comments. These are increasingly important and have to be included in touchpoint design. A breakdown from the company Accelerom shows that approximately 50% of a customer's impressions come from direct channels, while the other 50% come from indirect channels. As the impact of social media increases, we can expect this split to move more toward indirect touchpoints. It's worth bearing in mind, though, that almost all indirect touchpoints can be traced back to direct touchpoints originally. A good or bad experience with a service that is communicated via word of mouth was originally experienced directly through a touchpoint.

A third kind of touchpoint has also emerged: a *partner-controlled* touchpoint. This is increasingly common in digital services (for example, how many solutions use Google Maps these days?), but it can also be a subcontracted service provider used as part of your offering (for example, an electrical installer connecting broadband at a customer's home, or a baggage handler for a flight). Customers consider these third-party subcontractors a part of the service, so your organization should choose them with great care. A fantastic experiential journey can be ruined by a poor subcontractor who does not understand the design you have developed for the whole experience. At the same time, a partner-controlled touchpoint offers great potential in terms of B2B (business-to-business) provision if it is used by others. If you can understand the experiential journey that your customer wishes to achieve, and you can enable it, then you can create a strong relationship with them. This points to an increasing segmentation of, and an increased experiential focus in, B2B services. As an example, I have been working with a large postal organization that is adapting its offering to improve the customer experience of ordering and receiving packages. This new focus can help provide consistent experiences from the ordering phase through shipping and tracking to delivery and unboxing. In this way, the postal organization offers an experiential advantage over its competitors when competing for contracts.

Choose Touchpoints Appropriate to Your Context

All touchpoints are equal, but some touchpoints are better at certain things than others. This might sound obvious, but each touchpoint is unique in terms of its characteristics, meaning that different touchpoints are good at different things. Some are good at short, personalized, informational messages (e.g., SMS), others are good at transactions (internet), and still others are good at adding human value (telephone).

This realization, although obvious, is quite recent, and is leading companies to review their touchpoint strategies so that they utilize each touchpoint in the best way possible. When you're starting with the experience, it is easier to choose one preferred touchpoint over another based on its experiential characteristics. A text message, for example, has an immediacy about it, but lacks visual content and the ability to discern tone of voice. An email offers much more potential visually and content-wise, while a printed letter can give you undivided attention (although it can be very slow to compose). Choosing the right touchpoint for the experience desired therefore starts with the experience, and then works backward to find the best fit.

Keep Innovating to Stay Relevant

As technology develops, it is natural that some touchpoints will become more important for experience fulfillment than others. The rise of the smartphone app, for example, shows how the small, portable, handheld personal device has become a major touchpoint in our lives.

This also has a flip side, since some touchpoints that have fallen out of favor can now be used in different ways. The humble letter is a touchpoint crying out for a renaissance, simply due to the fact that our postboxes are empty many days of the week and yet we still have our emotional ritual pilgrimage to check the mail. This is a great opportunity for developing and nurturing a relationship with a customer, because physical mail now has an experiential weight to it and when they receive it they are likely to be alone, have time, and be able to give it their undivided attention. The same is true of the packing slips that come with the many packages customers order online. They offer fantastic potential for customer contact, simply because most packing slips are crappy; just a company-centric check-offs that something has occurred, rather than a note supporting the pleasurable act of opening a package. The CD Baby letter (see Chapter 6) shows how to take advantage of this opportunity to improve the customer's experience of buying something.

This change in relevance over time means that you need to keep innovating in your experiential journey design, always looking for new touchpoints and perhaps bringing in some old ones. Think about it as remixing a great song.

Ways of Innovating Through Touchpoints

Touchpoints are a key component of service design and offer several possibilities for innovation, from choosing based on their qualities to orchestrating them as a whole. Next I outline the four main ways you can innovate using touchpoints. The main thing to keep in mind is "Which touchpoints will ensure customers receive the target experience we want to give as an organization?"

Understand and Exploit the Unique
Qualities of Individual Touchpoints

Identify the relevant touchpoints for your service, and note the positive and negative qualities of each. The positive and negative aspects should be from an experiential journey perspective, but you can also add your company perspective to this, since each touchpoint comes with a cost, be that technology, development, integration, or maintenance. Understanding how the array of touchpoints fit together for your specific service takes you halfway to orchestrating them. This brings advantages both for your customers and for you.

Map Touchpoints over Time from
the Customer Perspective

Map touchpoints along a timeline to construct several possible experiential journeys and show which touchpoints are available to the customer at each stage. As discussed earlier, this gives you a way to see your service through the customer's eyes. From this starting point, you can gain many insights—for example, you can identify touchpoints that customers like to use, those that are painful for them (pain points), those that are rising stars, those that are dying out, and more.

Create Desirable Customer Experiences
by Orchestrating Your Touchpoints

Working with touchpoints combines *curation*, because you are choosing touchpoints with an experiential value that fit together, and *orchestration*, because you are designing a collaboration between many touchpoints and their corresponding parts of the organization. In musical terms, the touchpoints are notes on a score (timeline) with a conductor (design team). The musical metaphor also extends to touchpoints in the foreground and those in the background, and how they can change over time to create strong experiences.

When you have mapped the touchpoint terrain, you are ready to start orchestrating. Do the touchpoints flow together as a whole? Do you have a common tone of voice? Are there touchpoints that are missing? Is there potential to be had from adding or removing a touchpoint? Who has responsibility for the orchestration? How do you coordinate a touchpoint strategy?

Change the Service Experience Through Touchpoint Innovation

Sometimes focusing on touchpoints for existing services leads to an incremental innovation approach: you will improve what is already there, but are unlikely to create something radically new. However, it is possible to use touchpoints as a starting point for radical innovation. There are multiple examples of how a new touchpoint has created lasting competitive advantage. Uber, for example, exploited the abilities of the smartphone to create a taxi experience that was totally different from and more desirable than the alternative.

To take a more radical approach to touchpoint innovation, you can rip up what is there and start from scratch with the question, "How can we create the experience we want to give?" This can be done in-house or together with customers, and preferably both. Companies often have a habit of using the same touchpoints over and over again, and this kind of touchpoint "lock-in" leads to underperforming services. Starting from scratch and rethinking your offerings can help you create innovative design roadmaps and concept services.

The Principle of Frequency, Sequence, and Importance

One of the key principles of design relates to how things are used over time. The principle of *designing for frequency* requires that you identify and focus on the touchpoints that occur most frequently for customers. The more often something is used, the more you should work at and polish it to provide the right experience. Ensuring good flow for 90% of users makes sense, but spare a thought for the times where it goes wrong, because you'll need that little extra to recover the experiential level customers expect.

Designing for sequence means identifying and focusing on touchpoints that happen in a specific order. This can be recognizing sequences in people's everyday lives (for example, we usually pay after we choose something in a shop or restaurant, not before) and designing the journey to follow that sequence. The other aspect is to recognize sequences of touchpoints and smooth the handover between them during an experiential journey. For example, an online order is often followed up by an email confirmation. Seeing these two touchpoints together allows you to add design cues from one to the other to aid recognition from customers.

Designing for importance means identifying key touchpoints, or steps on the journey, and focusing your efforts to design these to deliver a specific experience. Important touchpoints might be when you leave a website to pay, when you confirm an order, or when you abandon a form that you have spent considerable time filling out.

These three principles reflect how people expect things to be designed, and they are not mutually exclusive. A frequent touchpoint, for example, may also be a part of an important sequence. If you recognize these touchpoints and design with them in mind, you will cover about 75% of touchpoint experiences in a journey.

Tips and Techniques for Experience Fulfillment

In addition to the three core design principles just described, there are some other tips and techniques that will help your organization ensure it fulfills customer expectations over the course of the experiential journey.

Avoid Journeys that Reflect Your Organizational Silos

As discussed earlier in the book, the Porter value chain way of thinking was highly influential in the '90s and led to a wave of business process reengineering. This, in turn, created strong silos in organizations. Unfortunately, the value chain was more suited to products than services, and since then, silos have often been found to be more of a hindrance than a help in an organization. An experiential journey will often cross many silos, and customers can be left confused after talking to different parts of an organization over time. Beware the journey where each step is handled by a different silo. First, you can be pretty sure that it's a structure that fits the organization better than the customer. Second, you will face handover problems between silos. And finally, KPIs will be optimized within silos, rather than encouraging cross-silo collaboration, leaving managers happy and customers frustrated. Journey designs have organizational consequences, and can influence formal and informal organizational structures such as empowerment, reward systems, selection, and training. Therefore, you need to consider your organization as an experience enabler—one that supports the customer experience—instead of trying to get the journey to fit around your organization.

Allow Handover Between Touchpoints

Although it is good to have a preferred journey through a series of touchpoints for the majority of your customers, some customers always find their own route. This means that you need to design for your preferred route, but also enable alternative routes through a journey. One organization I have been working with had a problem because different touchpoints for ordering products were a part of different silos within the company. They hired Livework, a design company, to look at the problem, and they found that it was simply not possible for an online customer to pick up a product in a physical shop, or for a person who was out shopping to order in store for home delivery (e.g., if they had too much to carry, or a product was sold out). This was primarily because there was no handover between touchpoints, and secondly because bonus payments to sellers would be lost if the sale was handed over from the physical store to the online one or vice versa.

Livework solved this problem by allowing a handover between the physical and online worlds, and renegotiating the company's bonus structure. By redesigning the experiential journey, they ensured that customers could find their own way through it, and they enabled the organization to support this alternative, thereby increasing sales completion rates.

Consider the Experience Across Analog and Digital

Germany's largest retail chain by revenue, dm-Drogerie Markt, restructured itself to provide a better customer experience by releasing its employees from the company's systems, functionality, and processes.

So, instead of having one team for the online store and a separate team for the physical store, the company has both teams work together to provide a seamless experience for customers.

"We have over 1,800 stores and have an online shop as well; the idea is to provide additional services for customers and combine both channels," said Jochen Kieninger, head of customer relationship management at dm Drogerie Markt.[2]

"Organizations used to think that for a local store, if the manager does not have the product and tells the customer to look for it online, he is giving the store's income to the online store. We cannot think like that in the future."

Be Specific About the Experiences a Customer Should Have Along the Journey

I often find project teams don't ask themselves how the customer will feel during the journey they are working on. If there is a customer focus in a project, I often see a thumbs up or down, good or bad, placed on each step of the journey to identify potential pain points and positives. Others might go further and use a set of emoticons ranging from rage to delight so that there is some grading of the experience. In an experience-centric organization it's necessary to be more precise and to put words to experiences as part of the journey design. Organizations that have a rich set of manager jargon but a poor vocabulary for emotions and experiences will struggle to become experience-centric and urgently need to develop this terminology. To help, Ted Matthews (guest author of Chapter 9) and I have developed a set of cards that describe possible emotions to spark nuanced discussion within a project team about the emotional experience the organization wants customers to have (see Figure 8-3). The cards can also be used at other times with customers to help them describe the emotions they have experienced during a service encounter.

Figure 8-3. Using emotion cards gives the project team a vocabulary to discuss specific emotions. These can be the emotions customers feel now as part of an existing service, and also the emotions you would like them to have in a new service. (Available at the book's website: www.experience-centric.com.)

Using these cards helps organizations give the customer experience the attention it deserves, and develop a vocabulary for experience, which assists with alignment and infusion throughout the organization.

Check Service Recovery in Your Journeys

As services become more and more digitalized, there is a tendency for journeys to become more like flow diagrams than experiential journey maps, since everything happens within the interface. I have heard people argue that the need for journey design is diminishing because of this. This is dangerous for three reasons. First, it tempts you to take the easy route and optimize for the organization by taking a system view, rather than the customer's view. Second, it ignores the before and after stages of the journey, which are key to any journey design. Third, and more importantly, it ignores situations of service breakdown, in which the customer needs help, often from a person. By considering service breakdown and service recovery, you are designing for flows where things do not always go as expected. Remember that customers create scenarios for what happens next, so a service breakdown is also a breakdown of their scenario. Bear this in mind, since customers are taken out of their comfort zones when their scenarios don't work out as expected, and they can easily become stressed and start to panic, in which case they develop wilder scenarios. You have to be prepared to stay calm and handle these situations before they explode. To summarize, consider a system breakdown a customer scenario breakdown, one where your customer needs special treatment, and develop recovery journeys that they'll remember positively.

Experience Prototyping: Fake It 'til You Break It

You can only experience an experience by experiencing it. Unfortunately, the experience only comes together when it is delivered as a completely developed service, and at that time it's too late and too expensive to change in any major way. The challenge, then, is to provide a project team with a realistic experience so they can evaluate its experiential aspects early enough to be able to make changes. This brings us back to design thinking (see Chapter 4) and the prototyping approach often called "failing fast but forward." By prototyping early, you discover areas that can be improved before you have spent resources on development.

There are five main ways to prototype a service experience, and each has its own advantages and disadvantages. They are often used in parallel to explore different aspects of the service in question. The next sections go through the five approaches, describing how they can be used to prototype the experience you want your customers to have. The last of these, virtual and augmented reality, has excellent potential for experience prototyping; however, this is cutting-edge technology at the moment and not for the faint-hearted or thin-walleted quite yet.

The Walkthrough

The walkthrough uses a physical scale model of your service, often using LEGO or DUPLO figures in a timeline. It sounds very much like going back to kindergarten, because you take a figure and walk it through the experiential journey (see Figure 8-4). This might seem trivial, but it is incredibly useful for getting a feel for the service flow, since we naturally have an ability (probably learned in kindergarten!) to put ourselves into a story and into the characters.

Figure 8-4. The walkthrough allows you to test the service flow and identify pain points along the journey. (Source: Johan Blomkvist.)

Walkthroughs are really good at allowing you to evaluate your service journey and the logistics related to it. For example, for a restaurant visit, we could use a floor plan of the restaurant and move the figure toward the entrance. The story would continue as follows: *from the main street, the customer sees the sign (Where is the sign, and what does it look like?), and walks to the restaurant. They open the door and immediately see (What do they see and how does it make them feel?). They stand and wait to be seated (How do they know that they have to stand? Where do they stand? Is there a sign? If so, what is the tone of voice?). They are greeted (Who greets them, how do they check a reservation? How are they dressed? What do they say?) before being shown to an area to hang their coats (Do we need one or many areas? Where is it? How safe is it perceived to be? How large is it?) and then to the table (What does the guide say while waiting for them to hang their coats and on the way to the table?)...*

Walkthroughs are not so good at letting you experience the experience, so in this context they are a bit coarse. They are also not so helpful for giving you an idea of the brand relevance of the experience, or of the detailed interactions involving specific touchpoints. We are, after all, using models here, so it requires a leap of the imagination to experience the experience. However, walkthroughs are quick and easy to use, easily reconfigured, and work well as part of co-design processes, since everyone can take part. They are also really good at identifying and working with the logical and functional flow of a service, and ironing out disconnects that you might not find from just looking at an experiential journey map.

Enactment

We have already mentioned the similarities between experiential journeys and film, and enactment (see Figure 8-5) uses precisely this mechanism to prototype the customer experience. Enactment is a method where you act out the service, and can be anything from simple *bodystorming* (brainstorming using spontaneous enactment) to very staged real-life run-throughs of a service (where the designers simulate the service for real customers in real settings). As with the walkthrough, it uses your innate abilities to put yourself into a context, but this method gives you a more realistic experience of the experience.

Enactment places emphasis on the tone of voice and behaviors of people and technology, and quickly allows you to see where this breaks down. That's one of its major benefits: it's easy to redo the enactment and change it (in film language, "do another take") until it works. This makes enactment perfect for quickly evaluating and perfecting personality, tone of voice, and behaviors. It is also fun, but with serious intent. Another advantage of enactment is that you can use props as alternatives to fully developed solutions. So, for example, when a customer is interacting with a tablet computer, you can use a piece of cardboard instead of the tablet to enter information, and this

Figure 8-5. Enactment allows you to quickly get a feel for a new solution, without expending a lot of resources to prototype it. Props work well in lieu of finished designs, and within a few minutes you can prototype several alternatives. (Source: author.)

is realistic enough for the circumstances. You use your innate abilities to role-play (or create scenarios) to get close to experiencing the experience. But, since enactment is often used early in the design process and many touchpoints are not yet fully developed, it means that the brand experience and holistic experience are less represented. For example, if you are prototyping a customer using a new bank building, you will be able to enact customer interactions, tone of voice, and behaviors, but you won't get the experiential effect that newly designed furniture, the interiors, the exterior of the bank, and the like will give.

Evidencing

Evidencing is one of my favorite approaches to experience prototyping because it describes the future as if it exists today, by assembling carefully faked photographs and tangible prototypes of the future service in a compelling narrative (see Figure 8-6). It gets its name from the term *tangible evidence from the future*, in which you are transported into a future world where the service exists. This method presents the offering and the customer experience through the experiential journey as a believable series of photographs or a stop-motion video.

Evidencing allows for a precision in terms of design detail and journey steps, giving you a good overall sense of the service experience for a new concept, right down to the detailed interactions.

Figure 8-6. Evidencing allows you to create relevant future contexts for your service in a way that makes them feel real. This allows you to almost experience the experience you want the customer to have at a very early stage of development. Source: author.

Evidencing a Fake Competitor Offering to Provoke a Service Innovation

One of the best service designers I have met, Lavrans Løvlie from Livework, told me how he was having trouble getting a client to see the potential in a new online service concept. This was a client Livework had worked with a lot, and they had a high degree of trust, but this time the client was too fond of their existing offering and was reluctant to adopt the new direction. They needed a bit of a jolt to see the benefits of the new offering. So, Livework produced a slick PowerPoint presentation showing a carefully faked description and review of a fictitious new service from a competitor, , and presented it in a slightly shocked way: "Have you seen the cool new service just launched by X?"

When this was presented, the leadership suddenly paid attention, and could see all of the experiential benefits that they earlier had been unable to see, because they now perceived the offering as a threat to their own business. When they learned what Livework had done, they realized the potential of the new offering, and knew they had to be first to deliver it. This led them to immediately commission a project to explore the new direction. Sometimes, you just need to experience the experience to see its value.

Evidencing can take several forms, but often it is a series of photos that realistically represent the touchpoints along the experiential journey. This allows you to show how the customer becomes aware of the service—for example, through realistic ads or even (faked) reviews in magazines. When you create physical versions of particular items, such as a gas bill or welcome package, it makes you feel that the service actually exists. However, evidencing doesn't let you interact with the service itself, so you cannot experience the interactions with touchpoints or the tone of voice of a service.

Graphic Experiential Evidencing

Graphic Experiential Evidencing (GEE) is an experiential extension to evidencing that uses the visual language of the comic book to accentuate the customer experience (see Figure 8-7). It was developed by Ted Matthews, the guest author for Chapter 9, who was trying to find a way of getting rich experiences across to others.

Figure 8-7. GEE accentuates the customer experience through the use of comic book graphics. (Source: Ted Matthews and Syver Lauritzsen.)

While evidencing provides a realistic representation of service encounters, GEE highlights the experiential outcome of the experiential journey. It was developed as part of a project designing experiences for a national football federation, to express the strong emotions people feel when watching a football match. Ted found comics offer a shared visual language that we can use to express these rich emotions (for more about this, have a look at Scott McCloud's book *Understanding Comics* [William Morrow]). GEE focuses on the emotions and the experience and is more a call to arms for the service offering than a neutral representation. It says, "This is how it can be; this is how it ought to feel," and in many ways forms a target for design within a team. It can then be used to specify a service offering, to explain what experience the project wants to attain.

GEE is not necessarily realistic, nor does it assist with the flow or logistics of a service. However, it highlights the experiential highs and lows, conveying the dramatic arc of a service, which makes it an important tool in the experience-centric organization.

Augmented and Virtual Reality

I am really excited about the potential of augmented reality (AR) and virtual reality (VR) to revolutionize experience prototyping, but at the moment this area has a lot of limitations. I have been working with two brilliant AR/VR designers, Kjetil Nordby (at AHO) and Stian Børresen (at HoloCap), who have been combining gaming engines and other technology to create realistic experience prototypes. Their work has the potential to bring the missing piece into experience prototyping, because they have found a way to bring real people into virtual spaces in real time with amazingly realistic results. I am not talking about simply representing people, but actually inserting real-time video into a virtual space so that you can greet, talk to, and interact with people in a realistic 3D space, so their behavior and tone of voice will be natural and not preprogrammed.

Earlier I mentioned that it is difficult to create a realistic prototype of a new flagship bank, since you can't fake the building, the interior, the lighting, the employees' behavior, and so on, without expending lots of effort and money. Well, in AR/VR you can do this in a realistic way and have people to interact with. It combines the advantages of the other approaches, but at this stage requires a lot of technological support. Sometime soon, an experience prototyping platform will be made available that allows you to input 3D models of the service environment, add a detailed library of touchpoints, and insert people into the scene so you can enact the experience in a realistic experiential way. I, for one, am looking forward to that.

The Top Experience Design Principles

In this section I present some basic design principles based on what we know about designing for experiences, emotions, and customer behavior. These principles are taken from both basic and applied research, and as with everything, there are exceptions to the rules.

As with everything, there are exceptions to all rules. Generally, it is agreed that we have to make things easy to use, but if that were a universal law, nobody would learn to play the piano or drive a car. Both require a steep learning curve, but because we expect our experience of the end result to be worthwhile, we choose to invest time in them. We also know that people generally like to be middle of the road and choose a mid-price offering, banded between low and high. However, when emotionally aroused, people sometimes break this rule, because we are gripped by an internal logic that encourages us to "go all in." Therefore, keep in mind that these principles are helpful guides, not laws, and should be seen in their context. Sometimes breaking a rule can be better than following one, especially when you are becoming masters of experience delivery.

Involve Customers

The whole essence of this book is that you need to be able to see through your customer's eyes. That doesn't always mean doing what they say, and sometimes delight comes from a service provider being proactive about unmet and unseen (by the customer) needs. So, rule number 1 is to involve customers. Be curious about what they want, like, and desire before you start designing, during the design process, and after you have designed. At the same time, reflect on what your customers are saying and place it in a larger perspective.

Be Relative, Not Absolute in Your Judgments

We have difficulty relating to something unless we have a comparison to judge it by. This can apply to everything from understanding metaphors and analogies for your solution right down to the need to relate amounts and sizes to units we know. This can work to your advantage when launching something new, because you can decide what it should be compared to and use it in your design through detailed design cues. On the flip side, be careful in your price range, as your price will be judged relative to others.

Start Strong, Finish Stronger

Customers enter the service journey with expectations, and you have to immediately relate to those expectations or exceed them. This requires a strong start with expression of intent, but don't forget to end on a high note, because people remember the end of an encounter more vividly than the start or its midpoint. In addition, make sure there is a high point somewhere along the way to create a "start-high-end" set of peaks (see the next principle).

Ensure Noticeable Peaks and Avoid Troughs

Peaks and troughs are memorable, so you need to focus on having a noticeable peak during the service journey. Obviously, avoiding a deep trough is important, but remember that service experiences are relative to expectations, so if something terrible happens during service delivery, your response in the recovery phase should be relative to expectations.

Be Benevolent

Make the customer feel that you have their best interests at heart, that you have made an effort to think about their needs, and that what you are doing is for their benefit (this is, after all, the essence of service).

Remember, Looks Can Seduce and Looks Can Kill

How things look, how people look, and how you look at people all communicate something. Always. And it is context-dependent. If you go into a mountain gear shop, you don't expect people to wear suits; you expect ruggedness. On the other hand, if you go to a funeral parlor, you don't expect people to wear mountain gear. This matters right down to the smallest detail—for example, it's why packaging is important. The way the package looks tells you about what is inside. This principle is so basic you might be scratching your head about why it is included, but of course you can choose to use it to your advantage, or to your loss. The design mantra of god and the devil both being in the details is true, even for how things look.

Use the Photocopier Principle to Hide (but Structure) Complexity

I worked for Xerox in the '90s, simplifying the use of copy machines. It was during this period that the principle of hiding complexity was implemented and the machines went from being complex products for the few to simple products accessible to most users. From observing the use of machines, the company realized that people often just wanted a single copy of something, so a big green button was placed on the control panel to do just that. The complex functions were not removed, but they were placed under a flap so they'd be easy to access during those rare times they were needed. At the time, it radically changed how we related to copy machines. Hiding complexity can make the ordinary become an extraordinary ordinary experience (see Chapter 6), with the iconic Google search page being a prime example.

Give the Bad News First

This principle relates to designing experiential journeys that start strong and finish stronger. People prefer to end on a high note, so if you have any bad news, give it first, and save the good news for last. In fact, create a dramatic curve for your service that takes this tip into account, and in times of service breakdown, make sure you somehow end on a happy note.

Use All of the Senses

There seems to be a fixation on the visual in our everyday lives, but interactions with touchpoints are tangible, audible, and olfactory too. When working with a tourist experience in Thailand, Ted Matthews and I designed in a breeze for when customers were waiting for a ferry, because a breeze is an experiential touchpoint of value when you're waiting in a hot, humid environment. Supermarkets have introduced in-store baking to give shoppers that homey feeling of freshly baked bread. And Apple understood the power of touch when innovating first the iPod, then the iPhone and iPad. Make sure to use all of the senses in your organization's touchpoints to appeal to your customers as they progress through the experiential journey.

Put the Customer in Control of Their Choices

This is a key finding from behavioral research: if the customer feels in control, they are willing to accept uneven service or even service breakdowns. Offering alternatives is a good way of giving them control (e.g., would you prefer a or b?), or you can even provide a slider, where they can choose the level themselves. Self-service is another solution, and in online services, real-time "what-if" solutions all shift the locus of control to the customer.

IKEA is a good example of customer co-production—that is, the customer is central to the construction of the product. This gives customers an increased attachment to the final product and the service provider, especially when it comes to IKEA, which has always had a focus on the customer experience.

Avoid Procrastination

I do it and my kids do it and we all hate it, but everyone procrastinates. Therefore, try to avoid letting your customers put things off, and if it can't be helped, keep in contact through gentle reminders. If you have already used the principle of benevolence, then your reminders will be seen as friendly and build trust.

Engage Customers and They Will Be Reluctant to Switch

Lock-in results not just from having a lot of data stored, but also from expending a lot of effort and engagement using something. People prefer to stay with something they've invested effort and energy into, and there is an inertia that builds over time as a result. Use this to your advantage and engage customers with relevant experiential activities, and it will reap rewards.

Heighten Emotional Arousal to Engage Customers

Our emotional state influences our behavior. Arousal makes a difference. If, for example, we are enjoying ourselves on vacation, we are willing to pay extra to buy souvenirs. We are less critical when aroused emotionally and are more willing to try things. If you design for emotional arousal, not only can you differentiate yourselves from your competitors, but you can charge a little more too.

Limit the Number of Choices, or Group into Chunks

Too much choice leaves us unable to choose anything. For example, offering 24 variants of the same kind of jam in a supermarket trial area resulted in only 3% of tasters buying jam, whereas offering only 6 variants led to 30% purchasing a jar. In a famous article from 1956, psychologist George Miller described the phenomenon of the magical number seven, noting that our information-processing skills all seem to be limited to about seven items (plus or minus two). So, if you are presenting a lot of alternatives, group them together so that people can process and relate to the options. If they have to remember options, you might have to go as low as four items.

Group Painful Processes to Get Them Over With

Grouping negative processes together gets the unpleasantness over with, while dividing them up prolongs the negative associations. The recent negativity about flying short distances is a typical example, and we can see how rail travel, which might take longer, is becoming preferred over short-haul flights. Air travel now is broken up into a series of uncomfortable steps: travel to the airport, check in, check your luggage, go through security, line up at the gate, board, find your cramped seats, and so on. Rail travel, on the other hand, takes longer, but the negative aspect is shortened, so people are often pleasantly surprised by the train journey and find it comparable.

Use Upper Bands to Help Customers Choose the Mid-Level Offerings

We tend to choose options relative to what is available, and place ourselves in a band, or range. For example, on a wine list, a particular wine might seem pricey when shown alone. However, the addition of some higher-priced wines will convince us that the same wine now is reasonable, and therefore an easier choice. Use upper bands in your organization to encourage your customers to choose the midpriced offerings.

Make the Invisible Visible

A lot of service provision is invisible—for example, cleaning and maintenance services in a hotel. Recently, a friend of mine, when working from his hotel room, dropped something that rolled under the bed. When he went to retrieve it, he found a card proudly proclaiming, "Yes, we even clean under here!" This made a great impression on him and he recounted the story many times over as a great experience. When working for a property management organization, my team and I designed small calling cards that could be attached to items that had been maintained, pointing out that the work had been done, when it had been done, and by whom. Not only did this make the invisible visible, but it improved pride among employees, as it made them visible too. Do the same in your organization to recognize employee efforts and reward those often-unsung heroes.

Use Pledging to Earn Your Customers' Trust

Pledging, as a clearly defined activity, has a strong effect on how people behave and makes us less likely to cheat. It creates a desire to follow social norms of trustworthy behavior, including after the event. This is especially true when the pledge is ritualized (see Chapter 9) or takes place in a social context—for example, in front of others. Use pledging as a way to publicly assure your customers that your word is your bond and you are worthy of their trust.

Follow the Rules of Frequency, Sequence, and Importance

Although this seems like common sense, it is amazing how many organizations break these rules in their designs. Make frequent operations easy (remember, easy can also be memorable if you design it that way). Put activities that happen in sequence into that sequence. And make sure that important activities are given the importance they deserve, even though they might not happen frequently.

Never Mention a Near Miss

Customers react negatively when reminded that they almost achieved some benefit from a service (e.g., "We're sold out now, but if only you had come five minutes earlier, we had plenty of them"). This indirectly criticizes the customer's behavior by putting the blame for the missed opportunity on them. Not mentioning the near-miss, or reframing it (e.g., "There has been huge demand for this"), is a better alternative.

Show Customers They're in Good Company

People often seek confirmation from others about our behaviors and choices. Seeing what others choose can help us make a decision ourselves and reassure us. Seeing the text "80% of our customers choose this option" will help guide your customers' decisions and make them happier with the choices they make.

Always Combine Advice with Action and Triggers

When you're advising people, the advice alone might not be enough to change their behavior. Thus, you should always combine it with clear, targeted action that supports the advice. In addition, you should add triggers in your experiential journey at relevant points that help prompt the desired behavior. For example, telling people they have to reduce energy consumption alone will probably not lead to much change, but adding three examples of how to do it and a "do it now" button will improve the chances of change.

Amazon uses these rules to good effect and in a clever way. Not only does it show that you are in good company when you buy something, but it also tempts you to look at some outliers, basically saying, "Hey, others are buying this, and you'd be stupid not to do the same."

Endnotes

1   "Hidden Fees Top Survey of What Annoys Americans Most," *Consumer Reports*, December 1, 2009, *http://bit.ly/2XfJ4b9*.

2   Shawn Lim, "Why Investing in Customer Experience Is Essential to Brand Survival," The Drum, September 5, 2017, *http://bit.ly/2wA2WtL*.

PART III

Going Further

9

D4Me: Designing for Meaningful Experiences

This guest chapter by Ted Matthews explains how meaningful experiences are made and why they are especially memorable and powerful. It describes how we, as a society, have developed behavioral and experiential patterns such as rituals and myths. It will also introduce his method, D4Me, which explains how these mechanisms can be systematically used in your design as a way of creating memorable and heightened customer experiences.

Meaningful and Memorable Moments

Recently I heard an interview with a young fan talking about Burnley Football Club's return to European football ("soccer," if you prefer) after an absence of 51 years. In his excitement he explained that his dad had actually been at "The Orient Game." Burnley was therefore in their blood, and neither could believe that the team was now back playing top-flight football. I too was at "The Orient Game" (see Figure 9-1). I felt a curious sense of pride and belonging that I could say I was there. The experience of that game was one of those meaningful and, indeed, memorable experiences in my life.

It was May 9, 1987. I was 16 years old. My friend Tony had nipped out during school lunch break to get us tickets. My parents didn't like me going to football games. However, this game was important; if we didn't win, we would be thrown out of the football league forever!

So damn it, I had to go, despite parental protestations and the £1.10 entrance fee. The stadium was absolutely packed. Tony and I wore claret and blue scarves and sang along to songs that had been sung

Figure 9-1. The Orient Game, 1987. I'm near the back with a mullet.
(Source: *Lancashire Telegraph*.)

there for a century. We were just 16 but felt like grown-ups now. We swore and shouted like wild things, moving helplessly with the crowd, which swayed and swelled like a rough sea on the packed terraces. We had Haffner's meat and potato pies at half time.

I have no recollection of the game itself other than us winning. But I remember with exceptional clarity all the other elements of the day. After the match we stormed the pitch to join the happy throng of supporters. Grown men cried, strangers hugged each other, and a run-down Lancastrian town came together in hope and relief.

In the 30 years since this game, the term "The Orient Game" has become a meaningful symbol of struggle, woven into the narrative of the club and the town. It is meaningful for me and to fellow fans when I say I was there. It was meaningful then and has become understood as more meaningful with time.

But Why Was It Meaningful?

This experience was meaningful because of the larger cultural back-drop, the culture to which Tony and I belonged: that of a working-class northern English mill town. This game, like most football games, was a form of ritual where we could express this belonging—a ritual that included symbols such as club scarves, songs, and even food (it would have included beer, but we were too young to get served). The larger context of the game itself, relating to the town and club's history and the increased drama of relegation, also heightened our stake in the experience. Clearly the other important factor was the assembly of thousands of other fans. It was tribal, and the sheer volume of humanity focused on a single outcome supercharged the experience and amplified the meaning.

These kinds of experiences are remembered better and longer than the mundane. They leave an indelible mark in the brain. Such events imprint what is referred to as "flashbulb memories" and a key part of this is about the shared experience, about being part of something greater, and how significant these events are to our lives. Rituals, myths, and collective symbols are ways to bring meaning to the experience. These societal mechanisms act as passageways to meaning, creating, in turn, meaningful and memorable experiences.

In trying to understand why people, specifically millennials, are less and less inclined to attend church, Thurston and ter-Kuile of Harvard Divinity School explain in their report *How We Gather* that while people are still looking for meaning, they are doing so outside of religion.[1] They argue that people are seeking community, personal transformation, social transformation, purpose, creativity, and accountability. One of the strongest urges, they argue, is that of community and the shared meaningful experience. Future trend innovation company TrendWatching suggests that "consuming means participating in networks that are both personally and socially valuable," freeing consumers to "dive in and embrace more meaningful and positive consumerism."[2]

The experience-centric organization can use these societal mechanisms as material to design deep connections with customers and memorable experiences that transcend the everyday. In the next section I describe these mechanisms and then go on to show how you can use them to deliver really great experiences.

Consuming Meaning

Smart organizations such as Harley Davidson and Apple have used these mechanisms for many years and have built a strong, loyal following. Just like football fans, they assemble for events where they engage in ritualized behavior, expressing their belonging through actions and symbols like logos, products, and the language they use. In assembly they further supercharge their experiences.

Source: *The Economist*.

Despite some cooling in the ardor of Apple devotees since Steve Jobs's death in 2011, the brand is still a good example of how some companies seem to generate meaningful experiences for their customers. "Macheads," as they have been called, attend Apple Store openings with the same verve and excitement Tony and I had at "The Orient Game." They hold unboxing parties and invite friends, engaging in ritualized activity. They wear symbols of the brand on their clothes, with subtle hierarchies of meaning, from the "vintage" striped logos to the modern versions. Macheads feel like they belong to a community and want to express that belonging. Through their consumption they have meaningful experiences. If you don't believe me, do a Google image search for "Apple tattoo;" you'll find hundreds of images. Do the same search for "Microsoft tattoo" and there are just a handful.

It's difficult to know how active Apple has been in encouraging customer rituals and related meaningful activity. What is clear, however, is that they are very good at their own myth and symbol making around their products, the origins of the company, and, not least, their shaman, Steve Jobs. Launches of new products are surrounded with the secrecy of papal appointments, and the events themselves are ritualized proceedings with sermons from their heads of tech, design, and finally from the current master of ceremonies, Tim Cook. Despite the fact that Apple is the world's biggest brand, many of those who consume it buy into a mythology of the creative, renegade outsider, and this is what they celebrate when they engage in its rituals, symbols, stories, and, of course, its products.

Meaningful Is the New Black

We are now in a meaning-based economy where consumers are actively seeking products or services that not only match their likes and interests but also deliver something authentic and meaningful in their lives. Consumers want to be transformed through their consumption. Consumers want to hit that self-actualizing top tier of Maslow's hierarchy of needs through what they consume. Simona Rocchi, Senior Director of Innovation and Design-for-Sustainability Studies at Philips, suggests that to be successful in today's market, businesses have to "enhance meaning" in their customer experiences. The meaning economy is on us now! (See Figure 9-2.)

All experiences have meaning, but some are more meaningful to customers than others. Meaning is how we read the world around us, and something that is meaningful to us matters to us and gets noticed. The experience-centric organization knows which meanings need to be taken into account as part of its offering, and can design this into everything it does.

Source: Jaguar.

Figure 9-2. What will cars mean in the future when they are self-driving? The move to automation will have to be about more than technology. It will also have to be about a renegotiation of what cars have meant in our culture for the last 100 years. How does this fit with a self-driving car?

The experience-centric organization is able to understand the broader cultural context and dig into those things that are meaningful to customers. Exact meaning might differ from one person to the next; however, we often find shared meanings within a group, a phenomenon known as *intersubjectivity*. Most Christians would agree that the cruciform is a meaningful symbol of suffering and hope. Most members of the Harley Davidson owners group, known as HOGS, would agree that their annual meetups are meaningful events, celebrating a machine that has come to mean freedom, America, and the rebel.

Incorporating meaning into the core of your offering should be a key part of your innovation and design work. It adds powerful shared context for experiences and creates deeply meaningful experiences for customers through use. However, a central part of this is the shared experience that customers have through use as part of a feeling of togetherness. If we want the experiences we design for to be meaningful and increase value for our customers, then we have to infuse our actual service experiences with shared meaningful cultural material. We need to go from *me* to *we*.

Worshipping at the Temple of WE

As much as we would like to think of ourselves as individuals, our individuality can be assessed only in its relation to everybody else and to society at large. We are in reality driven by relations and our connections to others.

The mantra of big data is that it makes it possible to target and personalize information to a fine degree so that our consumption can be tailored to us and we can get exactly what we want. The truth, however, is that at the moment, this is so coarsely targeted that we get ads based on what we have already bought (do I need to buy another toaster straight after researching and buying one?), or we get targeted ads that are still way off the mark (Simon recently bought some new speakers, and I searched the net to see what they look like; now, I can't avoid seeing them on every site I go to). Understanding peoples needs from their data, and individualizing for them, is incredibly difficult.

Consumers are actively seeking out shared meaningful experiences and this represents real opportunities for value creation. Companies that deliver meaningful experiences will be the winners in the next decade.

However, there is another approach that offers immense value to customers, and delivers what people deeply need—meaningful, shared experiences.

What we are witnessing is a move from the "me" in consumption to the "we" of shared experiences. Consumers are actively seeking out shared meaningful experiences and this represents real opportunities for value creation. Companies that deliver meaningful experiences will be the winners in the next decade. We are actively seeking the kinds of experiences Tony and I had on May 9, 1987, and are willing to pay for them, because they add meaning to our everyday. We are social animals, and recent research shows that the greatest influence on our happiness and longevity is related more to what we do with others than our diets or the amount we exercise.[3]

This shared "we" can be harnessed for areas outside big events and/or religion. In fact, the mechanisms can be decoded and used for everything from banking services to public transport. It's about celebrating a sense of self via others, gaining meaning, and belonging to something bigger (see Figure 9-3).

Figure 9-3. Come together, right now—over we. (Source: Alex Hoffard.)

You Just Couldn't Make It Up. Or Could You...

Many of the things we consider eternal and authentic traditions have been invented. Two good examples of this are the Scottish kilt and the Pledge of Allegiance.

In their well-researched 1983 book *The Invention of Tradition* (Cambridge University Press), Hobsbawn and Ranger highlight how the item of clothing we now know as the kilt was invented. It was the Englishman Thomas Rawlinson who first designed the kilt, to prevent his factory workers from getting the rough rags that they wore stuck in machines. But at this stage the kilt was a neutral-colored, cheap piece of clothing; there was no tartan. The tartan patterns were invented by industrialists to fit a sweeping romanticism started by Sir Walter Scott in the early 1800s. Together, this combination turned the relatively new invention of the kilt into a symbol of the ancient garb of the Highlanders that later became embedded in history.

The rituals, symbols, and stories that were created around an invented garment for the purpose of Scottish identity show how traditions can be fabricated and have lasting power not just over years but over centuries.

Now, the kilt feels as authentic and ancient as the hills of the Highlands themselves. When it is worn, not least at festivals, it becomes part of meaningful experiences for wearers and others in the community (see Figure 9-4).

The other example is the Pledge of Allegiance ritual played out each morning in US schools across the country. The Pledge of Allegiance was penned by Christian pastor Francis Bellamy in 1892 to mark the 400th anniversary of the arrival of Columbus on the shores of America.[4] It was conceived as a patriotic drive among school kids and was published in the magazine *Youth Interest*, encouraging children and their schools to affirm their allegiance to the American flag. To do this, the school would need to buy a flag. Luckily, the magazine also sold American flags. The ritual was good for patriotism but also good for business.

The Pledge of Allegiance was designed for commercial gain, but it succeeded because it gave meaning at the right time. During this period, immigration to the US was changing the country's demographic and character, which caused a push to reaffirm a sense of

Figure 9-4. A modern Gay Pride hybrid kilt. Symbols on symbols for new traditions and meanings. (Source: Verillas.)

"Americanness" among citizens. The Pledge of Allegiance arrived at just the right moment. Timing is everything with such things (a point that Claire Dennington takes up in Chapter 10).

Such invented symbols and rituals can be found across the globe, from National Days like Singapore's, which only dates back to the mid-1960s, to the Olympics, invented in the early 1900s, with all its pomp and ritual performance. Some symbols, rituals, and myths that deliver on meaningful experiences are also borrowed. Where I live in Norway, the Halloween tradition is only around 15 years old, but it has become established as a traditional high point in autumnal calendars with all the consumer ritual trappings borrowed from our American cousins.

If others can invent rituals, so can you. The experience-centric organization understands how to invent tradition, create myths, design rituals, and use symbols. You understand the huge potential that lies in creating deeper meaning through this process.

Myths, Rituals, and Symbols

In this section I'll give some further explanation to show how myths, rituals, and symbols are relevant to the experience-centric organization, to prevent you from thinking of religion and/or ancient civilizations. They are important to Apple and Harley Davidson, and they need to be important to you too.

When we think of myths, we often think they mean that something is untrue. However, in fields like sociology, myths are understood as stories that a community tells about itself, that speak to a very real sense of who its members think they are. They are not lies; they are shared metaphors of group identity. Myths, therefore, are potent devices in connecting people and helping create meaningful experiences. Myths also have a tendency to be heroic.

Harley Davidson is built around a hero myth. The brand is about the spirit of freedom, of America, of the outlaw and the rebel. This narrative helps the Harley Davidson community construct its identity and bonds people together and to the brand. The Harley myth is not based on a lie, but at the same time, it is not totally true either. It is a shared story, that is strongly believed in, pieced together from many small truths and placed in a relevant context for our times. Myths are very powerful—just ask the Marlboro Man.

Rituals, on the other hand, allow us to *perform* these identity myths. They are passageways to meaningful experiences that include anticipation and delivery using strong emotional engagement. Recent research from Harvard shows that a small ritual before eating makes the food taste better.[5]

Rituals transport us to changed states. A wedding transforms a bachelor to a husband. A simple handshake moves us from strangers to acquaintances. Graduation rituals put a spotlight on our meaningful achievements, but also act as rites of passage from student life to professional life: the event is full of symbolic acts (e.g., handshakes, songs, speeches, and processions) and symbolic objects (such as scrolls of paper and mortarboard hats).

Symbols are representative for people and for communities as an indication of who they think they are and their bond. I recently stopped and chatted with a stranger in the center of Oslo because he was wearing a Burnley football shirt. The shirt was a symbol of his connection to the club and in turn a symbolic bond between us. Two people of different generations and different nationalities found kinship over a symbol, and all the meaning that lies behind it. Community is not just about belonging to a local place, but can also be about connection to other forms of identity.

Picture how thin our experiences would be without myths, rituals, and symbols. Imagine removing origin myths and narratives about ancestors, elders, and kids from our families. They have been embellished over the years and construct a picture of who we are and what bonds us together. Imagine removing anniversary rituals, Sunday dinners, birthdays, and high season celebrations. Imagine having no family heirlooms that are symbolic of important moments in the family's history, both ancient and modern.

This material is all around us. It can also be invented and borrowed, and you can design with it to create fantastic impact. Let's see how it can be systematically applied to deliver increased value for your customers.

The Design for Meaningful Experiences Method

The Design for Meaningful Experiences, or D4Me, method is a structured approach to understanding and using the cultural material described in the previous pages. The method has been tried and tested in areas as diverse as professional football, telecoms, and the financial sector, and formed the basis of a national strategy for tourism in Norway.

It has four stages (illustrated on the next page):

1. Cultural scoping and mapping
2. Translation into meaning
3. Designing the offering as a service myth
4. Designing the experiential journey as a ritual journey through meaningful service encounters

I have found the method to be a strong add-on to the wheel of experience centricity described in Chapter 3, although it is an approach for organizations that already have some degree of experiential maturity.

Stage 1: Cultural Scoping and Mapping

Cultural scoping and mapping helps you to identify important cultural elements that are relevant for your market. Once you've identified them, you map to identify the materials to design your experiential offering and find key transition points in the service that will make it stand out. Once this is done, you design in detail for its delivery. This all sounds logical and linear, but like all design work, it follows the design thinking approach of being a mix of iterations, messiness, and repeatedly zooming in and out (this is explained in Chapter 4).

Cultural scoping is a bit like going to the optician for an eye test. The big letters are the larger shared cultural elements that are easy for anyone to read, but the smaller letters need a few different lenses and some expertise to help you get things into focus.

Cultural scoping is a form of actor mapping in some ways, but it's more about the layers of culture and identifying with communities. Understanding these layers also makes it easier to understand where you will draw from to map cultural material.

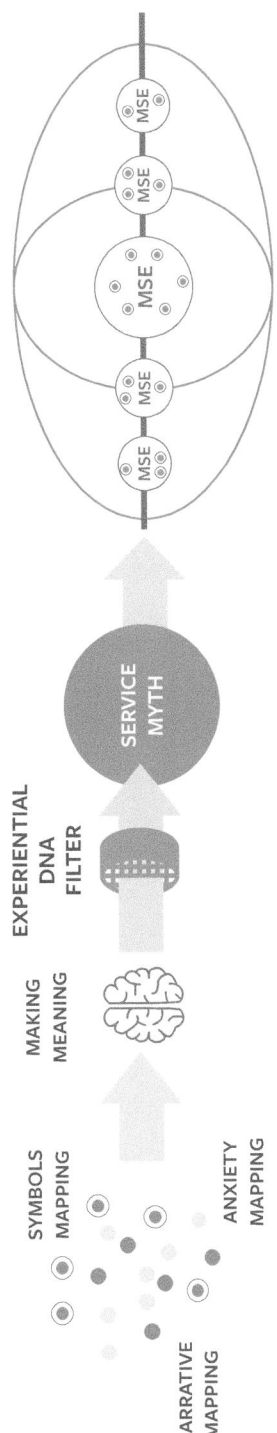

The output of cultural scoping is a clearly defined cultural focus area. Once you have done this, you can go into detail and start mapping symbols, narratives, and anxieties:

Symbols mapping

If you assemble the symbols from a ritual such as a graduation ceremony, then you can analyze them to understand their meaning. Some of the symbols are more meaningful than others; in the graduation ritual, the mortarboard, gowns, and roll of paper are perhaps the most distinctive and specific. The handshake and processions become important only when connected to the other symbols. By mapping these symbols and their relationship, we start to gather meaningful material to design with, but we also start to see an emerging narrative or myth that can be understood by others. This process will also help you identify where there are no existing symbols, opening opportunities for design.

Narrative mapping

What are the pervading stories and myths that seem to whirl around certain cultural groups or ideas? What are they telling us about that group's identity? In the case of Apple, the stories about Steve Jobs are telling us about a unique individual who dared to think differently, who was a renegade, a creator. These are still pervasive "myths" (and I use the term as a sociologist might) that many Mac users feel also represent them and their creative identity.

Anxiety mapping

Anxiety mapping can help you find narratives that are used to alleviate anxiety, and that create a kind of equilibrium through their telling. These anxieties are often present in society, but are rarely explicitly expressed. Instead they are commented on, indirectly, through media, art, and journalism. Holt and Cameron, in their 2010 book *Cultural Strategy: Using Innovative Ideologies to Build Breakthrough Brands* (Oxford University Press), suggested that in the early 1960s comfortable, middle-class suburban American men turned to the myth created around Jack Daniel as the frontier original male in response to their own anxiety and sense of emasculation due to their comfortable living. At the time, this was not part of everyday conversation, but it was referenced in TV, journalism, art, and literature. It could be argued that the strategy to alleviate this anxiety worked. Now Jack Daniel's is the best-selling spirit in the world, and the brand was valued by Interbrand in 2016 at $5,332 million.

Let's look at an example of some work my company did with a Norwegian bank that, for the sake of anonymity, I'll call Scandinavian Nordic.

Scandinavian Nordic has a service called Royal Gold (also a pseudonym). It is a privilege service for customers with incomes over an upper threshold or considerable savings. The service provides better rates, care, queue prioritization, and offers than those provided to standard customers. The reason the bank cited for why these customers receive better treatment was pretty blunt (to paraphrase): "Because you earn lots of money we'll treat you nicer than standard customers." This immediately seemed to clash with the traditional Norwegian aversion to privilege (though this is changing). In addition, many of the customer journeys designed by the bank were rather functional and did not give a Royal Gold user experience.

We undertook cultural mapping to look at Norwegians' attitudes toward privilege in general, and banking privilege (albeit within the larger Norwegian perspective). Through narrative mapping it became clear that Norway's long-held values and historical cultural sense of self still influence social attitudes. This sense of self is influenced by Norway's history as a Lutheran society with a "non-flashy" Protestant work ethic and the distinctly Norwegian and untranslatable *Jante Loven* (a term that describes culturally understood rules of not feeling or expressing that you are better than anyone else).

Stage 2: Translation into Meaning

When we analyzed the cultural symbols, we started to get an idea that privilege in the Norwegian narrative was not about wealth but about hard work and social contribution. This meaning was extracted from the narratives, symbols, and anxieties that we had collected, and each supported the others. This gave us a strong indication that the meaning we needed to work with lay with the Norwegian cultural conflict with the definition of privilege.

In mapping symbols of privilege in a banking context, we found that in Norway there were no clear intersubjective symbols. When we ran a similar process in the context of professional football, we found a rich canvas of symbols that spoke volumes about national, player, and supporter sense of self. In banking this was a little more limited. We would in the end borrow symbols of privilege from other contexts, but I will tell you about that shortly.

What was clear from the mapping exercise was a growing anxiety that a national sense of self was being eroded by increased selfishness and materialism. This could be seen in a TV drama that ridiculed privilege in West End Oslo, in a reality show that followed rich kids, and in countless newspaper articles that worried about Norway's new anonymous upper class.

This gave us material to be able to develop a service myth that could fit well with the Norwegian sense of self as a community, but could also act as a narrative to soothe the nerves of a nation facing an identity crisis (or at least for the wealthy customers who the Royal Gold service is for).

Stage 3: Designing the Offering as a Service Myth

How do you design a myth?

Well, as luck would have it (or thanks to the endeavor of tireless scholars), there seem to have been only a handful of great narratives through the ages, albeit told in the distinctive style of the cultures that produced them. Scholars differ as to the exact number, but Christopher Booker argues that there are just seven great narratives that all cultures tell in one form or another: Overcoming the Monster, Rags to Riches, The Quest, Voyage and Return, Comedy, Tragedy, and Rebirth.[6] These narratives seem to capture much of the human condition and experience in seven plots. They are therefore useful as a starting point to develop a service myth that fits with what the symbols and narratives you have mapped tell you about the consumer community you are developing experiences for. You may also find other possible inspiring story lines if you just do a Google search for "great plot lines."

There is no hard-and-fast science to choosing the right myth. It comes from the material identified during the cultural mapping process together with what fits your experiential DNA. As the service myth starts to emerge, use your experiential DNA as a means to help you clarify it further: the myth has to fit with that DNA as well as with the cultural context. In fact, you will tell the myth in the style of your organization.

Let's go back to the Scandinavian Nordic banking example to describe how we developed the service myth.

As the cultural mapping made things clearer, it seemed that we needed to find a service myth that could encapsulate and make peace with a concept of Norwegian privilege. We felt that a variation of the rags-to-riches story would work well for this purpose. The narrative tells the story of a poor protagonist who acquires, for example, power, wealth, and a mate before losing it all and gaining it back upon growing as a person, when they really appreciate the value of what they have acquired. This theme was adapted to become a service myth of Norwegian privilege for those qualified to use the Royal Gold service, while still reflecting brand values:

> You've worked hard and been smart. You will be rewarded and shown the appreciation that you deserve. You have success that transcends money, and you understand the value of what this success brings. Scandinavian Nordic understands this, too, and appreciates the fact that you have chosen us to look after your finances.

This contrasted starkly with: "Because you earn lots of money we'll treat you nicer than standard customers."

Creating a service myth in the D4Me process forms the basis for your offering, and for creating meaningful service encounters as part of the ritual experiential journey. This is where the service myth plays out, using many of the symbols that you have collected as part of the mapping process, together with ones designed specifically for your offering. But before you develop these, you need to identify key transition points where these meaningful service encounters can be designed.

Stage 4: Designing the Experiential Journey as a Ritual Journey Through Meaningful Service Encounters

Arise, Sir Lancelot!

Rituals act as passageways to meaning and thresholds into a heightened experiential state. Examples in a service context could be picking up a new car, signing a contract, upgrading a service, receiving a package, checking in and checking out, leaving a service, renewing a lease, and more—the list is potentially endless. Rituals, therefore, have the potential to change an ordinary service encounter into a meaningful service encounter (or MSE for short).

Rituals give meaningful structure to time, and have three phases: separation, transition, and reincorporation. Each has a purpose with regard to moving people emotionally to something meaningful and then cementing it in their memory. *Separation* works as a way to leave something behind and to build up anticipation. *Transition* is the core of the experience and should be full of symbols and meaningful actions. *Reincorporation* is about reaffirming the experience and bringing people back to the everyday, albeit changed by their experience.

Rituals can be grand rites of passage, and they can also be small, everyday actions and interactions. Handshakes are good examples of these smaller happenings. We separate by opening our hand to the other person, we are in transition while our hands come together in a shake, and we reincorporate when our hands are retracted. Voilà! We are together!

The grander rites of passage, such as weddings, graduations, and awards ceremonies, also follow the three phases of separation, transition, and reincorporation, and are filled with chains of smaller rituals and meaningful interactions that further build and energize the experience. These are the basis for developing MSEs.

This means that when we design for MSEs using ritual structures, we can go big or we can go small, and sometimes both. Nested chains of MSEs can be used for grand experiences, or just a handful might be used to add meaning to a shorter experiential journey. Whatever we choose, we are designing for deep and significant meaning that transcends the superficial.

Going back to the example of Royal Gold, we designed ritual into the experiential journey. This service experience was designed as a ritual journey with the three phases of separation, transition, and reincorporation, but one that also included a build-up period of "before" and a phase "after" the service experience. This resulted in a five-act ritual journey. This experience would be constructed around a chain of eight meaningful service encounters that would build anticipation and meaning into the onboarding process.

This was supplemented by the use of strong and clear symbols. We had found during the cultural mapping process that the current service did not have anything that connected banking to a Norwegian sense of privilege. Therefore, we decided to make the (Royal Gold) credit card a symbol of privilege and to use the touchpoint of a carefully designed letter as a central symbolic representation of ascension in status. The communication strategy, designed for the before phase of the customer journey, would connect the receipt of the letter and the letter itself to something meaningful as a symbol of Norwegian privilege, while still setting the tone of the service myth.

The separation phase would be kick-started with the MSE of receiving a letter whose beautiful design is intended to communicate its importance. It would officially invite the customer to become a Royal Gold member, because they have earned membership due to their hard work and endeavor. After this, a series of smaller MSEs would lead to a transition phase that included card-cutting ceremonies and artifacts, and a one-time embellished login process. The experience was brought to a close with a reincorporation ceremony that allowed for assembly, gifting, and emphasis on the meaning of the experience.

The resulting design did not require great funds from the bank to deliver the new service journey, only reordering, re-emphasis, and slight redesign of certain artifacts. The main expense was the introduction and subsequent establishment of a physical letter that would communicate new meaning about the value of an invitation to be part of the service.

Conclusion/Reincorporation

Before I close this chapter and you can be reincorporated into the rest of this book, I'd like to reflect on the use of this process.

Whether it's riding a Harley, dressing up in cosplay costumes, gathering for openings of Apple Stores, or just singing with total strangers at a football game, consumers are finding important meaning, joy, and significant connections with others through shared consumption. They demonstrate ritual behavior, tell myths about their favorite brands, and use experiential offerings. Facilitating for such experiences through design is something that should increasingly become part of the experience-centric organization.

Using the D4Me method will help you understand, find, and design the meaningful into your offerings and services. This will connect people to each other and to you, and provides heightened and more memorable experiences. By using broader cultural mechanisms such as rituals, myths, and symbols, you can tap into effective ways to influence experiences and build a stronger connection with your customers.

Having said this, it is not about *manipulating* customers, it is about using cultural mechanisms to improve their experiences and create shared mutual value. Customers are looking for shared meaningful experiences, and the question is whether you can provide them. It is not for us to judge if people find meaning through what they consume.

D4Me is about giving customers the opportunity to use established cultural concepts in a way that connects them to your experiential DNA. If your solution doesn't fit with your experiential DNA, or is out of step with culture, then it will feel inauthentic and forced. Therefore, it is important that the meaningful experiences you design for are considered genuine. In this way you provide exceptional and memorable customer experiences that both use and strengthen your experiential DNA and create mutual value. This distinguishes you from your competition and creates sustainable competitive advantage, and value for your customers, while cementing your role as an experience-centric organization.

Endnotes

1   Casper ter Kuile and Angie Thurston, *How We Gather* (Cambridge, MA: Harvard Divinity School, 2015) *https://www.howwegather.org/new-page.*

2   Henry Mason et al., *Trend-Driven Innovation: Beat Accelerating Customer Expectations,* (Hoboken, NJ: John Wiley & Sons , 2015).

3   Julianne Holt-Lunstad, Timothy B. Smith, and J. Bradley Layton, "Social Relationships and Mortality Risk: A Meta-Analytic Review," *PLoS Medicine* 7, no. 7 (2010): e1000316.

4   Richard J. Ellis, *To the Flag: The Unlikely History of the Pledge of Allegiance* (Lawrence: University Press of Kansas, 2005).

5   Katherine D. Vohs et al., "Rituals Enhance Consumption," *Psychological Science* 24, no. 9 (2013): 1714–21.

6   Christopher Booker, *The Seven Basic Plots: Why We Tell Stories* (London: Bloomsbury Press, 2004).

10

Trendslation

This second guest chapter is written by Claire Dennington, who has been working on her PhD in the field of translating trends into experience. Claire has been doing fantastic work in using *trendslation,* a method she has developed together with large and small organizations. But she is better at explaining this than I am...

In this chapter I'm going to tell you why cultural trends matter as part of the move to becoming an experience-centric organization. You will learn how to use this cultural material as a source for innovation, and through examples I will discuss culture and meaning-making. I will also introduce you to the method of trendslation, which offers a way to design for more meaningful service experiences in line with cultural trends and experiential DNA.

Hachiji Dachi!

Understanding Cultural Trends to Design for More Meaningful Service Experiences

In the aftermath of Superstorm Sandy in 2012, thousands of people in the Mid-Atlantic states were left displaced from their homes. Wanting to help, an Airbnb host got in touch with the company, asking how she could share her home for free to help some of those in need of temporary shelter. Airbnb was built on a commercial context, in which it was assumed that there would always be payment involved, and it turned out to be an extreme challenge for them to make free rental possible. Instead of turning their backs on the project, however, the company spent an intense weekend rebuilding their platform around this new service offering of sharing homes for free, in times of crisis. They then developed this capacity further and launched a new service offering, called Open Homes, which is now an established part of Airbnb (see Figure 10-1). Open Homes offers meaningful experiences to people in need of temporary housing due to natural disaster, conflict, and illness. At the time I'm writing this, nearly 300,000 people have been evacuated from their homes due to wildfires in California, and the Open Homes initiative is contributing to finding a place of sanctuary for evacuees. Airbnb's unique ability to swiftly deliver innovative and meaningful experiences in line with their core offering of sharing homes is not rooted in the quest for solely making more money. It comes from the company's strong organizational alignment and experience centricity, from deep compassion and values, and from a unique sense of how to translate cultural conversations into new service experiences.

Figure 10-1. The Airbnb Open Homes initiative, which allows hosts to share their space for free, is a good cultural fit for Airbnb. It doesn't have any commercial intent, but is a strong fit with the personality and experiential DNA of the organization. (Source: Airbnb.)

Earning Your Cultural Black Belt

As you are reading this chapter, hopefully your organization is getting close to the top of the experience-centricity maturity scale. You have carefully crafted and discussed your experiential DNA, built an internal experience team, hired an experience manager, and put experience at the heart of your organization. The time has come for you to further refine and advance this experience centricity by reflecting on and understanding your position within the contemporary cultural domain your company exists within or relates to. You may be wondering how the introductory story is relevant to your organization. Well, if you want to fulfill your true potential as a black belt experience-centric organization, you need to focus on delivering culturally relevant service experiences. You need to design for experiences that are in line with your customers' current worldviews and cultural context. You need to design for experiences that offer emotional value, ones that make sense and matter, ones that help customers fulfill their external identity projects. You need to design new services your customers not only have to use but really *want* to use.

Understanding Why Culture Matters

As customer experience becomes increasingly important, the way you choose to reinforce and influence your cultural position will become a key differentiating factor. By developing and nurturing your organizational ability to respond to cultural trends, you will be able to offer your customers new service experiences that are aligned with cultural movements and conversations. Your organization will gain competitive advantage and attain stronger customer loyalty through service experiences that customers perceive as attuned to their lifestyles and attitudes. Cultural alignment allows you to become a front-runner in your industry. Through this approach, you will be able to design new services that your customers love.

A black belt experience-centric organization understands that culture matters because:

- When you are proactively involved with culture, you are seen as a leader rather than a follower. You stand out in the market by standing for something that resonates with customers at a deep level.
- You create a connection between your experiential DNA and culture that is unique to you, and difficult for competitors to copy.
- Culture and cultural context frames meaning, and what is perceived as meaningful to people has great value. We interpret meaning through our cultural context, and through interpreting cultural codes.
- Cultural understanding relates to people's sense of self and extended identity. Through cultural codes—like how we dress, what we eat, and our leisure activities—we display our

preferences and taste through expression of self. This relates to individual identity creation and communication, and to a community of people.

- The more you focus on the customer experience, the more you develop a service personality. This personality is viewed by your customers in terms of expected behaviors, and these behaviors go beyond the experiential journey through the use of a particular service. Customers therefore view your behaviors through a cultural lens, meaning they expect your organization to behave in ways that reflect current cultural movements and to act according to cultural contexts.

- Being aware of culture, and linking it to your experiential DNA, gives a clarity of purpose that makes you stand out as both a service provider and an employer. Thus it assists in the development of internal culture and in recruitment of relevant staff.

To become a black belt you need to build cultural sensitivity and fully embrace the fact that cultural alignment can push you in the direction of becoming a front-runner in your industry. Through this approach, you will be able to design new services that your customers love.

Defining Culture: I Say Po-tay-to, You Say Po-tah-to

"Culture" is one of those terms that can be somewhat slippery and vague. No wonder, as it is a term used in several ways, in different contexts. You may use it to refer to high culture, as in the fine arts and going to the opera. Or you mean corporate culture, as in how your workplace has certain shared values, rules, and rituals, like Black-Tie Mondays or Casual Fridays. Or perhaps you mean pop culture, describing popular preferences and expressions, like trending Netflix series or the latest music craze. Or you may mean "culture" as in the unique and specific cultures of individual countries. In this chapter, when I talk about culture, I use it in terms of contemporary culture—a shared set of current values, practices, behaviors, and beliefs that exist in everyday life, shared by people within a community, as defined by cultural theorist Stuart Hall.[1]

Being Attuned to Culture

Let's go back to the introductory story for a minute. Airbnb, as a dynamic and innovative experience-centric organization, is inherently attuned to societal and cultural movements. One could say that the whole concept behind it was based on a strong cultural trend of people traveling more and wanting to experience new places, but not in the way many of us traveled for years and years, like tourists. No, now we want to travel like locals—not merely visiting a city, but living the authentic life in a local neighborhood, visiting the local café, having a friendly chat with a neighbor, being part of the community and imagining that this new place is your home away from home. This is, after all, Airbnb's experiential value proposition, to "live like a local." From the very first air mattress the Airbnb founders started renting out, the local experience was enhanced by sprinkles of small cultural clues (like leaving a few quarters for visitors to use for public transportation).

As an experience-centric organization, Airbnb has developed a unique sense of cultural movement, and an understanding of how to translate this into new experiential offerings and touchpoints. They continuously adjust, fine-tune, and innovate around their core offering of affordable rental accommodation, in line with cultural influences. They also strongly align this to their experiential DNA and their vision to "help create a world where you can belong anywhere." By translating cultural influence and brand DNA into experience, they are able to offer more meaningful experiences, like that of the Open Homes initiative. Through this initiative they created a meaningful experience not only for people in crisis and their families, but also for people wanting to help and for the whole community.

Airbnb didn't initiate Open Homes because they wanted to earn a few more bucks (the service is, of course, free). They did it as an act of benevolence because it was the right fit for their experiential DNA. This initiative was truly in line with their service personality as a friendly open-minded neighbor, building on the personal values of the founders. What would you do if your friends, family, or neighbors were in need? You would open your home to them.

Cultural influence shapes service personality and people's expectations of behavior. Now, imagine if Trump Hotels offered rooms for free in a time of crisis. Would you question their motives? Would you think that they were commercially (in some way) trying to exploit a vulnerable situation? The cultural reaction from Airbnb was the right fit for their experiential DNA, but it would be wrong for Trump Hotels. Having an experiential focus creates expectations of behavior, and actively taking part in relevant cultural conversations is therefore key to delivering meaningful experiences.

Let's look at another example. French supermarket Intermarché identified cultural trends regarding a growing awareness around food waste and sustainable food. They translated this into a meaningful experience through the design and development of a new and successful service offering. Intermarché turned what could have been a marketing stunt into a full experience. Focusing on the imperfect fruit and vegetables that are usually discarded for their looks, they used humorous characterizations based around the concept of "inglorious fruits and vegetables" (see Figure 10-2). They translated this into an experience through a strong design profile, a tongue-in-cheek tone of voice, and a full service ecology, comprising in-store happenings, inglorious smoothies, and inglorious soups, as well as by selling the disfigured produce. The results were beyond belief: products were sold out, new customers visited the stores, and Intermarché received national admiration. The key success factor was that they translated the trend into a strong experiential offering and implemented it right down to the individual touchpoints.

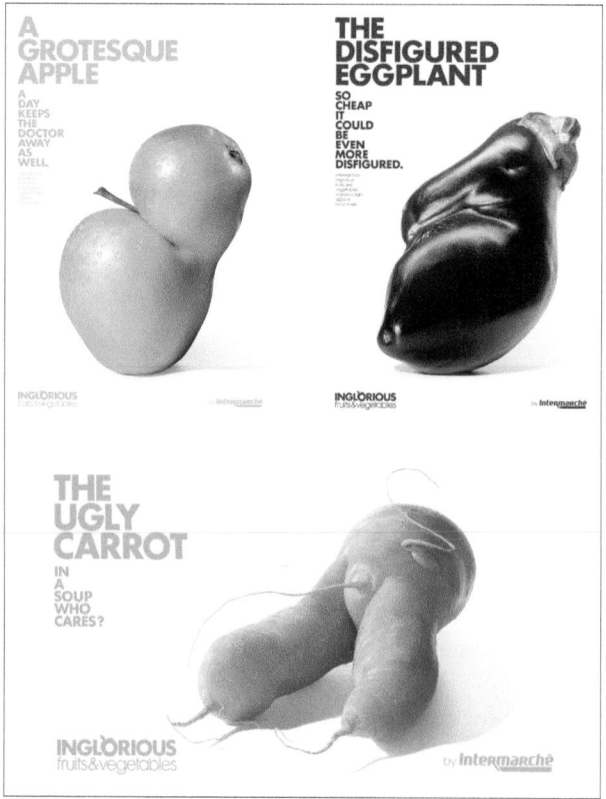

Figure 10-2. The French supermarket Intermarché translated the growing awareness around food waste into a highly successful new service offering: "the inglorious fruits and vegetables" that offered a meaningful experience for their customers. (Source: Intermarché.)

How to Trendslate

To successfully trendslate culture into service experiences, you need to first identify which cultural trends are relevant to your organization, and then build on this as a key part of the experience you are offering. This cultural affinity needs to be embedded throughout your organization, as part of the company backbone, and it needs to be embedded in your experiential DNA. You need to go beyond tokenism, minimum Corporate Social Responsibility (CSR) standards, add-ons, or clever marketing stunts. You need to design for experiences around issues that your customers engage with, on an emotional level. And you have to mean it. Why? Because if you don't, the people you care about, and the people that care about you, will see straight through you. As with the Airbnb example, when designing for meaningful service experiences, you need to embrace the act of benevolence—that people believe you have their best interests at heart. And you need to be brave.

When Airbnb acquired a Super Bowl advertising spot, just 10 days before kickoff, they decided to use the opportunity this touchpoint offered to culturally relate to President Trump's recent travel ban, and at the same time launch the initiative #weaccept. In an interview, CEO Brian Chesky recalls how he almost decided to pull the ad two days before it aired, fearing the consequences it might have on the business. Instead, it became one of the most shared Super Bowl ads ever. It was timely, it was radical, it related to the company's experiential DNA, and it was in tune with the sociocultural and political movements of the time. It worked because it was a good fit with Airbnb's personality and the behaviors that its customers expected.

Patagonia is a clothing brand that is built on a kind of bravery, in that it takes a stance against the mainstream fashion industry. With its activist personality, the brand embraces a philosophy and vision around building long-lasting and durable products, without causing unnecessary harm to the environment. This is embedded in the company's experiential DNA, extends throughout the whole organization, and permeates every detail of the Patagonia experience. The close connection to nature and outdoor sports experiences translates into their products, as well as into their anti-marketing approach (don't buy more than necessary), and more recently into their new services, such as clothing repair and their hub for worn Patagonia wear.

When Nike, in September 2018, hired former San Francisco quarterback Colin Kaepernick (famous for kneeling in protest of racial injustice during the US national anthem before NFL games) as head of its campaign, it risked igniting a blaze of controversy. Social media filled with images of Nike shoes going up in flames (#justburnit). Mainstream media predicted the brand's fall, but instead Nike stocks skyrocketed. The company was seen as taking a stance for something it believed in. The experience of Nike presenting a personality that believes in and defends equal rights for all was perceived as meaningful (for those who didn't burn their sneakers) and in tune with the experiential DNA of the company. Its bravery was repaid many times over.

Understanding Cultural Trends: The Importance of the Zeitgeist

As a black belt experience-centric organization, you need to become aware of and attuned to the cultural spirit of the moment—the *zeitgeist*. This is the essence of the era, which is invisible to most people at the time, but obvious when they look back on it in the future. The experience-centric organization is in tune with the zeitgeist, and always manages to adapt the customer experience to the underlying shifts in culture (see Figure 10-3).

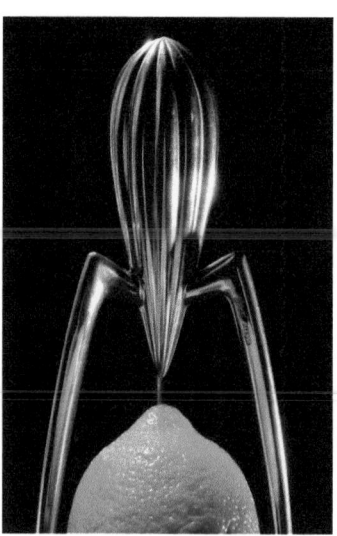

Figure 10-3. This iconic fruit juicer, designed by Philippe Starck, is a perfect example of a product catching the spirit of the times—the zeitgeist. It was one of a series of products that poked fun at functionalism and spawned a period of "quirky and fun" post-modern products in the 1990s. (Source: Wikimedia, Creative Commons.)

"Rip. Mix. Burn." was Apple's message to fans in the early 2000s, when the company completely disrupted the music market. By introducing the music download service iTunes and launching the new iMac with features for both ripping and burning CDs, they were offering the customer the lead role as orchestrator and owner of their own mix of music. Apple had picked up on the zeitgeist of independence and freedom of choice in society, and had translated this into an ecology of products and services. Together with the design of the desirable iMac machines in colorful translucent plastic, this transformed and saved Apple (see Figure 10-4). The combination of the (at the time radical) iMac design and a focus on disrupting the music business turned Apple's fortunes around, and one could argue that this was all due to perfect trendslation.

For most consumer-oriented and product-focused organizations, understanding and translating cultural trends is a key factor for delivering the right products at the right time, to the right customer. This means providing meaningful and desirable products in line with your customers' values, needs, and expectations. It means having a team of design professionals keeping up to date with trends and using their design skills to translate them into new service experiences. You need to invest time in finding service designers with a strong organizational fit, and knowledge in branding, service design, and cultural translation.

Figure 10-4. In the early 2000s, Apple understood the spirit of the times and chose to launch products and services that gave people the experience of freedom, individuality, and choice. This disrupted the music business and at the same time relaunched Apple as a culturally relevant brand. (Source: Apple.)

You need to develop dynamic organizational structures that take into account this cultural knowledge, and have a team that can not only identify which trends are relevant, but also reflect on and extract the underlying meaning of these cultural shifts. Why are these trends happening? What are they signaling? What are the main reasons a trend has manifested? What is the underlying meaning behind this trend? And, more importantly, what does this mean for us?

Delivering a Fabulous Aesthetic Experience: Aesop

Aesop is an organization that is founded on responding to the cultural trend of beauty (see Figure 10-5). It is a high-price luxury experience that frames its experiential offering through beautiful, highly aesthetic, and poetic experiences. Aesop is an example of a company that has captured the zeitgeist of beauty. It has created an aesthetic world that goes a long way beyond the product, such that when you enter into a relationship with Aesop, you are not buying cosmetics, you are appreciating beauty.

For over 30 years the brand has been "offering skin, hair, and body care formulations created with meticulous attention to detail, and with efficacy and sensory pleasure in mind." There is a strong focus on design and experience throughout the entire organization. Every single touchpoint and element in the customer's experiential journey has been beautifully crafted. With close links to art, design, and architecture, and an immense interest in and understanding of materials and ingredients, Aesop offers products, packaging, a graphic profile, and shop interiors that both look and feel divine. The company's experiential DNA is continuously translated into highly stylistic and aesthetic elements such as carefully curated artist collaborations, a friendly yet professional tone of voice, and invitations that combine

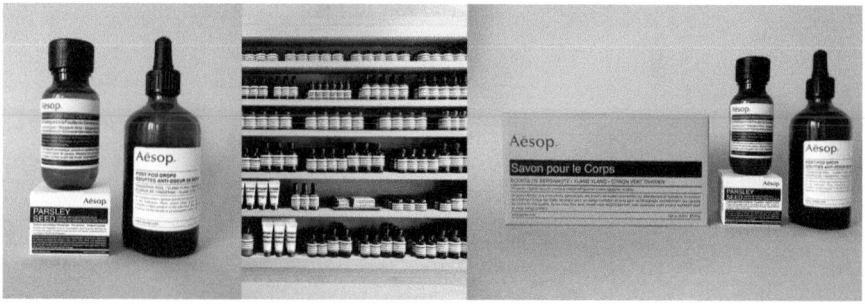

Figure 10-5. Aesop has transformed buying and using beauty products into a pilgrimage and sacred aesthetic experience. (Source: Claire Dennington.)

poetry and beautiful illustrations. Aesop is not for everyone, but in the target group their customers feel that the brand adds value to their lives, through the aesthetic experiences it provides. Every time they wash their hands or faces, they associate the experience with the wondrous world of Aesop. And, of course, they are willing to pay for this experience. Aesop's ability to successfully identify and translate a cultural theme of beauty into a world of aesthetic experiences has been highly successful, and has resulted in 40% year-on-year growth.

Linking Experiential DNA and Culture

"Where there is a disconnect in authenticity, people will feel cheated and react negatively."
   – TAI TRAN, FORBES 30 UNDER 30 CEO

When you are designing new services, it is key that new offerings are not only attuned to cultural trends, but also tightly aligned to your experiential DNA. The Aesop example describes an experience-centric organization that has successfully aligned its experiential DNA to cultural trends and infused this throughout the whole organization. With cultural awareness and cultural alignment, you can more easily identify the direction to develop your new service offerings and what fits your company best. That is, cultural awareness and alignment give you a clarity of vision and invisible boundaries. And just as important, they help you understand what does *not* fit your company. If Aesop wanted to move into a new fast food space in a suburban mall, most of the company's loyal fans would probably gasp in disbelief and turn their backs on both this initiative and the brand. However, if Aesop instead launched a pop-up bar at a local music festival, providing healthy beauty- and skin-enhancing vitamin-infused juice shots, most fans would applaud it and not even think twice about using, or promoting it. In other words, there is a specific cultural opportunity that fits Aesop's experiential DNA, and the same is true for all organizations. Knowing this and using it to your advantage is key to trendslation.

When IKEA launched the social kitchen Kutchnia Spotkan in Warsaw—a large, fully equipped kitchen in a spacious city apartment—they were not only offering a space for people to get together to make and enjoy a meal, they were simultaneously addressing the issue of small, expensive living spaces in larger cities. It seemed IKEA was not just trying to sell furniture, but also exploring how to create opportunities for customers to get involved in valuable and meaningful experiences, in an innovative way that aligns with the brand proposition of "affordable solutions for better living." Similarly, when dating service Match.com saw that 3.1 million of its users listed "coffee and conversation" as an interest, they teamed up with Starbucks and introduced "Meet at Starbucks," a one-click-coffee-date invitation feature with a chat function. That function enabled users visiting Starbucks to chat directly with other users there, creating experiential opportunity for people in our digital age to meet up in real life and adding individual value to the customer experience.

In 2016 Starbucks founder Howard Schultz encouraged employees to use their vote in the US election, and the company teamed up with the voting service TurboVote to enable employees to register via computer or mobile device. In 2018, Starbucks employed 8,000 veterans and pledged to employ 10,000 refugees. Rather than just adding a marketing campaign, the company is aligning initiatives to its DNA and fully embedding this into the organization. This is a new direction for Starbucks, and has not always been a success. Its #racetogether initiative aimed at stimulating discussion about race was a failure, not because of the idea, but due to its implementation. However, it's clear that Starbucks has recognized that it is not only an economic actor in the market, but also a cultural actor in society, and that this comes with both responsibilities and consequences.

The Trendslation Method: Three Steps of Translation

After working with several brands and companies on service design research projects, I saw the need to assist companies with trendslation—that is, translating cultural trends into new services. I have worked for several years developing the trendslation method (see Figure 10-6), and have used it with local, national, and global organizations with great success. The aim of the trendslation method is to offer a way of designing for more holistic and trend-driven service innovation, and for more meaningful and highly experiential service encounters. The trendslation method explores how trends can be factors for conveying intrinsic meaning, and how organizations can capture this meaning and use it to develop new experiential offerings in line with their experiential DNA. The three steps of trendslation are:

1. Understanding and exploring the trend to extract the underlying meaning and its relationship to your experiential DNA
2. Ideating to translate meaning into experiential value propositions (EVPs)
3. Defining and detailing the service concept through an experiential journey and experiential elements

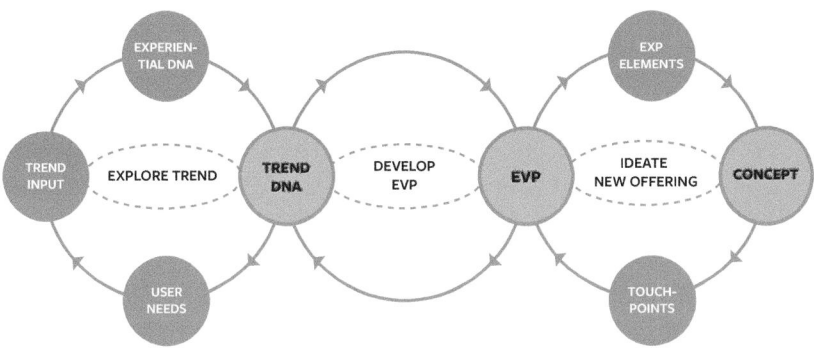

Figure 10-6. The trendslation method is a three-step process that translates trends into new service experiences. (Source: Claire Dennington.)

1. Explore the Trend

The first step of the trendslation process is to gain a clear understanding of the underlying meaning behind a trend. This means reflecting on what the trend actually means, to whom, and how, why the trend is happening, and if/how/why the trend is relevant to your organization. In my work with partners, the mere act of mapping, discussing, and then putting the trend into words and visual representations makes this underlying meaning more clear. In essence, you will be decoding and encoding the intangible nature of trends, and making them relevant to your experiential DNA. The five-step DCODE process enables this exploration:

D – DISCUSS
What are the implications of this trend, on a personal, individual, societal, and organizational level? Discuss what the key features and characteristics of the trend are, and what level of relevance it may have to your organization. Discuss the extent of the trend. Is it a micro, meta, or mega trend?

C – CONSIDER

Why is this trend emerging now? Are there larger movements impacting culture and society, such as technological, political, sociocultural, environmental, or economical shifts? Consider in what way attitudes are changing, and why these issues are important to people. Consider whether your organization could and should relate to this trend. Is it relevant? Why? In what way? Remember that the trends need to fit your organization, experiential DNA, and service personality in a good way.

O – OBSERVE

Notice where you find "clues" or evidence manifesting the trend in different sectors. Go on a city safari or research trip, look to news, social media, new product ranges, art, movies, literature, best-selling lists, trending hashtags. Observe new innovations, services, and start-ups. Start gathering examples of these clues and create a visual repository of them.

D - DEFINE

Articulate what new needs and opportunity spaces can arise in light of this trend and in relation to your experiential DNA.

E – EXPLAIN

Capture the core, the bloodline, the underlying meaning of the trend in one simple phrase.

For each step it can be helpful to note down keywords, short statements, and ideas along the way. You may look into several relevant trends that you merge together—anything that can help pinpoint and reveal what you and your company view as the underlying meaning. This is not an exact science, and it helps to co-create a visual, experiential code map. When working with desirability and experience, thinking in visual terms can lead to a more coherent and holistic representation of the underlying meaning through the evidence, or codes that are emerging. Such visualizations can help give you immediate feedback about whether the experience looks and feels right, and create shared ownership in a project team. Your goal should be to synthesize this process down to a short sentence summarizing the underlying meaning, which serves as a baseline for further concept ideation.

2. Develop an Experiential Value Proposition

Now that you have explored a trend and understand its inherent meaning, you are ready to translate this knowledge into alternative experiential value propositions (EVPs). To do this, you need to map out new opportunity spaces, and start ideating around what new offerings you could provide that cater to them. Consider how a new offering could impact or build on your existing offering, and if and how these new offerings align with your experiential DNA. Try to imagine near-future scenarios based on the insights in the first trendslation step. Start discussing what a completely new offering could be, what a modified version of your existing offering might be, and what could be a future offering. As you start framing new offerings, go into more detail about the experience. What would the new service be called? What is your elevator pitch? Which images would you use to represent the experience? By doing this, you and your team will start developing a coherent interpretation and aligned expectations. This is also a great way to start building a concept library for later use and inspiration.

3. Detail the New Service Concept

It's crucial to stay open-minded at this step of the trendslation process. There is always a lot of can't, won't, wouldn't, shouldn't do, but you must resist that way of thinking and be open to new ideas. Ask yourself what your customers will dream of, fear, anticipate, and need help with solving in light of the trends you have identified. What will be meaningful to them? Focus on the cultural context of your new offering and on the experience you want to offer.

To further refine the offerings/ideas into service concepts, develop a stylistic experiential journey map (Figure 10-7). The stylistic experiential journey is like the experiential journey (see Chapter 8) crossed with a mood board. It takes the experiential service journey a step further and communicates a richer view of the experience by adding stylistic images that relate to the experience at different stages of the journey. In this way cultural and style aspects are linked to the customer experience, thereby ensuring cultural relevance right down to the individual touchpoints.

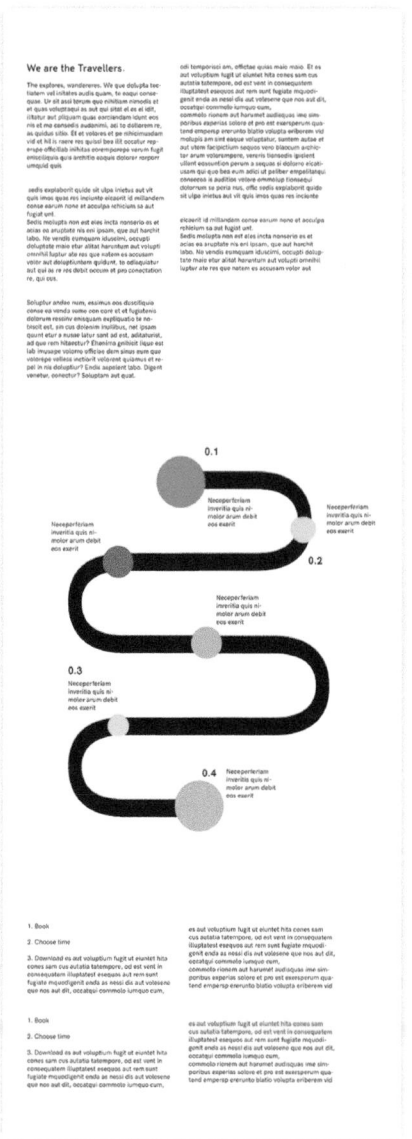

Figure 10-7. The stylistic experiential journey adds culturally relevant images to the experiential journey mapping described in Chapter 8. In doing so, it gives you a richer experiential view of the journey, and ensures cultural relevance right down to individual touchpoints. (Source: Claire Dennington.)

Through developing the stylistic experiential journey, you may identify new opportunity areas, and this can lead you to develop other and better experiential value propositions. To engage customers through-out the service journey every touchpoint and detail needs to have a high level of style, including service-specific details such as tone of voice, sensory elements, gestures, and rituals.

To reinforce the journey, add specific experiential elements to touch-points to reinforce your organization's intended experience/mean-ing, and to help you develop a specific service style. Experimental elements could include sensory, symbolic, gestural, physical, digital, material, aesthetic, and spatial details, such as tone of voice, interior design, graphic elements, taste, sound, lighting, fonts, colors, illustra-tions, photos, branding, and form or geographic location, to mention a few. By understanding and detailing these elements, you can shift, alter, or even curate the experience

Conclusion

This chapter has described how cultural awareness needs to be a core competency in the black belt experience-centric organization. By hav-ing an understanding of the zeitgeist, the spirit of the times, you will be able to trendslate cultural trends into relevant experiences that sur-prise and delight your customers. In doing so, you will be able to sat-isfy needs that customers have not yet recognized, build long-term relationships with them, and create experiences that they consider desirable.

Trendslation is a method developed to help organizations monitor trends, identify those that are relevant for their services, and trans-form them into desirable experiences. The method is straightfor-ward and has been used successfully in large and small organizations, ranging from supermarkets to global clothing brands. Trendslation is an approach that requires a high degree of experience maturity, and therefore builds on a core competency in organizational experience centricity.

To round out this chapter, I'd like to say a few words about value perception that will influence all organizations during the next years. Throughout the past years, and in my PhD work, I have worked with many brands and businesses that are product-focused. Their main aim was to sell products, and they concentrated on the point of sale. As we are shifting to a service-dominant society, with a focus on experience, they have all had to contemplate the meaning of value. This means moving from a point-of-sale focus to a service experience focus, while also developing an experience-centric culture. Value is now derived from interactions and relationships rather than through the point of sale alone, and this has consequences for the organizational mindset. Following the trajectory toward experience centricity changes this mindset, and the trendslation approach becomes a natural further step for the organization.

Finally, there is one huge trend that we cannot ignore. Customers increasingly feel that we have come to a point in history where we need to acknowledge that our resources are not unlimited, and that today's consumption patterns need to be left in the past. Customers are more and more critical of the "use and dispose" mentality of the past, and believe that this way of thinking needs to be ceremoniously discarded, for good. Longevity, social responsibility, and sustainability will be key trends for the next decade as customers look to develop long-term relationships with organizations taking a lead in this area. Being an experience-centric organization requires that you relate to these important issues. As people start consuming fewer products, or shift to using services that offer more sustainable solutions (like rental, reuse, and repair), you need to position yourself through new service offerings that create value beyond the point of sale. How can you become front-runners in your industry by offering emotional value, experiential value, educational value, or social value? In my opinion, a good start is embracing your new role as a fully developed experience-centric organization and delivering new service experiences that add value and meaning to people's lives. In this way, you become a part of current cultural conversations, and that is a good place to be.

Endnotes

1   Stuart Hall, "Gramsci's Relevance for the Study of Race and Ethnicity," *Journal of Communication Inquiry* 10, no. 2 (1986): 5–27.

2   Tai Tran, "#RaceTogether: 3 Reasons Behind Starbucks' Plunder," LinkedIn, March 21, 2015, *http://bit.ly/2JR0bNo*.

Conclusion

Becoming an experience-centric organization is not a choice you make, but an imperative driven by the market. Where there is competition, all organizations are competing on experience in one way or another, and all are inevitably on a trajectory toward experience centricity. You can choose to move quickly along this trajectory and gain competitive advantage, or you can wait and watch others speed past you.

In this book I have shown what it means to be experience-centric as an organization, and the steps that you need to take to reach experience centricity. You can obtain quick wins by embracing an experiential journey approach, so that is a good place to start. However, this is something your competitors will also be doing, and my experience is that you need to think long-term and start an organizational transformation. Key to this transformation is experience thinking, a way of thinking that is powered by design. If there is one discipline that can accelerate your transformation to experience centricity, it is design—but not design in the traditional sense. Experience centricity requires that you embrace design thinking as a way of thinking, and design doing as a way of doing. A central part of this design-driven experiential competence is being one step ahead of your customers by being able to see them, hear them, and be them. This understanding is not enough on its own, though; you have to translate it into experiences in order to deliver a combination of an experientially desirable offering and touchpoints along the experiential journey. This requires an organizational competence that connects you to trends, meaning, and culture on the one hand, and to experiential fulfillment, technology, and organization on the other.

The wheel of experience centricity should form the backbone of your understanding of experience centricity. It is a powerful model that describes how the various parts of your organization have to fit together to be able to deliver on your experiential offerings. I cannot overemphasize the importance of your experiential DNA in this, because knowing yourself takes you halfway toward being able to create and deliver great experiences. This is not to undermine the other parts of the wheel, since all are vital to make the approach work effectively and efficiently. But if you do not know yourself well, then how can you expect your customers to know you and want to develop a relationship with you? The wheel helps you understand the roles of various parts of your organization in making great experiences happen, and it allows you to align them to the goal of providing desirable experiences. It equips you to ask the right questions of each part of your organization, such as "How will this software platform support experience fulfillment and the experience we want to provide?" or "How will this strategic collaboration improve the customer experience?" These questions have unfortunately been lacking in the past, leading to a blurring of lines around the customer experience. Now you have the structure to ask them, and to bring everything into focus. I recommend you make the wheel of experience centricity your own, and use it actively as you develop your own experience-centric organization.

It is my sincere hope that by employing the approaches presented in this book that you will create more value not only for your organization but also for your customers, and will build a long-term competitive advantage in the marketplace. In the years to come, I hope you will be able to look back on the journey you have embarked on and check off the stages toward experience centricity. Your customers will thank you for it, your employees will thank you for it, and your investors will cheer you on.

Further Reading

It is always difficult to recommend further reading without knowing more about the reader who wants to learn more. So, with that in mind, I have listed books here that I recommend based on my own interests and the theme of this book. Please point me to other books if you have suggestions, as these are key areas of reading for me.

Design Thinking

Resources in the field of design thinking are a mix of consultant-based books and research-based ones. From the consultant point of view, Tim Brown's book *Change by Design: How Design Thinking Transforms*

Organizations and Inspires Innovation (HarperBusiness) was a kick-starter to the wave of design thinking and is therefore worth a read. His articles in the *Harvard Business Review* are also good, and fairly easy to find online. I have always been a fan of Jeanne Liedtka too, and can recommend her book *Designing for Growth: A Design Thinking Tool Kit for Managers* (Columbia University Press). From the research point of view, Hasso Plattner's book *Design Thinking Research: Taking Breakthrough Innovation Home* (Springer) is a good research summary. To gain a good understanding about how designers design, I recommend *Design Expertise* by Bryan Lawson (Taylor & Francis) as a good start.

Service Design

To my mind, service design takes design thinking a step further by applying it to innovation in services. Service design has not expanded as much in the US as in Europe, but I really recommend the thinking and approaches behind service design as a pragmatic and successful approach to using design thinking to innovate. For me, *This is Service Design Doing*, by Marc Stickdorn et al. (O'Reilly), is the best book by far, standing head and shoulders above all others at the moment.

Customer Experience

This is a minefield of an area, and is partly the reason why I wrote this book. There are a lot of books that preach about the importance of the customer experience, but I don't find them very useful. I did find Chip Heath and Dan Heath's book *The Power of Moments* (Simon & Schuster) to be a good read, even though its aim is to convince you of the power of experiences, not show how you can harness it yourself. In terms of understanding experiences, Daniel Kahneman's book *Thinking, Fast and Slow* (Farrar, Straus, and Giroux) is a classic. I recommend *How Emotions Are Made* by Lisa Feldman Barrett (Mariner Books) to explain the neuropsychological basis of emotions and experiences. Finally, I recommend *Embodied Mind, Meaning, and Reason* by Mark Johnson, who also co-wrote a classic called *Metaphors We Live By* with George Lackoff (both published by University of Chicago Press).

Nudging

Linked to customer experience, the area of nudging is interesting and the books *Predictably Irrational* by Dan Ariely (HarperCollins) and *Nudge* by Richard Thaler and Cass Sunstein (Penguin) are good resources. The website *Coglode.com* has a nice collection and clear interpretation of many nudging or behavioral biases we have. There is little background on the site explaining why nudges work, but it offers some useful summaries of what they are.

Designing for Experience

To be able to design for experience, you will have to learn how to map experiences, and *Mapping Experiences* by Jim Kalbach (O'Reilly) is a fantastic book that tells all you need to know. I would complement this with *Orchestrating Experiences* by Chris Risdon and Patrick Quattlebaum (Rosenfeld).

Organizational Transformation

I have struggled to find good books that relate to organizational design from the perspective of this book. So, I have gone back to the basics of organization. *Designing Dynamic Organizations* by Jay Galbraith, Diane Downey, and Amy Kates (AMACOM) is a good book on this topic. *Reinventing Organizations* by Frederic Laloux (Nelson Parker) is also good choice; and I can't discuss organization design without pointing you to *Holacracy* by Brian J. Robertson (Holt, Henry & Company).

Culture and Meaning

This field is crying out for a book that applies cultural theory to design, but until it arrives, then I suggest the following. *How Brands Become Icons: The Principles of Cultural Branding* by Douglas Holt (Harvard Business Review Press) is very good and shows how consumption and branding can respond to cultural need. His follow-up book with Douglas Cameron, *Cultural Strategy: Using Innovative Ideologies to Build Breakthrough Brands* (Oxford University Press) is also worth a read. If you are interested in rituals and the design of tradition, *The Invention of Tradition* by Eric Hobsbawm and Terence Ranger (Cambridge University Press) is a classic and full of aha moments where you realize that cultural pillars (including the kilt) were actually invented.

Biographies

Simon Clatworthy is a professor at the Oslo School of Architecture and Design (AHO). He has worked with design for experience and the strategic use of design for over 20 years, and has worked with large global service organizations such as Lufthansa, Telenor, Visa, and Adidas. Simon has a PhD in service design and was central in forming two eight-year national initiatives: the Norwegian Centre for Service Innovation and Centre for Connected Care.

Ted Matthews, the author of Chapter 9, *4Me: Designing for Meaningful Experiences*, is a service designer, speaker, trainer, and researcher. He is Chair of Service Design at AHO and recently delivered his PhD on the potential of ritual and myth in the design of meaningful service experiences. This work has been applied to a diverse range of areas, including professional football, banking, and meaningful tourism experiences in Norway.

Claire Dennington, the author of Chapter 10, *Trendslation,* is an experienced and recognized designer who has worked in design and fashion for many years, together with national and global fashion brands such as BikBok and Adidas. She is currently carrying out her PhD at AHO in the area of trendslation—translating cultural trends into service experiences.

Colophon

The cover design and illustration are by Simon Clatworthy and Graham John Mansfield. The cover fonts are FreightSans Pro and Guardian Sans Condensed. The text fonts are FreightSans Pro and Garamond.

Index

A

Aaker, David, 128
Aaker, Jennifer, 128, 138, 150
Aarstiderne food delivery service, 15–18
abductive logic/thinking, 81
Accenture Interactive consultancy, 10, 94
actor ecology, experience structure and, 48, 50
actor network, 36, 58–60, 59
Aesop (company), 20, 220–222
The Aesthetic Brain (Chatterjee), 117, 131
Airbnb rental site, 14–15, 154, 211–212, 215, 217
alignment
  about, 24
  creating within organization, 96–99
  customer-centric organization and, 38
  experience centricity and, , 98–99, 67
  experience-centric organization and, 28, 41–42, 67, 76, 81
  experience fulfillment and, 175
  experiential translation and, 141, 149, 155
  trendslation on, 212–214, 221
Allianz Arena, 55–56

Amabile, Teresa, 90
Amazon.com, 21, 51, 136, 188
American Management Association, 101
anxiety mapping (D4Me), 204–205
Apple (company)
  creating postboxes in our minds, 120
  cultural zeitgeist and, 147, 219–220
  as experience-focused, 20–21
  meaningful experiences and, 194–195
  myths, rituals, and symbols, 200
  narrative mapping, 203
  power of touch, 184
  product desirability and, 124
  "Rip.Mix.Burn" campaign, 29, 219
  working from experience backward, 51
AR (augmented reality), 181
Ariely, Dan, 113, 137
The Art of War (Sun Tzu), 134–135
Audi (company), 148
augmented reality (AR), 181
authenticity of purpose, 73, 91
Azoulay, Audrey, 150

B

Bailey, Christopher, 86–87
Barrett, Lisa Feldman, 113, 116–117, 120, 137
BASF consulting group, 78–79
beauty, receiving pleasure from, 117
behavioral authenticity, 25
Beil, Christian, 78–79
belief, importance of, 159
Bellamy, Francis, 199
benevolence, 183, 215, 217
best practices, experience-centric organization, 20–21
Bezos, Jeff, 21
big data, 197
BMW (company), 5
Body Shop (company), 125
body-storming, 177
Booker, Christopher, 205
Børresen, Stian, 181
branding. *See also* experiential DNA
    Aaker on, 128
    brand experience, 73
    brand personality and, 128, 150–152
    Burberry example, 86–87
    customer-centric organization and, 36–37
    customer experiences, 7–8, 19, 232
    customer-oriented organization and, 29
    D4Me and, 195, 200
    experience-centric organization and, 18, 41–42
    experience-oriented organization and, 39–40
    experiential focus and, 142
    Filho on, 156–157
    Ind on, 30–31, 146–147

journey-oriented organization and, 34
meaningful experiences and, 195
postboxes metaphor for, 120–121
trendslation and, 215–223
brand personality, 128, 138, 150–152
British Airways, 120
Brown, Tim, 88
Buick Model Y, 76
Burberry rainwear brand, 86–87
business model, experience structure and, 47, 48, 59–60

C

Cameron, Douglas, 204
Carlzon, Jan, 67, 68
CB Insights platform, 21
CD Baby (company), 120, 138
CEO (Chief Executive Officer), 74, 91, 98
Chatterjee, Anjan, 117, 131
Chesky, Brian, 217
Claure, Marcelo, 11
CNET, 13
co-design processes, 83–84, 90, 105, 177
commoditization of services, 5
competition in marketplace, 7–8
Competitive Advantage (Porter), 43
complexity, hiding, 183–184
concept cars, 76–77
CONSIDER (DCODE process), 224
Consumer Reports survey, 161
Cook, Tim, 195
coolhunting for experiences, 83–84

E

Hunt, Elle, 12

I

IDEO design company, 88
IKEA (company), 184, 221
importance, designing for, 172, 187
indirect touchpoints, 167–168
Ind, Nicholas, 30–31, 146–147
informal culture, 58
infusion
    about, 24, 98
    design strategy and, 98
    experience centricity and, 90, 93, 106
    experience-centric organization and, 76
    experience fulfillment and, 175
institutional logics, 18, 106
interaction-out approach in organizations, 96–97
interactions
    as central to who we are, 113
    customer experience requiring, 118–120
    experience fulfillment through, 47, 48, 57–58
Intermarché supermarkets, 216
intersubjectivity, 196
iTunes service, 219

J

Jack Daniel brand, 204
Jante Loven, 204
job promotions, customer contact and, 85
Jobs, Steve, 21, 195–196, 203
Jordan toothbrushes, 109–111
journey-oriented organization, 28, 32–37

just-in-time production system, 100–101

K

Kaepernick, Colin, 43, 218
Kahneman, Daniel, 123
Kalbach, Jim, 164
Kapferer, Jean-Noël, 150
key performance indicators. *See* KPIs (key performance indicators)
keywords, experiential transformation, 21–25
Kieninger, Jochen, 173
Kierkegaard, Soren, 8
kilts, tradition of, 198–199
kindness as contagious, 116
KPIs (key performance indicators)
    for customer centricity, 37–38
    for experience centricity, 43
    measuring progress with, 103–104
    Schybergson on, 10
    for silos, 101, 172
    targeting experience, 6

L

leadership, 42, 96, 213
Lee, Harper, 88
LEGO (company), 146, 176
lifetime value metric, 5, 21
listening to customers, 71, 84–85
LiveWork designer company, 173, 179
Løvlie, Lavrans, 179
loyalty, concept of, 11

M

Mapping Experiences (Kalbach), 164

off-script experiences, 55–56, 99–100, 135–136
O'Leary, Michael, 137
Open Homes initiative (Airbnb), 212, 215
optimism as core behavior, 77–80
Orange telco, 30–31
orchestration, 23–24, 90, 170
orchestrator, 23–24
organizational DNA
    customer-centric organization and, 37
    customer experience fitting, 145
    experience-centric organization and, 40–41
    having story that resonates, 71
    Hunsaker on, 118
    internal logics and, 18
    interpreting, 91
    Schybergson on, 11
    service personality and, 150
    understanding one's, 22
organizational logics
    about, 92, 106
    customer-centric organization and, 35, 37
    designing, 89–90, 92–93
    experience-centric organization and, 41–42
    experience-oriented organization and, 39
    experiential DNA and, 61
    subjective evaluation of, 103
    transforming, 98
organizational structures
    aligning around customer experience, 8
    cultural knowledge and, 220

customer-centric organization and, 18, 37
customer-oriented organization and, 29
designing for experience, 125, 140
experience-centric organization and, 18, 41–43
experience enablers through, 47, 48, 58–59
experience fulfillment and, 172–173
experience-oriented organization and, 39
formal and informal culture in, 58
journey-oriented organization and, 34
organizing for experience centricity
    about, 89–90
    doing what you love, 90–91
    gap analysis, 102–103
    interaction-out approach, 96–97
    measuring progress, 102–103
    owning customer experience, 91
    top-up approach, 96–99
"The Orient Game", 191–192, 195
ownership
    about, 24–25
    experience centricity and, 90–92
    experience-centric organization and, 73
    trendslation on, 224

P

pain points, 162, 165, 170, 174, 176

utility, customer experience and, 130–131

V

value chains, 29, 43, 59, 101, 172
value in use, 52
value maximization, 74–75
value networks, 43, 51, 59, 101
value perception, 227
value proposition (offer-
ing), 22. *See also* experiential offering
values. *See* experiential DNA
Virgin Atlantic airway, 120, 125
virtual reality (VR), 181
VR (virtual reality), 181

W

walkthroughs, 176–177
Wall Street Journal, 6
washing machines, 8–9
wheel of experience centricity
about, 45, 49–51, 62
customer experience and, 45–
54
experience enablers, 47, 49,
57–58, 50
experience fulfillment, 47–49,
54–57, 97, 50
experience structure, 47, 49,
59–60, 50
experiential DNA and, 62–65
experiential offering, 50–53
innovating service experience
with, 66–68
restaurant example, 45–48
service personality, 50–53
"Why We Gather" report, 193
winking, 128–129

X

Xerox (company), 183

Y

Y-Job, 76
Youth Interest magazine, 199

Z

zeitgeist, 71, 147, 218–220
zooming out/in, 82
ZOZO service, 83–84

O'REILLY®

There's much more where this came from.

Experience books, videos, live online training courses, and more from O'Reilly and our 200+ partners—all in one place.

Learn more at oreilly.com/online-learning